Other People's Mail

Other People's
 Mail

AN ANTHOLOGY OF
LETTER STORIES

*Edited with an
Introduction by Gail Pool*

UNIVERSITY OF MISSOURI PRESS

COLUMBIA AND LONDON

Copyright © 2000 by
The Curators of the University of Missouri
University of Missouri Press, Columbia, Missouri 65201
Printed and bound in the United States of America
All rights reserved
5 4 3 2 1   04 03 02 01 00

Library of Congress Cataloging-in-Publication Data

Other people's mail : an anthology of letter stories / edited with an introduction by
    Gail Pool.
        p.   cm.
    Includes bibliographical references.
    ISBN 0-8262-1246-8 (alk. paper)
    1. Letter writing—Fiction.   2. Epistolary fiction.   I. Pool, Gail, 1946–
PN6071.L48 086 1999
    808.83'1—dc21   99-049609

⊗™ This paper meets the requirements of the
American National Standard for Permanence of Paper
for Printed Library Materials, Z39.48, 1984.

Designer: Stephanie Foley
Typesetter: Bookcomp, Inc.
Printer and Binder: Thomson-Shore, Inc.
Typefaces: Adobe Garamond, Optima, and Poppl Laudatio

FOR JEREMY

CONTENTS

Other People's Mail

Letter writing, both as art and pastime, has steadily declined over the past hundred years. Before our lively involvement with e-mail, it seemed that written correspondence might entirely disappear. Yet in fiction, throughout the era, letters have held their own. Long after we were all on the telephone and long before we were all on the Internet, letter stories thrived. Cast as love letters and Dear John letters, as thank-you notes and suicide notes, as memos, letters to the editor, and exchanges with the IRS, these stories have been published by the hundreds, the work of many of our best-known authors. Clearly, writers have found the letter tale compelling, and they know that readers do as well: Who, after all, is immune to the seduction of reading other people's mail?

My interest in modern letter stories was sparked several years ago by Nadine Gordimer's "Letter from His Father" and Torgny Lindgren's "Water"—each a tour de force—and led me to explore works by writers as disparate as Vladimir Nabokov, Alice Munro, Ralph Ellison, Ring Lardner, Joyce Carol Oates, Mark Helprin, Louis Auchincloss, Doris Lessing, Rosellen Brown, André Maurois, and Paul Bowles. That so many such stories had been written took me by surprise. Like many people, I expect, I had associated epistolary fiction mainly with the past. The very word *epistolary* has an old-fashioned sound. The term does not evoke Alice Walker's *The Color Purple* or Stephanie D. Fletcher's *E-Mail: A Love Story,* though both are certainly composed of letters. Nor does the word readily link to the short story, which is such a modern form. "Epistolary" conjures up Samuel Richardson's vast novels-in-letters, *Pamela* and *Clarissa,* and the letter-fiction vogue they triggered in the eighteenth century, which ended as the nineteenth began. I hadn't realized that this literary mode, which had flourished in a bygone era, had been so widely used in our own.

Its modern use intrigued me. After all, epistolary fiction enjoyed its greatest popularity at a time when letter writing was an art and letters central to daily life. It emerged in an era when letters were becoming increasingly a part of the literary world—as letters to the editor, as epistolary essays and poems; when letter-writers aspired to the eloquence achieved by Lady Mary Wortley Montagu, whose correspondence from Turkey, written between 1716 and 1718, is still reprinted in travel anthologies today; when letters themselves were so important that publishers produced letter-writing manuals—such as the one Richardson himself was compiling when he first saw the novelistic potential of letters and turned his hand to fiction. In the eighteenth century, to cast fiction in letters was a logical choice. That so many writers had done so in more recent decades, when serious letter writing had declined, seemed to require an explanation: why, I wondered, would this mode appeal in modern times.

It is certainly a distinctive style. To start with, it is self-conscious, artistically—typographically—intrusive; it announces its presence, reminding us that we are reading fiction and playing with our suspension of disbelief.

Further, letter stories don't simply invite, they require participation. The salutation, the personal voice, the immediacy are enticing, and the stories engage us on at least two levels: the tale the letter tells and the tale of the letter itself, the larger context. Even in a one-way correspondence, we not only have to read between the lines written by a first-person narrator who is likely to be unreliable, we also have to look to the margins to discern the context that gives the story meaning. In an exchange of letters— a multiplicity of first-person voices—the sense of a narrator altogether disappears, and it is we who have to piece the tale together, gathering the different perspectives into a whole.

And yet, for all their enticement, these stories are distancing as well: the mode is not straightforward, but indirect. The narrator is always addressing someone who isn't us, crafting letters to elicit—to manipulate—*their* response, not, ostensibly, ours; we are only eavesdropping. Within these stories, we observe communication taking place—or failing to occur. These tales aren't simply forms of communication, they are also inherently *about* communication.

As I reflected on this literary style, its contemporary appeal became apparent: with its self-consciousness, its indirection, its audience involvement and its pose, its focus on communication and its capacity to play with viewpoint, the venerable epistolary mode has a decidedly postmodern air. Looking more deeply, I could see how these mechanisms

are effective in framing our modern concerns: the struggle to find meaningful stories, relationships, and lives amidst the social and moral disarray
of the era; the absence of the omniscient viewpoint and the limitations
of the relative perspective—not only in literature but in life; the blurred
boundaries between fact and fiction, artist and audience, private and
public domains. These are the themes of our time, and they are the
themes of the stories in this collection. As these tales make clear, the
letter mode has thrived because there are stories that demand it, stories
that can't be told as well another way.

Because the epistolary style is so distinctive, I decided, in selecting these
tales, to consider only those that were truly epistolary: no stories with
framing narrators were included. Because my focus was on the modern
uses of the form, I decided to consider only stories written after World
War II. And because I wanted to show the versatility of the mode—as well
as to provide interesting reading—I aimed for diversity, seeking a variety
of nationalities, cultures, voices, and themes. These guidelines, of course,
eliminated many stories, however excellent, that made use of letters
but were not in themselves letters. The guidelines also excluded many
epistolary stories, however significant, that fell outside the time frame—
such as Kressmann Taylor's World War II story "Address Unknown,"
which caused a stir when it was published in 1938, or Thomas Bailey
Aldrich's "Marjorie Daw," which was such a success when it appeared in
the *Atlantic* in 1873 that the editors claimed it helped resolve some of
the magazine's financial problems. And my emphasis on diversity led me
to reject many stories, however engaging, that were similar to others that
I preferred—such as André Maurois's "Ariane, My Sister . . . ," which,
with its exchange between first and second wives, too closely resembled
Gail Godwin's "False Lights." My aim was not to produce a history of
the epistolary story: these stories do not represent all that has been done
in the letter tale, but rather demonstrate what the letter tale, at its best,
can do.

Richardson characterized letters as being written "to the *moment*," and
there is no question that a strength of the letter story is its immediacy,
its intrinsic present tense. While the use of the present tense can seem
artificial in many narratives, in epistolary fiction it is appropriate—this
is the tense that letter-writers actually use; and the vivid image it carries,
of someone writing at a particular moment, is underscored by the date
that appears at the top of the page. Moreover, this immediacy seems
strengthened by the fact that the letter-writer is in one sense locked into

that moment: though he or she may write about events past, the future is unknown. As Natascha Würzbach observes in her study *The Novel in Letters* (1969), the epistolary narrator writing to the moment, unlike the autobiographical narrator looking back, does not know how events will turn out; and this fact, in a series of letters, can be used to generate suspense. In Mark Helprin's "Letters from the *Samantha*," for example, the ship's captain contending, morally and physically, with the ape he has taken on board does not know, from letter to letter, how the situation will be resolved. Each letter reads like an installment in a serial, in which the narrator, observing, speculating, but no more prescient than we are, arouses our curiosity and impels us toward the conclusion.

Further intensifying the letter mode's immediacy is the way in which it can directly replicate both the process of communication and the practice of storytelling, each with its failures and limitations. A letter story needn't merely tell us about those failures and limitations: it can embody them. In Virginia Moriconi's "Simple Arithmetic," the strained correspondence between a newly remarried father and his adolescent son—and the conspicuous silence of the mother—together become the broken communications in a broken family. In Stephen Dixon's "Man of Letters," Newt's successive epistolary efforts to break off his relationship with Mary, as they progress from simple statements through sprawling permutations and finally peter out, embody the rise and fall of his intentions. And in Alice Munro's "A Wilderness Station," the contradictory stories revolving around the eccentric Annie Herron, whose husband dies in the Canadian wilderness, leave us with an uncertainty that proves surprisingly satisfying, in part, I think, because it seems so much the point of the story, whose letters mimic so well the vagaries of storytelling and storytellers, and point us so wryly to the epigram from which the story takes its title: "This world is a wilderness, in which we may indeed get our station changed, but the move will be out of one wilderness station unto another."

A tale that uses letters to deal explicitly with the limitations of storytelling while replicating the storytelling process itself is Ghassan Kanafani's "The Death of Bed Number 12." In this story, a young man hospitalized for a stomach ulcer becomes unsettled by the death of a fellow patient. In the first of two letters to a friend, Ahmed, he relates how, following this death, he invented a complete story of the man's life. In the second, he reports that he has since found that only one tiny detail of his entire story proved to be true. "Oh, Ahmed, how imprisoned we are in our bodies and minds!" he laments, as he struggles with the gap between stories and reality, and the limitations of the single viewpoint. And yet, for all this young man's lamentation, we can see by the very form of the story that he is not someone likely to give up storytelling—which is for him a way of giving meanings to lives and life—not even if the meanings prove untrue. His letters themselves have already created a story for his friend.

Perhaps nothing so distinguishes the letter story from the conventional first-person narrative as that "other"—the letter's recipient, the correspondents—who can provide additional voices, viewpoints, or contexts to enhance disclosure, self-disclosure, or comment, without the author apparently intruding.

What makes stories like Donna Kline's "Correspondence," A. A. Milne's "The Rise and Fall of Mortimer Scrivens," and Michael Carson's "Peter's Buddies" so effective is the way that each correspondent has only a piece of the story, while the reader, who has all of the pieces, always knows more than the single character, is always just ahead, and enjoys becoming the omniscient observer. In a story like Gail Godwin's "False Lights," a second correspondent is used as a corrective to the single voice. In this exchange between a young woman and her husband's discarded older wife, the young woman's remarks are outrageous *because* of the person she is addressing. As Godwin has written this, we do not identify with the letter-writer, but neither do we feel she is addressing us. We read the letter through the eyes of the recipient and take satisfaction in the older woman's tart reply, which provides the story with the comment it needs.

Although the storytelling potential of multiple correspondents seems to me so much a virtue of the letter mode, by far the majority of letter stories consist of one-way correspondence, perhaps because authors find it more realistic. Nevertheless, even when the recipient is silent, his or her presence is always implicit, a dimension that can be used to shape the story and our response.

In Ray Russell's hilarious "Evil Star," for example, the real protagonist of the story is not the letter-writer but the person to whom he is writing; much of the story's humor derives from the contrast between the two. In Hubert Aquin's "Back on April Eleventh," the woman addressed never says a word, but she permeates every line of the letter. The narrator has not simply written this suicide note *to* his lover, a woman who has taken a trip abroad and left him feeling obsessed and abandoned; he has crafted the note entirely *for* her. "Someone really has to tell you, my love, that

I tried twice to take my life in the course of this dark winter," he writes. Someone really has to tell you, my love, that you are to blame, his letter so clearly says. The story here doesn't lie with the woman's response, which we never hear, nor with her behavior, which we can't really assess, but with the way in which this man has framed his experience for her and what we sense outside the frame.

Torgny Lindgren uses the letter form's capacity for contrasting contexts to give his unusual story "Water" its conceptual spin. In this tale, an old farmer, receiving a County Council request for information about his "water situation," replies that their questionnaire with only two lines for response is useless—since "water is like the sand on the shores of the sea, its numbers are countless." He proceeds to write them a long discourse about his quest to find water on his dry land and his longing for offspring in a childless marriage, intertwining the two threads into a life story. As we read this tale, it is easy to forget it is a letter. Yet it is the letter format that gives the story its ironic humor: juxtaposing the anonymous government request for information with the personal story it elicits, the literal question with the metaphorical response.

Few letter stories, it seems to me, handle the epistolary interplay among narrator, recipient, and audience more deftly than Nadine Gordimer's "Letter from His Father," which draws its resonance and humor from its relation both to Franz Kafka's famous "Letter to His Father" and to Franz Kafka himself. At one level, this is—like so many letter stories—a self-revelatory portrait. As Hermann Kafka responds—from the grave— to his son's charges, he exhibits the very behavior of which he is accused: imperiousness, condemnatory anger, spiteful laughter, self-pity, an ability to craft insults that induce feelings of worthlessness and guilt. But as Hermann attacks his son and his work, rails against the fame, adulation, and exposure, he also invites us to consider what it would be like to be the father of Franz Kafka, with your whole life laid bare for public display, and to have Franz Kafka as a child—a pale, melancholy boy, picking at his food; a young man writing about turning into a bug ("Your longing, Franz: ugh, for monsters, for perversion."). The effect is both arresting and funny: arresting because the perspective offers an unexpected glimpse of reality, funny because the perspective is, from our viewpoint, so inappropriate. If Lindgren's farmer is writing a personal response to a government form, Hermann is writing a personal response to a letter that is now literature and entirely public, "translated," as Hermann says, "into everything—I don't know what—Hottentot and

Icelandic, Chinese." Gordimer's story, like Lindgren's, turns upon the incongruence between the initial letter and the reply.

The authenticity and intimacy that give the first-person voice credibility are enhanced in the letter story, which identifies itself as genuine rather than fictive and addresses specific individuals rather than the world at large. In Julio Cortázar's "Letter to a Young Lady in Paris," the narrator's compellingly personal voice framed by the "realistic" letter addressed to a friend persuades us to go along with his wild, incredible story; disarmed, we are unable either to assess his strange tale or dismiss it. In Reginald McKnight's "Quitting Smoking," the narrator's lengthy, talky letter, with its nongrammatical colloquialisms, is so carefully crafted to seem artless that we feel we aren't reading a story but the real thing.

Doris Lessing plays deftly with the letter story's authentic voice in "A Letter from Home." Her narrator, an Afrikaaner university teacher and poet in southern Africa, sounds extremely personal and real as he writes to a former colleague. Yet what is strikingly real about this tale is literally its sound; we feel that we can hear the narrator talking to his friend. Lessing has achieved this effect by strewing colloquial phrases, such as "Ja," "Goed," and "Right," throughout. Upon reflection we may realize that we do not generally write such phrases in our letters, we only speak them. But that is only upon reflection. Within the story, if Lessing has taken the fictional letter further from the "real" letter, she has made it seem closer by creating, through voice, an intensely real effect.

Because the letter story always tells about telling, because it is never itself straightforward, it is well suited for telling stories that themselves cannot be told "straight"; stories, for example, of survival, of bearing witness to an experience that cannot really be grasped by those who have not endured it. In Tadeusz Borowski's "Auschwitz, Our Home (A Letter)," a series of letters written by an inmate of the concentration camp to his lover, also imprisoned, the narrator remarks on the need to bear witness. "Look carefully at everything around you," he writes, "and conserve your strength. For a day may come when it will be up to us to give an account of the fraud and mockery to the living—to speak up for the dead." But he comments as well on the difficulty of bearing witness to an experience that has so separated him from "civilians." "Today," he writes, "having become totally familiar with the inexplicable and the abnormal; having learned to live on intimate terms with the crematoria, the itch and the tuberculosis; having understood the true meaning of wind, rain and sun, of bread and turnip soup, of work to survive, of slavery and power; having, so to say, daily broken bread with the beast—I look at these civilians with a certain indulgence, the way a scientist regards a layman, or the initiated an outsider."

By casting his story in the form of letters, Borowski, a Pole who was a concentration camp survivor, can have his narrator write to the insider, his lover, while he himself addresses outsiders, us. The letters are at once a way for the writer within the camp to keep the memory of the past alive—the memory of his lover, of love itself, of himself as he was; and also a way for Borowski to keep a record of the camp experience alive, a memory preserved for the future. The story on different levels becomes a document of survival.

From Munro's story about what cannot really be known to Borowski's about what cannot really be said, the stories in this collection reflect the ways in which we frame our experience for others as they comment on those ways. It is this element of comment, implicit in the fictional letter, that distinguishes it from its "real" counterpart—no matter how eloquent or "literary"—and suggests the distance the letter story has traveled from its origins. No longer artifact, the letter story is an art form whose bonds to the actual letter began to weaken the moment it became "story"; each form has gone its own way. This is why even when few of us write letters or receive them, epistolary stories can survive; why even when letter writing has become old-fashioned, these tales can stay modern in their style and their concerns; why even when our actual letters have become largely formalistic, epistolary stories can be vital and necessary fiction. It is also why the letters in a story might be cast as telegrams, memos, or e-mail, without altering the basic nature of this fictional mode. These stories, after all, are not about the letters we write; they are not simply about the way in which we write letters. They are about correspondence in the very broadest sense: the ways in which we pose and position ourselves; the modes we use to share, persuade, confess, deceive, and lay blame; the strategies by which we explain and defend our lives. Beyond their artful format, these tales are stories about the stories we contrive as we struggle to comprehend, to present, to master, as best we can, ourselves, others, and the world.

Alice Munro published her first short-story collection in 1968, and apart from a single novel—*Lives of Girls and Women* (1971)—she has since devoted herself to short fiction. It may be that in English Canada, it is possible for a writer "to write nothing but short stories and be considered major," as Margaret Atwood once observed, citing Munro. But in the United States, this is seldom the case. Yet Munro has achieved a comparable literary stature here, winning acclaim, awards, and an increasingly large audience.

In "A Wilderness Station," we find many of the elements characteristic of Munro's stories: a rural Canadian landscape and small-town settings; a female protagonist; a fractured narrative digressively circling its subject; a conclusion at once unexpected and precisely right. Munro's narrative technique and worldview lend themselves extremely well to the epistolary form, and though "A Wilderness Station" is the only letter story in her collection *Open Secrets* (1994), letters figure in other stories in the volume. All these tales reflect the ways in which correspondence simultaneously reveals and conceals, and they suggest the gap between what is said and what is known. Munro has said of her work, "I want the stories to keep diminishing but not to be suddenly over with, so one is left with the central mystery of the story." In "A Wilderness Station," she leaves us with the mystery of storytelling itself.

A WILDERNESS STATION

I

Miss Margaret Cresswell, Matron, House of Industry, Toronto, to Mr. Simon Herron, North Huron, January 15, 1852.

Since your letter is accompanied by an endorsement from your minister, I am happy to reply. Requests of your sort are made to us frequently, but unless we have such an endorsement we cannot trust that they are made in good faith.

We do not have any girl at the Home who is of marriageable age, since we send our girls out to make a living usually around the age of fourteen or fifteen, but we do keep track of them for some years or usually until they are married. In cases such as yours we sometimes recommend one of these girls and will arrange a meeting, and then of course it is up to the two parties involved to see if they are suited.

There are two girls eighteen years of age that we are still in touch with. Both are apprenticed to a milliner and are good seamstresses, but a marriage to a likely man would probably be preferred to a lifetime of such work. Further than that cannot be said, it must be left to the girl herself and of course to your liking for her, or the opposite.

The two girls are a Miss Sadie Johnstone and a Miss Annie McKillop. Both were born legitimately of Christian parents and were placed in the Home due to parental deaths. Drunkenness or immorality was not a factor. In Miss Johnstone's case there is however the factor of consumption, and though she is the prettier of the two and a plump rosy girl, I feel I must warn you that perhaps she is not suited to the hard work of a life in the bush. The other girl, Miss McKillop, is of a more durable constitution though of leaner frame and not so good a complexion. She has a waywardness about one eye but it does not interfere with her vision and her sewing is excellent. The darkness of her eyes and hair and brown tinge of her skin is no indication of mixed blood, as both parents were from Fife. She is a hardy girl and I think would be suited to such a life as you can offer, being also free from the silly timidity we often see in

11

girls of her age. I will speak to her and acquaint her with the idea and will await your letter as to when you propose to meet her.

II

Carstairs *Argus,* Fiftieth Anniversary Edition, February 3, 1907. Recollections of Mr. George Herron.

On the first day of September, 1851, my brother Simon and I got a box of bedclothes and household utensils together and put them in a wagon with a horse to pull it, and set out from Halton County to try our fortunes in the wilds of Huron and Bruce, as wilds they were then thought to be. The goods were from Archie Frame that Simon worked for, and counted as part of his wages. Likewise we had to rent the house off him, and his boy that was about my age came along to take it and the wagon back.

It ought to be said in the beginning that my brother and I were left alone, our father first and then our mother dying of fever within five weeks of landing in this country, when I was three years old and Simon eight. Simon was put to work for Archie Frame that was our mother's cousin, and I was taken on by the schoolteacher and wife that had no child of their own. This was in Halton, and I would have been content to go on living there but Simon being only a few miles away continued to visit and say that as soon as we were old enough we would go and take up land and be on our own, not working for others, as this was what our father had intended. Archie Frame never sent Simon to school as I was sent, so Simon was always bound to get away. When I had come to be fourteen years of age and a husky lad, as was my brother, he said we should go and take up Crown Land north of the Huron Tract.

We only got as far as Preston on the first day as the roads were rough and bad across Nassageweya and Puslinch. Next day we got to Shakespeare and the third afternoon to Stratford. The roads were always getting worse as we came west, so we thought best to get our box sent on to Clinton by the stage. But the stage had quit running due to rains, and they were waiting till the roads froze up, so we told Archie Frame's boy to turn about and return with horse and cart and goods back to Halton. Then we took our axes on our shoulders, and walked to Carstairs.

Hardly a soul was there before us. Carstairs was just under way, with a rough building that was store and inn combined, and there was a German named Roem building a sawmill. One man who got there before us and already had a fair-sized cabin built was Henry Treece, who afterwards became my father-in-law.

We got ourselves boarded at the inn where we slept on the bare floor with one blanket or quilt between us. Winter was coming early with cold rains and everything damp, but we were expecting hardship or at least Simon was. I came from a softer place. He said we must put up with it so I did.

We began to underbrush a road to our piece of land and then we got it marked out and cut the logs for our shanty and big scoops to roof it. We were able to borrow an ox from Henry Treece to draw the logs. But Simon was not of a mind to borrow or depend on anybody. He was minded to try raising the shanty ourselves, but when we saw we could not do it I made my way to Treeces' place and with Henry and two of his sons and a fellow from the mill it was accomplished. We started next day to fill up the cracks between the logs with mud and we got some hemlock branches so we would not be out money anymore for staying at the inn but could sleep in our own place. We had a big slab of elm for the door. My brother had heard from some French-Canadian fellows that were at Archie Frame's that in the lumber camps the fire was always in the middle of the shanty. So he said that was the way we should have ours, and we got four posts and were building the chimney on them, house-fashion, intending to plaster it with mud inside and out. We went to our hemlock bed with a good fire going, but waking in the middle of the night we saw our lumber was all ablaze and the scoops burning away briskly also. We tore down the chimney and the scoops being green basswood were not hard to put out. As soon as it came day, we started to build the chimney in the ordinary way in the end of the house and I thought it best not to make any remark.

After the small trees and brush was cleared out a bit, we set to chopping down the big trees. We cut down a big ash and split it into slabs for our floor. Still our box had not come which was to be shipped from Halton so Henry Treece sent us a very large and comfortable bearskin for our cover in bed but my brother would not take the favour and sent it back saying no need. Then after several weeks we got our box and had to ask for the ox to bring it on from Clinton, but my brother said that is the last we will need to ask of any person's help.

We walked to Walley and brought back flour and salt fish on our back. A man rowed us across the river at Manchester for a steep price. There were no bridges then and all that winter not a good enough freeze to make it easy going over the rivers.

Around Christmastime my brother said to me that he thought we had the place in good enough shape now for him to be bringing in a wife, so we should have somebody to cook and do for us and milk a cow when we could afford one. This was the first I had heard of any wife and I said that I did not know he was acquainted with anybody. He said he was not but he had heard that you could write to the Orphanage Home and ask if they had a girl there that was willing to think about the prospect and that they would recommend, and if so he would go and see her. He wanted one between eighteen and twenty-two years of age, healthy and not afraid of work and raised in the Orphanage, not taken in lately, so that she would not be expecting any luxuries or to be waited on and would not be recalling about when things were easier for her. I do not doubt that to those hearing about this nowadays it seems a strange way to go about things. It was not that my brother could not have gone courting and got a wife on his own, because he was a good-looking fellow, but he did not have the time or the money or inclination, his mind was all occupied with establishing our holding. And if a girl had parents they would probably not want her to go far away where there was little in comforts and so much work.

That it was a respectable way of doing things is shown by the fact that the minister Mr. McBain, who was lately come into the district, helped Simon to write the letter and sent word on his own to vouch for him.

So a letter came back that there was a girl that might fit the bill and Simon went off to Toronto and got her. Her name was Annie but her maiden name I had forgotten. They had to ford the streams in Hullet and trudge through deep soft snow after leaving the stage in Clinton, and when they got back she was worn out and very surprised at what she saw, since she said she had never imagined so much bush. She had in her box some sheets and pots and dishes that ladies had given her and that made the place more comfortable.

Early in April my brother and I went out to chop down some trees in the bush at the farthest corner of our property. While Simon was away to get married, I had done some chopping in the other direction towards Treeces', but Simon wanted to get all our boundaries cut clear around and not to go on chopping where I had been. The day started out mild and there was still a lot of soft snow in the bush. We were chopping down a tree where Simon wanted, and in some way, I cannot say how, a branch of it came crashing down where we didn't expect. We just heard the little branches cracking where it fell and looked up to see it and it hit Simon on the head and killed him instantly.

I had to drag his body back then to the shanty through the snow. He was a tall fellow though not fleshy, and it was an awkward task and greatly wearying. It had got colder by this time and when I got to the clearing I saw snow on the wind like the start of a storm. Our footsteps were filled in that we had made earlier. Simon was all covered with snow that did not melt on him by this time, and his wife coming to the door was greatly puzzled, thinking that I was dragging along a log.

In the shanty Annie washed him off and we sat still a while not knowing what we should do. The preacher was at the inn as there was no church or house for him yet and the inn was only about four miles away, but the storm had come up very fierce so you could not even see the trees at the edge of the clearing. It had the look of a storm that would last two or three days, the wind being from the northwest. We knew we could not keep the body in the shanty and we could not set it out in the snow fearing the bobcats would get at it, so we had to set to work and bury him. The ground was not frozen under the snow, so I dug out a grave near the shanty and Annie sewed him in a sheet and we laid him in his grave, not staying long in the wind but saying the Lord's Prayer and reading one Psalm out of the Bible. I am not sure which one but I remember it was near the end of the Book of Psalms and it was very short.

This was the third day of April, 1852.

That was our last snow of the year, and later the minister came and said the service and I put up a wooden marker. Later on we got our plot in the cemetery and put his stone there, but he is not under it as it is a foolish useless thing in my opinion to cart a man's bones from one place to another when it is only bones and his soul has gone on to Judgment.

I was left to chop and clear by myself and soon I began to work side by side with the Treeces, who treated me with the greatest kindness. We worked all together on my land or their land, not minding if it was the one or the other. I started to take my meals and even to sleep at their place and got to know their daughter Jenny who was about of my age, and we made our plans to marry, which we did in due course. Our life together was a long one with many hardships but we were fortunate in the end and raised eight children. I have seen my sons take over my wife's father's land as well as my own since my two brothers-in-law went away and did well for themselves in the West.

My brother's wife did not continue in this place but went her own way to Walley.

Now there are gravel roads running north, south, east, and west and a railway not a half mile from my farm. Except for woodlots, the bush is a thing of the past and I often think of the trees I have cut down and if I had them to cut down today I would be a wealthy man.

The Reverend Walter McBain, Minister of the Free Presbyterian Church of North Huron, to Mr. James Mullen, Clerk of the Peace, Walley, United Counties of Huron and Bruce, September 10, 1852.

I write to inform you, sir, of the probable arrival in your town of a young woman of this district, by the name of Annie Herron, a widow and one of my congregation. This young person has left her home here in the vicinity of Carstairs in Holloway Township, I believe she intends to walk to Walley. She may appear at the Gaol there seeking to be admitted, so I think it my duty to tell you who and what she is and her history here since I have known her.

I came to this area in November of last year, being the first minister of any kind to venture. My parish is as yet mostly bush, and there is nowhere for me to lodge but at the Carstairs Inn. I was born in the west of Scotland and came to this country under the auspices of the Glasgow Mission. After applying to know God's will, I was directed by Him to go to preach wherever was most need of a minister. I tell you this so you may know what sort I am that bring you my account and my view of the affairs of this woman.

She came into the country late last winter as the bride of the young man Simon Herron. He had written on my advice to the House of Industry in Toronto that they might recommend to him a Christian, preferably Presbyterian, female suitable to his needs, and she was the one recommended. He married her straightaway and brought her here to the shanty he had built with his brother. These two young lads had come into the country to clear themselves a piece of land and get possession of it, being themselves orphans and without expectations. They were about this work one day at the end of winter when an accident befell. A branch was loosed while chopping down a tree and fell upon the elder brother so as to cause instant death. The younger lad succeeded in getting the body back to the shanty and since they were held prisoner by a heavy snowstorm they conducted their own funeral and burial.

The Lord is strict in his mercies and we are bound to receive his blows as signs of his care and goodness for so they will prove to be.

Deprived of his brother's help, the lad found a place in a neighbouring family, also members in good standing of my congregation, who have accepted him as a son, though he still works for title to his own land. This family would have taken in the young widow as well, but she would have nothing to do with their offer and seemed to develop an aversion to everyone who would help her. Particularly she seemed so towards her brother-in-law, who said that he had never had the least quarrel with her, and towards myself. When I talked to her, she would not give any answer or sign that her soul was coming into submission. It is a fault of mine that I am not well-equipped to talk to women. I have not the ease to win their trust. Their stubbornness is of another kind than a man's.

I meant only to say that I did not have any good effect on her. She stopped appearing at services, and the deterioration of her property showed the state of her mind and spirit. She would not plant peas and potatoes though they were given to her to grow among the stumps. She did not chop down the wild vines around her door. Most often she did not light a fire so she could have oat-cake or porridge. Her brother-in-law being removed, there was no order imposed on her days. When I visited her the door was open and it was evident that animals came and went in her house. If she was there she hid herself, to mock me. Those who caught sight of her said that her clothing was filthy and torn from scrambling about in the bushes, and she was scratched by thorns and bitten by the mosquito insects and let her hair go uncombed or plaited. I believe she lived on salt fish and bannock that the neighbours or her brother-in-law left for her.

Then while I was still puzzling how I might find a way to protect her body through the winter and deal with the more important danger to her soul, there comes word she is gone. She left the door open and went away without cloak or bonnet and wrote on the shanty floor with a burnt stick the two words: "Walley, Gaol." I take this to mean she intends to go there and turn herself in. Her brother-in-law thinks it would be no use for him to go after her because of her unfriendly attitude to himself, and I cannot set out because of a deathbed I am attending. I ask you therefore to let me know if she has arrived and in what state and how you will deal with her. I consider her still as a soul in my charge, and I will try to visit her before winter if you keep her there. She is a child of the Free Church and the Covenant and as such she is entitled to a minister of her own faith and you must not think it sufficient that some priest of the Church of England or Baptist or Methodist be sent to her.

In case she should not come to the Gaol but wander in the streets, I ought to tell you that she is dark-haired and tall, meagre in body, not comely but not ill-favoured except having one eye that goes to the side.

Mr. James Mullen, Clerk of the Peace, Walley, to the Reverend Walter McBain, Carstairs, North Huron, September 30, 1852.

Your letter to me arrived most timely and appreciated, concerning the young woman Annie Herron. She completed her journey to Walley unharmed and with no serious damage though she was weak and hungry when she presented herself at the Gaol. On its being inquired what she did there, she said that she came to confess to a murder, and to be locked up. There was consultation round and about, I was sent for, and it being near to midnight, I agreed that she should spend the night in a cell. The next day I visited her and got all particulars I could.

Her story of being brought up in the Orphanage, her apprenticeship to a milliner, her marriage, and her coming to North Huron, all accords pretty well with what you have told me. Events in her account begin to differ only with her husband's death. In that matter what she says is this:

On the day in early April when her husband and his brother went out to chop trees, she was told to provide them with food for their midday meal, and since she had not got it ready when they wanted to leave, she agreed to take it to them in the woods. Consequently she baked up some oat-cakes and took some salt fish and followed their tracks and found them at work some distance away. But when her husband unwrapped his food he was very offended, because she had wrapped it in a way that the salty oil from the fish had soaked into the cakes, and they were all crumbled and unpleasant to eat. In his disappointment he became enraged and promised her a beating when he was more at leisure to do it. He then turned his back on her, being seated on a log, and she picked up a rock and threw it at him, hitting him on the head so that he fell down unconscious and in fact dead. She and his brother then carried and dragged the body back to the house. By that time a blizzard had come up and they were imprisoned within. The brother said that they should not reveal the truth as she had not intended murder, and she agreed. They then buried him—her story agreeing again with yours—and that might have been the end of it, but she became more and more troubled, convinced that she had surely been intending to kill him. If she had not killed him, she says, it would only have meant a worse beating, and why should she have risked that? So she decided at last upon confession and as if to prove something handed me a lock of hair stiffened with blood.

This is her tale, and I do not believe it for a minute. No rock that this girl could pick up, combined with the force that she could summon to throw it, would serve to kill a man. I questioned her about this, and she changed her story, saying that it was a large rock that she had picked up in both hands and that she had not thrown it but smashed it down on his head from behind. I said why did not the brother prevent you, and she said, he was looking the other way. Then I said there must indeed be a bloodied rock lying somewhere in the wood, and she said she had washed it off with the snow. (In fact it is not likely a rock would come to hand so easily, with all such depth of snow about.) I asked her to roll up her sleeve that I might judge of the muscles in her arms, to do such a job, and she said that she had been a huskier woman some months since.

I conclude that she is lying, or self-deluded. But I see nothing for it at the moment but to admit her to the Gaol. I asked her what she thought would happen to her now, and she said, well, you will try me and then you will hang me. But you do not hang people in the winter, she said, so I can stay here till spring. And if you let me work here, maybe you will want me to go on working and you will not want me hanged. I do not know where she got this idea about people not being hanged in the winter. I am in perplexity about her. As you may know, we have a very fine new Gaol here where the inmates are kept warm and dry and are decently fed and treated with all humanity, and there has been a complaint that some are not sorry—and at this time of year, even happy—to get into it. But it is obvious that she cannot wander about much longer, and from your account she is unwilling to stay with friends and unable to make a tolerable home for herself. The Gaol at present serves as a place of detention for the Insane as well as criminals, and if she is charged with Insanity, I could keep her here for the winter perhaps with removal to Toronto in the spring. I have engaged for a doctor to visit her. I spoke to her of your letter and your hope of coming to see her, but I found her not at all agreeable to that. She asks that nobody be allowed to see her excepting a Miss Sadie Johnstone, who is not in this part of the country.

I am enclosing a letter I have written to her brother-in-law for you to pass on to him, so that he may know what she has said and tell me what he thinks about it. I thank you in advance for conveying the letter to him, also for the trouble you have been to, in informing me as fully as you have done. I am a member of the Church of England, but have a high regard for the work of other Protestant denominations in bringing an orderly life to this part of the world we find ourselves in. You may believe that I will do what is in my power to do, to put you in a position to deal with the soul of this young woman, but it might be better to wait until she is in favour of it.

The Reverend Walter McBain to Mr. James Mullen, November 18, 1852.

I carried your letter at once to Mr. George Herron and believe that he has replied and given you his recollection of events. He was amazed at his sister-in-law's claim, since she had never said anything of this to him or to anybody else. He says that it is all her invention or fancy, since she was never in the woods when it happened and there was no need for her to be, as they had carried their food with them when they left the house. He says that there had been at another time some reproof from his brother to her, over the spoiling of some cakes by their proximity to fish, but it did not happen at this time. Nor were there any rocks about to do such a deed on impulse if she had been there and wished to do it.

My delay in answering your letter, for which I beg pardon, is due to a bout of ill health. I had an attack of the gravel and a rheumatism of the stomach worse than any misery that ever fell upon me before. I am somewhat improved at present and will be able to go about as usual by next week if all continues to mend.

As to the question of the young woman's sanity, I do not know what your Doctor will say but I have thought on this and questioned the Divinity and my belief is this. It may well be that so early in the marriage her submission to her husband was not complete and there would be carelessness about his comfort, and naughty words, and quarrelsome behaviour, as well as the hurtful sulks and silences her sex is prone to. His death occurring before any of this was put right, she would feel a natural and harrowing remorse, and this must have taken hold of her mind so strongly that she made herself out to be actually responsible for his death. In this way, I think many folk are driven mad. Madness is at first taken on by some as a kind of play, for which shallowness and audacity they are punished later on, by finding out that it is play no longer, and the Devil has blocked off every escape.

It is still my hope to speak to her and make her understand this. I am under difficulties at present not only of my wretched corpus but of being lodged in a foul and noisy place obliged to hear day and night such

uproars as destroy sleep and study and intrude even on my prayers. The
wind blows bitterly through the logs, but if I go down to the fire there is
swilling of spirits and foulest insolence. And outside nothing but trees to
choke off every exit and icy bog to swallow man and horse. There was a
promise to build a church and lodging but those who made such promise
have grown busy with their own affairs and it seems to have been put
off. I have not however left off preaching even in my illness and in such
barns and houses as are provided. I take heart remembering a great man,
the great preacher and interpreter of God's will, Thomas Boston, who in
the latter days of his infirmity preached the grandeur of God from his
chamber window to a crowd of two thousand or so assembled in the yard
below. So I mean to preach to the end though my congregation will be
smaller.

Whatsoever crook there is in one's lot, it is of God's making. Thomas
Boston.

*This world is a wilderness, in which we may indeed get our station changed,
but the move will be out of one wilderness station unto another.* Ibid.

Mr. James Mullen to the Reverend Walter McBain, January 17, 1853.

I write to you that our young woman's health seems sturdy, and she
no longer looks such a scarecrow, eating well and keeping herself clean
and tidy. Also she seems quieter in her spirits. She has taken to mending
the linen in the prison which she does well. But I must tell you that she
is firm as ever against a visit, and I cannot advise you to come here as
I think your trouble might be for nothing. The journey is very hard in
winter and it would do no good to your state of health.

Her brother-in-law has written me a very decent letter affirming that
there is no truth to her story, so I am satisfied on that.

You may be interested in hearing what the doctor who visited her had
to say about her case. His belief is that she is subject to a sort of delusion
peculiar to females, for which the motive is a desire for self-importance,
also a wish to escape the monotony of life or the drudgery they may
have been born to. They may imagine themselves possessed by the forces
of evil, to have committed various and hideous crimes, and so forth.
Sometimes they may report that they have taken numerous lovers, but
these lovers will be all imaginary and the woman who thinks herself a
prodigy of vice will in fact be quite chaste and untouched. For all this
he—the doctor—lays the blame on the sort of reading that is available to
these females, whether it is of ghosts or demons or of love escapades with

Lords and Dukes and suchlike. For many, these tales are a passing taste given up when life's real duties intervene. For others they are indulged in now and then, as if they were sweets or sherry wine, but for some there is complete surrender and living within them just as in an opium-dream. He could not get an account of her reading from the young woman, but he believes she may by now have forgotten what she has read, or conceals the matter out of slyness.

With his questioning there did come to light something further that we did not know. On his saying to her, did she not fear hanging? she replied, no, for there is a reason you will not hang me. You mean that they will judge that you are mad? said he, and she said, oh, perhaps that, but is it not true also that they will never hang a woman that is with child? The doctor then examined her to find out if this were true, and she agreed to the examination, so she must have made the claim in good faith. He discovered however that she had deceived herself. The signs she took were simply the results of her going so long underfed and in such a reduced state, and later probably of her hysteria. He told her of his findings, but it is hard to say whether she believes him.

It must be acknowledged that this is truly a hard country for women. Another insane female has been admitted here recently, and her case is more pitiful for she has been driven insane by a rape. Her two attackers have been taken in and are in fact just over the wall from her in the men's section. The screams of the victim resound sometimes for hours at a stretch, and as a result the prison has become a much less pleasant shelter. But whether that will persuade our self-styled murderess to recant and take herself off, I have no idea. She is a good needlewoman and could get employment if she chose.

I am sorry to hear of your bad health and miserable lodgings. The town has grown so civilized that we forget the hardship of the hinterlands. Those like yourself who choose to endure it deserve our admiration. But you must allow me to say that it seems pretty certain that a man not in robust health will be unable to bear up for long in your situation. Surely your Church would not consider it a defection were you to choose to serve it longer by removing to a more comfortable place.

I enclose a letter written by the young woman and sent to a Miss Sadie Johnstone, on King Street, Toronto. It was intercepted by us that we might know more of the state of her mind, but resealed and sent on. But it has come back marked "Unknown." We have not told the writer of this in hopes that she will write again and more fully, revealing to us something to help us decide whether or not she is a conscious liar.

Mrs. Annie Herron, Walley Gaol, United Counties of Huron and Bruce, to Miss Sadie Johnstone, 49 King Street, Toronto, December 20, 1852.

Sadie, I am in here pretty well and safe and nothing to complain of either in food or blankets. It is a good stone building and something like the Home. If you could come and see me I would be very glad. I often talk to you a whole lot in my head, which I don't want to write because what if they are spies. I do the sewing here, the things was not in good repare when I came but now they are pretty good. And I am making curtains for the Opera House, a job that was sent in. I hope to see you. You could come on the stage right to this place. Maybe you would not like to come in the winter but in the springtime you would like to come.

Mr. James Mullen to the Reverend Walter McBain, April 7, 1853.

Not having had any reply to my last letter, I trust you are well and might still be interested in the case of Annie Herron. She is still here and busies herself at sewing jobs which I have undertaken to get her from outside. No more is said of being with child, or of hanging, or of her story. She has written once again to Sadie Johnstone but quite briefly and I enclose her letter here. Do you have an idea who this person Sadie Johnstone might be?

I don't get any answer from you, Sadie, I don't think they sent on my letter. Today is the First of April, 1853. But not April Fool like we used to fool each other. Please come and see me if you can. I am in Walley Gaol but safe and well.

Mr. James Mullen from Edward Hoy, Landlord, Carstairs Inn, April 19, 1853.

Your letter to Mr. McBain sent back to you, he died here at the inn February 25. There is some books here, nobody wants them.

III

Annie Herron, Walley Gaol, to Sadie Johnstone, Toronto. Finder Please Post.

George came dragging him across the snow I thought it was a log he dragged. I didn't know it was him. George said, it's him. A branch fell out of a tree and hit him, he said. He didn't say he was dead. I looked for him to speak. His mouth was part way open with snow in it. Also his eyes part way open. We had to get inside because it was starting to storm like anything. We dragged him in by the one leg each. I pretended to myself when I took hold of his leg that it was still the log. Inside where I had the fire going it was warm and the snow started melting off him. His blood thawed and ran a little around his ear. I didn't know what to do and I was afraid to go near him. I thought his eyes were watching me.

George sat by the fire with his big heavy coat on and his boots on. He was turned away. I sat at the table, which was of half-cut logs. I said, how do you know if he is dead? George said, touch him if you want to know. But I would not. Outside there was terrible storming, the wind in the trees and over top of our roof. I said, Our Father who art in Heaven, and that was how I got my courage. I kept saying it every time I moved. I have to wash him off, I said. Help me. I got the bucket where I kept the snow melting. I started on his feet and had to pull his boots off, a heavy job. George never turned around or paid attention or helped me when I asked. I didn't take the trousers or coat off of him, I couldn't manage. But I washed his hands and wrists. I always kept the rag between my hand and his skin. The blood and wet where the snow had melted off him was on the floor under his head and shoulders so I wanted to turn him over and clean it up. But I couldn't do it. So I went and pulled George by his arm. Help me, I said. What? he said. I said we had to turn him. So he came and helped me and we got him turned over, he was laying face down. And then I saw, I saw where the axe had cut.

Neither one of us said anything. I washed it out, blood and what else. I said to George, go and get me the sheet from my box. There was the good sheet I wouldn't put on the bed. I didn't see the use of trying to take off his clothes though they were good cloth. We would have had to cut them away where the blood was stuck and then what would we have but the rags. I cut off the one little piece of his hair because I remembered when Lila died in the Home they did that. Then I got George to help me roll him on to the sheet and I started to sew him up in the sheet. While I was sewing I said to George, go out in the lee of the house where the wood is piled and maybe you can get in enough shelter there to dig him a grave. Take the wood away and the ground is likely softer underneath.

I had to crouch down at the sewing so I was nearly laying on the floor beside him. I sewed his head in first folding the sheet over it because I had to look in his eyes and mouth. George went out and I could hear through the storm that he was doing what I said and pieces of wood were thrown up sometimes hitting the wall of the house. I sewed on, and every bit of him I lost sight of I would say even out loud, there goes, there goes. I had got the fold neat over his head but down at the feet I didn't have material enough to cover him, so I sewed on my eyelet petticoat I made at the Home to learn the stitch and that way I got him all sewed in.

I went out to help George. He had got all the wood out of the way and was at the digging. The ground was soft enough, like I had thought. He had the spade so I got the broad shovel and we worked away, him digging and loosening and me shovelling.

Then we moved him out. We could not do it now one leg each so George got him at the head and me at the ankles where the petticoat was and we rolled him into the earth and set to work again to cover him up. George had the shovel and it seemed I could not get enough dirt onto the spade so I pushed it in with my hands and kicked it in with my feet any way at all. When it was all back in, George beat it down flat with the shovel as much as he could. Then we moved all the wood back searching where it was in the snow and we piled it up in the right way so it did not look as if anybody had been at it. I think we had no hats on or scarves but the work kept us warm.

We took in more wood for the fire and put the bar across the door. I wiped up the floor and I said to George, take off your boots. Then, take off your coat. George did what I told him. He sat by the fire. I made the kind of tea from catnip leaves that Mrs. Treece showed me how to make and I put a piece of sugar in it. George did not want it. Is it too hot, I said. I let it cool off but then he didn't want it either. So I began, and talked to him.

You didn't mean to do it.

It was in anger, you didn't mean what you were doing.

I saw him other times what he would do to you. I saw he would knock you down for a little thing and you just get up and never say a word. The same way he did to me.

If you had not have done it, some day he would have done it to you.

Listen, George. Listen to me.

If you own up what do you think will happen? They will hang you. You will be dead, you will be no good to anybody. What will become of your land? Likely it will all go back to the Crown and somebody else will get it and all the work you have done will be for them.

What will become of me here if you are took away?

I got some oat-cakes that were cold and I warmed them up. I set one on his knee. He took it and bit it and chewed it but he could not get it down and he spit it on to the fire.

I said, listen. I know things. I am older than you are. I am religious too, I pray to God every night and my prayers are answered. I know what God wants as well as any preacher knows and I know that he does not want a good lad like you to be hanged. All you have to do is say you are sorry. Say you are sorry and mean it well and God will forgive you. I will say the same thing, I am sorry too because when I saw he was dead I did not wish, not one minute, for him to be alive. I will say, God forgive me, and you do the same. Kneel down.

But he would not. He would not move out of his chair. And I said, all right. I have an idea. I am going to get the Bible. I asked him, do you believe in the Bible? Say you do. Nod your head.

I did not see whether he nodded or not but I said, there. There you did. Now. I am going to do what we all used to do in the Home when we wanted to know what would happen to us or what we should do in our life. We would open the Bible any place and poke our finger at a page and then open our eyes and read the verse where our finger was and that would tell you what you needed to know. To make double sure of it just say when you close your eyes, God guide my finger.

He would not raise a hand from his knee, so I said, all right. All right, I'll do it for you. I did it, and I read where my finger stopped. I held the Bible close in to the fire so I could see.

It was something about being old and gray-headed, *oh God forsake me not,* and I said, what that means is that you are supposed to live till you are old and gray-headed and nothing is supposed to happen to you before that. It says so, in the Bible.

Then the next verse was so-and-so went and took so-and-so and conceived and bore him a son.

It says you will have a son, I said. You have to live and get older and get married and have a son.

But the next verse I remember so well I can put down all of it. *Neither can they prove the things of which they now accuse me.*

George, I said, do you hear that? *Neither can they prove the things of which they now accuse me.* That means that you are safe.

You are safe. Get up now. Get up and go and lay on the bed and go to sleep.

He could not do that by himself but I did it. I pulled on him and pulled on him until he was standing up and then I got him across the room to the bed which was not his bed in the corner but the bigger bed, and got him to sit on it then lay down. I rolled him over and back and got his clothes off down to his shirt. His teeth were chattering and I was afraid of a chill or the fever. I heated up the flat-irons and wrapped them in cloth and laid them down one on each side of him close to his skin. There was not whisky or brandy in the house to use, only the catnip tea. I put more sugar in it and got him to take it from a spoon. I rubbed his feet with my hands, then his arms and his legs, and I wrung out clothes in hot water which I laid over his stomach and his heart. I talked to him then in a different way quite soft and told him to go to sleep and when he woke up his mind would be clear and all his horrors would be wiped away.

A tree branch fell on him. It was just what you told me. I can see it falling. I can see it coming down so fast like a streak and little branches and crackling all along the way, it hardly takes longer than a gun going off and you say, what is that? and it has hit him and he is dead.

When I got him to sleep I laid down on the bed beside him. I took off my smock and I could see the black and blue marks on my arms. I pulled up my skirt to see if they were still there high on my legs, and they were. The back of my hand was dark too and sore still where I had bit it.

Nothing bad happened after I laid down and I did not sleep all night but listened to him breathing and kept touching him to see if he was warmed up. I got up in the earliest light and fixed the fire. When he heard me, he waked up and was better.

He did not forget what had happened but talked as if he thought it was all right. He said, we ought to have had a prayer and read something out of the Bible. He got the door opened and there was a big drift of snow but the sky was clearing. It was the last snow of the winter.

We went out and said the Lord's Prayer. Then he said, where is the Bible? Why is it not on the shelf? When I got it from beside the fire, he said, what is it doing there? I did not remind him of anything. He did not know what to read so I picked the 131st Psalm that we had to learn at the Home. *Lord my heart is not haughty nor mine eyes lofty. Surely I have behaved and quieted myself as a child that is weaned of his mother, my soul is even as a weaned child.* He read it. Then he said he would shovel out a path and go and tell the Treeces. I said I would cook him some food. He went out and shovelled and didn't get tired and come in to eat like I was waiting for him to do. He shovelled and shovelled a long path out of sight and then he was gone and didn't come back. He didn't come back until near dark and then he said he had eaten. I said, did you tell them about the tree? Then he looked at me for the first time in a bad way. It was the same bad way his brother used to look. I never said anything more to him about what had happened or hinted at it in any way. And he never said anything to me, except he would come and say things in my dreams. But I knew the difference always between my dreams and when I was awake, and when I was awake it was never anything but the bad look.

Mrs. Treece came and tried to get me to go and live with them the way George was living. She said I could eat and sleep there, they had enough beds. I would not go. They thought I would not go because of my grief but I wouldn't go because somebody might see my black and blue, also they would be watching for me to cry. I said I was not frightened to stay alone.

I dreamed nearly every night that one or other of them came and chased me with the axe. It was him or it was George, one or the other. Or sometimes not the axe, it was a big rock lifted in both hands and one of them waiting with it behind the door. Dreams are sent to warn us.

I didn't stay in the house where he could find me and when I gave up sleeping inside and slept outside I didn't have the dream so often. It got warm in a hurry and the flies and mosquitoes came but they hardly bothered me. I would see their bites but not feel them, which was another sign that in the outside I was protected. I got down when I heard anybody coming. I ate berries both red and black and God protected me from any badness in them.

I had another kind of dream after a while. I dreamed George came and talked to me and he still had the bad look but was trying to cover it up and pretend that he was kind. He kept coming into my dreams and he kept lying to me. It was starting to get colder out and I did not want to go back in the shanty and the dew was heavy so I would be soaking when I slept in the grass. I went and opened the Bible to find out what I should do.

And now I got my punishment for cheating because the Bible did not tell me anything that I could understand, what to do. The cheating was when I was looking to find something for Geroge, and I did not read exactly where my finger landed but looked around quick and found something else that was more what I wanted. I used to do that too when we would be looking up our verses in the Home and I always got good things and nobody ever caught me or suspected me at it. You never did either, Sadie.

So now I had my punishment when I couldn't find anything to help me however I looked. But something put it into my head to come here and I did, I had heard them talking about how warm it was and tramps would be wanting to come and get locked up, so I thought, I will too, and it was put into my head to tell them what I did. I told them the very same lie that George told me so often in my dreams, trying to get me to believe it was me and not him. I am safe from George here is the main thing. If they think I am crazy and I know the difference I am safe. Only I would like for you to come and see me.

And I would like for that yelling to stop.

When I am finished writing this, I will put it in with the curtains that I am making for the Opera House. And I will put on it, Finder Please Post. I trust that better than giving it to them like the two letters I gave them already that they never have sent.

IV

Miss Christena Mullen, Walley, to Mr. Leopold Henry, Department of History, Queen's University, Kingston, July 8, 1959.

Yes I am the Miss Mullen that Treece Herron's sister remembers coming to the farm and it is very kind of her to say I was a pretty young lady in a hat and veil. That was my motoring-veil. The old lady she mentions was Mr. Herron's grandfather's sister-in-law, if I have got it straight. As you are doing the biography, you will have got the relationships worked out. I never voted for Treece Herron myself since I am a Conservative, but he was a colorful politician and as you say a biography of him will bring some attention to this part of the country—too often thought of as "deadly dull."

I am rather surprised the sister does not mention the car in particular. It was a Stanley Steamer. I bought it myself on my twenty-fifth birthday in 1907. It cost twelve hundred dollars, that being part of my inheritance from my grandfather James Mullen who was an early Clerk of the Peace in Walley. He made money buying and selling farms.

My father having died young, my mother moved into my grandfather's house with all us five girls. It was a big cut-stone house called Traquair, now a Home for Young Offenders. I sometimes say in joke that it always was!

When I was young, we employed a gardener, a cook, and a sewing-woman. All of them were "characters," all prone to feuding with each other, and all owing their jobs to the fact that my grandfather had taken an interest in them when they were inmates at the County Gaol (as it used to be spelled) and eventually had brought them home.

By the time I bought the Steamer, I was the only one of my sisters living at home, and the sewing-woman was the only one of these old servants who remained. The sewing-woman was called Old Annie and never objected to that name. She used it herself and would write notes to the cook that said, "Tea was not hot, did you warm the pot? Old Annie." The whole third floor was Old Annie's domain and one of my sisters— Dolly—said that whenever she dreamed of home, that is, of Traquair, she dreamed of Old Annie up at the top of the third-floor stairs brandishing her measuring stick and wearing a black dress with long fuzzy black arms like a spider.

She had one eye that slid off to the side and gave her the air of taking in more information than the ordinary person.

We were not supposed to pester the servants with questions about their personal lives, particularly those who had been in the Gaol, but of course we did. Sometimes Old Annie called the Gaol the Home. She said that a girl in the next bed screamed and screamed, and that was why she—Annie—ran away and lived in the woods. She said the girl had been beaten for letting the fire go out. Why were you in jail, we asked her, and she would say, "I told a fib!" So for quite a while we had the impression that you went to jail for telling lies!

Some days she was in a good mood and would play hide-the-thimble with us. Sometimes she was in a bad mood and would stick us with pins when she was evening our hems if we turned too quickly or stopped too soon. She knew a place, she said, where you could get bricks to put on children's heads to stop them growing. She hated making wedding dresses (she never had to make one for me!) and didn't think much of any of the men that my sisters married. She hated Dolly's beau so much that she made some kind of deliberate mistake with the sleeves which had to be ripped out, and Dolly cried. But she made us all beautiful ball gowns to wear when the Governor-General and Lady Minto came to Walley.

About being married herself, she sometimes said she had been and sometimes not. She said a man had come to the Home and had all the girls paraded in front of him and said, "I'll take the one with the coal-black hair." That being Old Annie, but she refused to go with him, even though he was rich and came in a carriage. Rather like Cinderella but with a different ending. Then she said a bear killed her husband, in the woods, and my grandfather had killed the bear, and wrapped her in its skin and taken her home from the Gaol.

My mother used to say, "Now, girls. Don't get Old Annie going. And don't believe a word she says."

I am going on at great length filling in the background but you did say you were interested in details of the period. I am like most people my age and forget to buy milk but could tell you the color of the coat I had when I was eight.

So when I got the Stanley Steamer, Old Annie asked to be taken for a ride. It turned out that what she had in mind was more of a trip. This was a surprise since she had never wanted to go on trips before and refused to go to Niagara Falls and would not even go down to the Harbor to see the fireworks on the First of July. Also she was leery of automobiles and of me as a driver. But the big surprise was that she had somebody she wanted to go and see. She wanted to drive to Carstairs to see the Herron family, who she said were her relatives. She had never received any visits or letters from these people, and when I asked if she had written to ask if we might visit she said, "I can't write." This was ridiculous—she wrote those notes to the cooks and long lists for me of things she wanted me to pick up down on the Square or in the city. Braid, buckram, taffeta—she could spell all of that.

"And they don't need to know beforehand," she said. "In the country it's different."

Well, I loved taking jaunts in the Steamer. I had been driving since I was fifteen but this was the first car of my own and possibly the only Steam car in Huron County. Everybody would run to see it go by. It did not make a beastly loud noise coughing and clanking like other cars but rolled along silently more or less like a ship with high sails over the lake waters and it did not foul the air but left behind a plume of steam. Stanley Steamers were banned in Boston, because of steam fogging the air. I always loved to tell people, I used to drive a car that was banned in Boston!

We started out fairly early on a Sunday in June. It took about twenty-five minutes to get the steam up and all that time Old Annie sat up straight in the front seat as if the show were already on the road. We both had our motoring-veils on, and long dusters, but the dress Old Annie was wearing underneath was of plum-colored silk. In fact it was made over from the one she had made for my grandmother to meet the Prince of Wales in.

The Steamer covered the miles like an angel. It would do fifty miles an hour—great then—but I did not push it. I was trying to consider Old Annie's nerves. People were still in church when we started, but later on the roads were full of horses and buggies making the journey home. I was polite as all get-out, edging by them. But it turned out Old Annie did not want to be so sedate and she kept saying, "Give it a squeeze," meaning the horn, which was worked by a bulb under a mudguard down at my side.

She must not have been out of Walley for more years than I had been alive. When we crossed the bridge at Saltford (that old iron bridge where there used to be so many accidents because of the turn at both ends), she said that there didn't used to be a bridge there, you had to pay a man to row you.

"I couldn't pay but I crossed on the stones and just hiked up my skirts and waded," she said. "It was that dry a summer."

Naturally I did not know what summer she was talking about.

Then it was, Look at the big fields, where are the stumps gone, where is the bush? And look how straight the road goes, and they're building their houses out of brick! And what are those buildings as big as churches?

Barns, I said.

I knew my way to Carstairs all right but expected help from Old Annie once we got there. None was forthcoming. I drove up and down the main street waiting for her to spot something familiar. "If I could just see the inn," she said, "I'd know where the track goes off behind it."

It was a factory town, not very pretty in my opinion. The Steamer of course got attention, and I was able to call out for directions to the Herron farm without stopping the engine. Shouts and gestures and finally I was able to get us on the right road. I told Old Annie to watch the mailboxes but she was concerned with finding the creek. I spotted the name myself, and turned us in at a long lane with a red brick house at the end of it and a couple of these barns that had amazed Old Annie. Red brick houses with verandas and key windows were all the style then, they were going up everywhere.

"Look there!" Old Annie said, and I thought she meant where a herd of cows was tearing away from us in the pasture-field alongside the lane. But she was pointing at a mound pretty well covered with wild grape, a few logs sticking out of it. She said that was the shanty. I said, "Well, good—now let's hope you recognize one or two of the people."

There were enough people around. A couple of visiting buggies were pulled up in the shade, horses tethered and cropping grass. By the time the Steamer stopped at the side veranda, a number were lined up to look at it. They didn't come forward—not even the children ran out to look close up the way town children would have done. They all just stood in a row looking at it in a tight-lipped sort of way.

Old Annie was staring off in the other direction.

She told me to get down. Get down, she said, and ask them if there is a Mr. George Herron that lives here and is he alive yet, or dead?

I did what I was told. And one of the men said, that's right. He is. My father.

Well, I have brought somebody, I told them. I have brought Mrs. Annie Herron.

The man said, that so?

(A pause here due to a couple of fainting-fits and a trip to the hospital. Lots of tests to use up the taxpayers' money. Now I'm back and have read this over, astounded at the rambling but too lazy to start again. I have not even got to Treece Herron, which is the part you are interested in, but hold on, I'm nearly there.)

These people were all dumbfounded about Old Annie, or so I gathered. They had not known where she was or what she was doing or if she was alive. But you mustn't think they surged out and greeted her in any excited way. Just the one young man came out, very mannerly, and helped first her then me down from the car. He said to me that Old Annie was his grandfather's sister-in-law. It was too bad we hadn't come even a few months sooner, he said, because his grandfather had been quite well and his mind quite clear—he had even written a piece for the paper about his early days here—but then he had got sick. He had recovered but would never be himself again. He could not talk, except now and then a few words.

This mannerly young man was Treece Herron.

We must have arrived just after they finished their dinner. The woman of the house came out and asked him—Treece Herron—to ask us if we had eaten. You would think she or we did not speak English. They were all very shy—the women with their skinned-back hair, and men in dark-blue Sunday suits, and tongue-tied children. I hope you do not think I am making fun of them—it is just that I cannot understand for the life of me why it is necessary to be so shy.

We were taken to the dining-room which had an unused smell—they must have had their dinner elsewhere—and were served a great deal

of food of which I remember salted radishes and leaf lettuce and roast
chicken and strawberries and cream. Dishes from the china cabinet, not
their usual. Good old Indian Tree. They had sets of everything. Plushy
living-room suite, walnut dining-room suite. It was going to take them a
while, I thought, to get used to being prosperous.

Old Annie enjoyed the fuss of being waited on and ate a lot, picking
up the chicken bones to work the last shred of meat off them. Children
lurked around the doorways and the women talked in subdued, rather
scandalized voices out in the kitchen. The young man, Treece Herron,
had the grace to sit down with us and drink a cup of tea while we ate.
He chatted readily enough about himself and told me he was a divinity
student at Knox College. He said he liked living in Toronto. I got the
feeling he wanted me to understand that divinity students were not all
such sticks as I supposed or led such a stringent existence. He had been
tobogganing in High Park, he had been picnicking at Hanlan's Point,
he had seen the giraffe in the Riverdale Zoo. As he talked, the children
got a little bolder and started trickling into the room. I asked the usual
idiocies . . . How old are you, what book are you in at school, do you like
your teacher? He urged them to answer or answered for them and told
me which were his brothers and sisters and which his cousins.

Old Annie said, "Are you all fond of each other, then?" which brought
on funny looks.

The woman of the house came back and spoke to me again through
the divinity student. She told him that Grandpa was up now and sitting
on the front porch. She looked at the children and said, "What did you
let all them in here for?"

Out we trooped to the front porch, where two straight-backed chairs
were set up and an old man settled on one of them. He had a beautiful
full white beard reaching down to the bottom of his waistcoat. He did
not seem interested in us. He had a long, pale, obedient old face.

Old Annie said, "Well, George," as if this was about what she had
expected. She sat on the other chair and said to one of the little girls,
"Now bring me a cushion. Bring me a thin kind of cushion and put it at
my back."

I spent the afternoon giving rides in the Stanley Steamer. I knew enough
about them now not to start in asking who wanted a ride, or bombarding
them with questions, such as, were they interested in automobiles? I just
went out and patted it here and there as if it was a horse, and I looked in

the boiler. The divinity student came behind and read the name of the Steamer written on the side. "The Gentleman's Speedster." He asked was it my father's.

Mine, I said. I explained how the water in the boiler was heated and how much steam-pressure the boiler could withstand. People always wondered about that—about explosions. The children were closer by that time and I suddenly remarked that the boiler was nearly empty. I asked if there was any way I could get some water.

Great scurry to get pails and man the pump! I went and asked the men on the veranda if that was all right, and thanked them when they told me, help yourself. Once the boiler was filled, it was natural for me to ask if they would like me to get the steam up, and a spokesman said, it wouldn't hurt. Nobody was impatient during the wait. The men stared at the boiler, concentrating. This was certainly not the first car they had seen but probably the first steam car.

I offered the men a ride first, as it was proper to. They watched skeptically while I fiddled with all the knobs and levers to get my lady going. Thirteen different things to push or pull! We bumped down the lane at five, then ten miles an hour. I knew they suffered somewhat, being driven by a woman, but the novelty of the experience held them. Next I got a load of children, hoisted in by the divinity student telling them to sit still and hold on and not be scared and not fall out. I put up the speed a little, knowing now the ruts and puddle-holes, and their hoots of fear and triumph could not be held back.

I have left out something about how I was feeling but will leave it out no longer, due to the effects of a martini I am drinking now, my late-afternoon pleasure. I had troubles then I have not yet admitted to you because they were love-troubles. But when I had set out that day with Old Annie, I had determined to enjoy myself as much as I could. It seemed it would be an insult to the Stanley Steamer not to. All my life I found this a good rule to follow—to get as much pleasure as you could out of things even when you weren't likely to be happy.

I told one of the boys to run around to the front veranda and ask if his grandfather would care for a ride. He came back and said, "They've both gone to sleep."

I had to get the boiler filled up before we started back, and while this was being done, Treece Herron came and stood close to me.

"You have given us all a day to remember," he said.

I wasn't above flirting with him. I actually had a long career as a flirt ahead of me. It's quite a natural behavior, once the loss of love makes you give up your ideas of marriage.

I said he would forget all about it, once he got back to his friends in Toronto. He said no indeed, he would never forget, and he asked if he could write to me. I said nobody could stop him.

On the way home I thought about this exchange and how ridiculous it would be if he should get a serious crush on me. A divinity student. I had no idea then of course that he would be getting out of Divinity and into Politics.

"Too bad old Mr. Herron wasn't able to talk to you," I said to Old Annie.

She said, "Well, I could talk to him."

Actually, Treece Herron did write to me, but he must have had a few misgivings as well because he enclosed some pamphlets about Mission Schools. Something about raising money for Mission Schools. That put me off and I didn't write back. (Years later I would joke that I could have married him if I'd played my cards right.)

I asked Old Annie if Mr. Herron could understand her when she talked to him, and she said, "Enough." I asked if she was glad about seeing him again and she said yes. "And glad for him to get to see me," she said, not without some gloating that probably referred to her dress and the vehicle.

So we just puffed along in the Steamer under the high arching trees that lined the roads in those days. From miles away the lake could be seen—just glimpses of it, shots of light, held wide apart in the trees and hills so that Old Annie asked me if it could possibly be the same lake, all the same one that Walley was on?

There were lots of old people going around then with ideas in their heads that didn't add up—though I suppose Old Annie had more than most. I recall her telling me another time that a girl in the Home had a baby out of a big boil that burst on her stomach, and it was the size of a rat and had no life in it, but they put it in the oven and it puffed up to the right size and baked to a good color and started to kick its legs. (Ask an old woman to reminisce and you get the whole ragbag, is what you must be thinking by now.)

I told her that wasn't possible, it must have been a dream.

"Maybe so," she said, agreeing with me for once. "I did used to have the terriblest dreams."

MARK HELPRIN
(1947–)

Mark Helprin, who was born in New York City, is best known for such large, ambitious novels as *Winter's Tale* (1983) and *A Soldier of the Great War* (1990), but he has written short stories as well. "Letters from the Samantha," originally published in the *New Yorker,* appeared in his second collection, *Ellis Island and Other Stories* (1981), which won a PEN/Faulkner Award and the National Jewish Book Award and was nominated for the American Book Award. This story about a ship's captain grappling with his own "breach of regulations" is cast as a series of letters written to his superior: they are framed as confession, explanation, apology, and defense. Despite the epistolary mode, though, these strange letters read at times like a journal; in the end, Captain Low sounds very much like someone talking to himself. One of the questions this fablelike tale leaves readers to ponder is just what Low intended for these letters, which are ultimately found aboard ship, unmailed.

These letters were recovered in good condition from the vault of the sunken *Samantha,* an iron-hulled sailing ship of one thousand tons, built in Scotland in 1879 and wrecked during the First World War in the Persian Gulf off Basra.

20 August, 1909, 20° 14' 18" S,
43° 51' 57" E
Off Madagascar

Dear Sir:

Many years have passed since I joined the Green Star Line. You may note in your records and logs, if not, indeed, by memory, the complete absence of disciplinary action against me. During my command, the *Samantha* has been a trim ship on time. Though my subordinates sometimes complain, they are grateful, no doubt, for my firm rule and tidiness. It saves the ship in storms, keeps them healthy, and provides good training—even though they will be masters of steamships.

No other vessel of this line has been as punctual or well run. Even today we are a week ahead and our Madagascar wood will reach Alexandria early. Bound for London, the crew are happy, and though we sail the Mozambique Channel, they act as if we had just caught sight of Margate. There are no problems on this ship. But I must in conscience report an irregular incident for which I am ready to take full blame.

Half a day out of Androka, we came upon a sea so blue and casual that its waters seemed fit to drink. Though the wind was slight and we made poor time, we were elated by perfect climate and painter's colors, for off the starboard side Madagascar rose as green and tranquil as a well-watered palm, its mountains engraved by thrashing freshwater streams which beat down to the coast. A sweet upwelling breeze blew steadily from shore and confounded our square sails. Twenty minutes after noon, the lookout sighted a tornado on land. In the ship's glass I saw it, horrifying and enormous. Though at a great distance, its column appeared as thick as a massive tree on an islet in an atoll, and stretched at least 70 degrees upward from the horizon.

I have seen these pipes of windy fleece before. If there is sea nearby, they rush to it. So did this. When it became not red and black from soil and debris but silver and green from the water it drew, I began to tighten ship. Were the typhoon to have struck us directly, no preparation would have saved us. But what a shame to be swamped by high waves, or to be dismasted by beaten sea and wind. Hatches were battened as if for storm, minor sails furled, and the mainsail driven down half.

It moved back and forth over the sea in illegible patterning, as if tacking to changing winds. To our dismay, the distance narrowed. We were afraid, though every man on deck wanted to see it, to feel it, perhaps to ride its thick swirling waters a hundred times higher than our mast—higher than the peaks inland. I confess that I have wished to be completely taken up by such a thing, to be lifted into the clouds, arms and legs pinned in the stream. The attraction is much like that of phosphorescent seas, when glowing light and smooth swell are dangerously magnetic even for hardened masters of good ships. I have wanted to surrender to plum-colored seas, to know what one might find there naked and alone. But I have not, and will not.

Finally, we began to run rough water. The column was so high that we bent our heads to see its height, and the sound was greater than any engine, causing masts and spars to resonate like cords. Waves broke over the prow. Wind pushed us on, and the curl of the sea rushed to fill the depression of the waters. No more than half a mile off the starboard bow, the column veered to the west, crossing our path to head for Africa as rapidly as an express. Within minutes, we could not even see it.

As it crossed our bows, I veered in the direction from which it had come. It seemed to communicate a decisiveness of course, and here I took opportunity to evade. In doing so we came close to land. This was dangerous not only for the presence of reefs and shoals but because of the scattered debris. Trees as tall as masts and much thicker, roots sucked clean, lay in puzzlement upon the surface. Brush and vines were everywhere. The water was reddish brown from earth which had fallen from the cone. We were meticulously careful in piloting through this fresh salad, as a good ram against a solid limb would have been the end. Our cargo is hardwoods, and would have sunk us like granite. I myself straddled the sprit stays, pushing aside small logs with a boat hook and calling out trim to the wheel.

Nearly clear, we came upon a clump of tangled vegetation. I could not believe my eyes, for floating upon it was a large monkey, bolt upright and dignified. I sighted him first, though the lookout called soon after. On impulse, I set trim for the wavy mat and, as we smashed into it, offered the monkey an end of the boat hook. When he seized it I was almost pulled in, for his weight is nearly equal to mine. I observed that he had large teeth, which appeared both white and sharp. He came close, and then took to the lines until he sat high on the topgallant. As he passed, his foot cuffed my shoulder and I could smell him.

My ship is a clean ship. I regretted immediately my gesture with the hook. We do not need the mysterious defecations of such a creature, or the threat of him in the rigging at night. But we could not capture him to throw him back into the sea and, even had we collared him, might not have been able to get him overboard without danger to ourselves. We are now many miles off the coast. It is dark, and he sits high off the deck. The night watch is afraid and requests that I fell him with my rifle. They have seen his sharp teeth, which he displays with much screaming and gesticulating when they near him in the rigging. I think he is merely afraid, and I cannot bring myself to shoot him. I realize that no animals are allowed on board and have often had to enforce this rule when coming upon a parrot or cat hidden belowdecks where some captains do not go. But this creature we have today removed from the sea is like a man, and he has ridden the typhoon. Perhaps we will pass a headland and throw him overboard on a log. He must eventually descend for want of food. Then we will have our way. I will report further when the matter is resolved, and assure you that I regret this breach of regulations.

Yours & etc.,
Samson Low
Master, S/V Samantha

23 August, 1909, 10° 43' 3" S,
49° 5' 27" E
South of the Seychelles

Dear Sir:

We have passed the Channel and are heading north-northeast, hoping to ride the summer monsoon. It is shamefully hot, though the breeze is less humid than usual. Today two men dropped from the heat but they resumed work by evening. Because we are on a homeward tack, morale is at its best, or rather would be were it not for that damned ape in the rigging. He has not come down, and we have left behind his island and its last headland. He will have to have descended by the time we breach passage between Ras Asir and Jazirat Abd al-Kuri. The mate has suggested that there we throw him into the sea on a raft, which the carpenter has already set about building. He has embarked upon this with my permission, since there is little else for him to do. It has been almost an overly serene voyage and the typhoon caused no damage.

The raft he designed is very clever and has become a popular subject of discussion. It is about six feet by three feet, constructed of spare pine dunnage we were about to cast away when the typhoon was sighted. On each side is an outrigger for stability in the swell. In the center is a box, in which is a seat. Flanking this box are several smaller ones for fruit, biscuit, and a bucket of fresh water, in case the creature should drift a long time on the sea. This probably will not be so; the currents off Ras Asir drive for the beach, and we have noted that dunnage is quickly thrown upon the strand. Nevertheless, the crew have added their own touch—a standard distress flag flying from a ten-foot switch. They do not know, but I will order it replaced by a banner of another color, so that a hapless ship will not endanger itself to rescue a speechless monkey.

The crew have divided into two factions—those who wish to have the monkey shot, and those who would wait for him to descend and then put him in his boat. I am with the latter, since I would be the huntsman, and have already mentioned my lack of enthusiasm for this. A delegation of the first faction protested. They claimed that the second faction comprised those who stayed on deck, that the creature endangered balance in the rigging, and that he produced an uncanny effect in his screeching and bellicose silhouettes, which from below are humorous but which at close range, they said, are disconcerting and terrifying.

Since I had not seen him for longer than a moment and wanted to verify their complaint, I went up. Though sixty years of age, I did not use the bosun's chair, and detest those masters who do. It is pharaonic, and smacks of days in my father's youth when he saw with his own eyes gentlemen in sedan chairs carried about the city. The sight of twenty men laboring to hoist a ship's rotund captain is simply Egyptian, and I will not have it. Seventy feet off the deck, a giddy height to which I have not ascended in years, I came even with the ape. The ship was passing a boisterous sea and had at least a twenty-degree roll, which flung the two of us from side to side like pendula.

I am not a naturalist, nor have we on board a book of zoology, so the most I can do is to describe him. He is almost my height (nearly five feet ten inches) and appears to be sturdily built. Feet and hands are human in appearance except that they have a bulbous, skew, arthritic look common to monkeys. He is muscular and covered with fine reddish-brown hair. One can see the whiteness of his tendons when he stretches an arm or leg. I have mentioned the sharp, dazzling white teeth, set in rows like a trap, canine and pointed. His face is curiously delicate, and covered with orange hair leading to a snow-white crown of fur. My breath nearly failed when I looked into his eyes, for they are a bright, penetrating blue.

At first, he began to scream and swing as if he would come at me. If he had, I would have fared badly. The sailors fear him, for there is no man on board with half his strength, no man on the sea with a tenth his agility in the ropes, and if there is a man with the glacierlike pinnacled teeth, then he must be in a Scandinavian or Eastern European circus, for there they are fond of such things. To my surprise, he stopped his pantomime and, with a gentle and quizzical tilt of the head, looked me straight in the eyes. I had been sure that as a man I could answer his gaze as if from infallibility, and I calmly looked back. But he had me. His eyes unset me, so that I nearly shook. From that moment, he has not threatened or bared his teeth, but merely rests near the top of the foremast. The crew have attributed his conversion to my special power. This is flattering, though not entirely, as it assumes my ability to commune with an ape. Little do they suspect that it is I and not the monkey who have been converted, although to what I do not know. I am still thoroughly ashamed of my indiscretion and the trouble arising from it. We will get him and put him adrift off Ras Asir.

This evening, the cook grilled up some beef. I had him thoroughly vent the galley and use a great many herbs. The aroma was maddening. I sat in near-hypnotic ease in a canvas chair on the quarterdeck, a glass of wine in hand, as the heat fell to a cool breeze. We are all sunburnt and have been working hard, as the ape silently watches, to trim regularly and catch the best winds. We are almost in the full swift of the monsoon, and shortly will ride it in all its speed. It was wonderful to sit on deck and smell the herb-laden meat. The sea itself must have been jealous. I had several men ready with cargo net and pikes, certain that he would come down. We stared up at him as if he were the horizon, waiting. He smelled the food and agitated back and forth. Though he fretted, he did not descend. Even when we ate we saw him shunting to and fro on a yardarm. We left a dish for him away from us but he did not venture to seize it. If he had, we would have seized him.

From his impatience, I predict that tomorrow he will surrender to his stomach. Then we will catch him and this problem will be solved. I truly regret such an irregularity, though it would be worthwhile if he could only tell us how far he was lifted inside the silvered cone, and what it was like.

Yours & etc.,
Samson Low

25 August, 1909, 2° 13' 10" N,
51° 15' 17" E
Off Mogadishu

Dear Sir:
Today he came down. After the last correspondence, it occurred to me that he might be vegetarian, and that though he was hungry, the meat had put him off. Therefore, I searched my memory for the most aromatic vegetable dish I know. In your service as a fourth officer, I called at Jaffa port, in Palestine, in January of 1873. We went up to Sfat, a holy town high in the hills, full of Jews and Arabs, quiet and mystical. There were so many come into that freezing velvet dome of stars that all hostelries were full. I and several others paid a small sum for private lodging and board. At two in the morning, after we had returned from Mt. Jermak, the Arabs made a hot lively fire from bundles of dry cypress twigs, and in a great square iron pan heated local oil and herbs, in which they fried thick sections of potato. I have never eaten so well. Perhaps it was our hunger, the cold, the silence, being high in the mountains at Sfat, where air is like ether and all souls change. Today I made the cook follow that old receipt.

We had been in the monsoon for several hours, and the air was littered with silver sparks—apparitions of heat from a glittering afternoon. Though the sun was low, iron decks could not be tread. In the rigging, he appeared nearly finished, limp and slouching, an arm hanging without energy, his back bent. We put potatoes in a dish on the forecastle. He descended slowly, finally touching deck lightly and ambling to the bows like a spider, all limbs brushing the planks. He ate his fill, and we threw the net over him. We had expected a ferocious struggle, but his posture and expression were so peaceful that I ordered the net removed. Sailors stood ready with pikes, but he stayed in place. Then I approached him and extended my hand as if to a child.

In imitation, he put out his arm, looking much less fearsome. Without a show of teeth, in his tired state, crouched on all fours to half our heights, he was no more frightening than a hound. I led him to the stern and back again while the crew cheered and laughed. Then the mate took him, and then the entire hierarchy of the ship, down to the cabin boys, who are smaller than he and seemed to interest him the most. By dark, he had strolled with every member of the crew and was miraculously tame. But I remembered his teeth, and had him chained to his little boat.

He was comfortable there, surrounded by fruit and water (which he ate and drank methodically) and sitting on a throne of sorts, with half a dozen courtiers eager to look in his eyes and hold his obliging wrist. Mine is not the only London post in which he will be mentioned. Those who can write are describing him with great zeal. I have seen some of these letters. He has been portrayed as a "mad baboon," a "man-eating gorilla of horrible colors, muscled but as bright as a bird," a "pygmy man set down on the sea by miracle and typhoon," and as all manner of Latin names, each different from the others and incorrectly spelled.

Depending on the bend of the monsoon and whether it continues to run strongly, we will pass Ras Asir in three days. I thought of casting him off early but was implored to wait for the Cape. I relented, and in doing so was made to understand why those in command must stay by rules. I am sure, however, that my authority is not truly diminished, and when the ape is gone I will again tighten discipline.

I have already had the distress flag replaced by a green banner. It flies over the creature on his throne. Though in splendor, he is in chains and in three days' time will be on the sea once more.

Yours & etc.,
Samson Low

28 August, 1909, 12° 4' 39" N,
50° 1' 2" E
North of Ras Asir

Dear Sir:

A most alarming incident has occurred. I must report, though it is among the worst episodes of my command. This morning, I arose, expecting to put the ape over the side as we rounded Ras Asir at about eleven. (The winds have been consistently excellent and a northward breeze veering off the monsoon has propelled us as steadily as an engine.)

Going out on deck, I discovered that his boat was nowhere to be seen. At first, I thought that the mate had already disposed of him, and was disappointed that we were far from the coast. Then, to my shock, I saw him sitting unmanacled atop the main cargo hatch.

I screamed at the mate, demanding to know what had happened to the throne (as it had come to be called). He replied that it had gone overboard during the twelve-to-four watch. I stormed below and got that watch out in a hurry. Though sleepy-eyed, they were terrified. I told them that if the guilty one did not come forth I would put them all in irons. My temper was short and I could have struck them down. Two young sailors, as frightened as if they were surrendering themselves to die, admitted that they had thrown it over. They said they did not want to see the ape put to drift.

They are in irons until we make Suez. Their names are Mulcahy and Esper, and their pay is docked until they are freed. As we rounded the Cape, cutting close in (for the waters there are deep), we could see that though the creature would have been immediately cast up on shore, the shore itself was barren and inhospitable, and surely he would have died there. My Admiralty chart does not detail the inland topography of this area and shows only a yellow tongue marked "Africa" thrusting into the Gulf of Aden.

I can throw him overboard now or later. I do not want to do it. I brought him on board in the first place. There is nothing with which to fashion another raft. We have many tons of wood below, but not a cubic foot of it is lighter than water. The wind is good and we are making for the Bab al-Mandab, where we will pass late tomorrow afternoon—after that, the frustrating run up the Red Sea to the Canal.

The mate suggests that we sell him to the Egyptians. But I am reluctant to make port with this in mind, as it would be a victory for the two in chains and in the eyes of many others. And we are not animal traders. If he leaves us at sea the effects of his presence will be invalidated, we will touch land with discipline restored, and I will have the option of destroying these letters, though everything here has been entered in short form in the log. I have ordered him not to be fed, but they cast him scraps. I must get back my proper hold on the ship.

Yours & etc.,
Samson Low

30 August, 1909, 15° 49' 30" N,
41° 5' 32" E
Red Sea off Massawa

Dear Sir:

I have been felled by an attack of headaches. Never before has this happened. There is pressure in my skull enough to burst it. I cannot keep my balance; my eyes roam and I am drunk with pain. For the weary tack up the Red Sea I have entrusted the mate with temporary command, retiring to my cabin with the excuse of heat prostration. I have been in the Red Sea time and again but have never felt apprehension that death would follow its heat. We have always managed. To the east, the mountains of the Hijaz are so dry and forbidding that I have seen sailors look away in fright.

The ape has begun to suffer from the heat. He is listless and ignored. His novelty has worn off (with the heat as it is) and no one pays him any attention. He will not go belowdecks but spends most of the day under the canvas sun shield, chewing slowly, though there is nothing in his mouth. It is hot there—the light so white and uncompromising it sears the eyes. I have freed his champions from irons and restored their pay. By this act I have won over the crew and caused the factions to disappear. No one thinks about the ape. But I dare not risk a recurrence of bad feeling and have decided to cast him into the sea. Where we found him, a strong seaward current would have carried him to the open ocean. Here, at least, he can make the shore, although it is the most barren coast on earth. But who would have thought he might survive the typhoon? He has been living beyond his time. To be picked up and whirled at incomprehensible speed, carried for miles above the earth where no man has ever been, and thrown into the sea is a death sentence. If he survived that, perhaps he can survive Arabian desert.

His expression is neither sad nor fierce. He looks like an old man, neutral to the world. In the last two days he has become the target of provocation and physical blows. I have ordered this stopped, but a sailor will sometimes throw a nail or a piece of wood at him. We shall soon be rid of him.

Yesterday we came alongside another British ship, the *Stonepool*, of the Dutch Express Line. On seeing the ape, they were envious. What is it, their captain asked, amazed at its coloring. I replied that he was a

Madagascar ape we had fished from the sea, and I offered him to them, saying he was as tame as a dog. At first, they wanted him. The crew cried out for his acceptance, but the captain demurred, shaking his head and looking into my eyes as if he were laughing at me. "Damn!" I said, and went below without even a salute at parting.

My head aches. I must stop. At first light tomorrow, I will toss him back.

Yours & etc.,
Samson Low

3 September, 1909
Suez

Dear Sir:

The morning before last I went on deck at dawn. The ape was sitting on the main hatch, his eyes upon me from the moment I saw him. I walked over to him and extended my arm, which he would not take in his customary manner. I seized his wrist, which he withdrew. However, as he did this I laid hold of the other wrist, and pulled him off the hatch. He did not bare his teeth. He began to scream. Awakened by this, most of the crew stood in the companionways or on deck, silently observing.

He was hard to drag, but I towed him to the rail. When I took his other arm to hoist him over, he bared his teeth with a frightening shriek. Everyone was again terrified. The teeth must be six inches long.

He came at me with those teeth, and I could do nothing but throttle him. With my hands on his throat, his arms were free. He grasped my side. I felt the pads of his hands against my ribs. I had to tolerate that awful sensation to keep hold of his throat. No man aboard came close. He shrieked and moaned. His eyes reddened. My response was to tighten my hold, to end the horror. I gripped so hard that my own teeth were bared and I made sounds similar to his. He put his hands around my neck as if to strangle me back, but I had already taken the inside position and, despite his great strength, lessened the power of his grip merely by lifting my arms against his. Nevertheless he choked me. But I had a great head start. We held this position for long minutes, sweating, until his arms dropped and his body convulsed. In rage, I threw him by the neck into the sea, where he quickly sank.

Some of the crew have begun to talk about him as if he were about to be canonized. Others see him as evil. I assembled them as the coasts began to close on Suez and the top of the sea was white and still. I made my views clear, for in years of command and in a life on the sea I have learned much. I felt confident of what I told them.

He is not a symbol. He stands neither for innocence nor for evil. There is no parable and no lesson in his coming and going. I was neither right nor wrong in bringing him aboard (though it was indeed incorrect) or in what I later did. We must get on with the ship's business. He does not stand for a man or men. He stands for nothing. He was an ape, simian and lean, half sensible. He came on board, and now he is gone.

Yours & etc.,
Samson Low

A Palestinian leader, Ghassan Kanafani was born in Acre, Palestine, in 1936, but he and his family were exiled in 1948. He worked in Kuwait as a teacher and journalist, became a spokesman for the Marxist Popular Front for the Liberation of Palestine, and was editor of the organization's weekly in Beirut when he was assassinated in 1972. Kanafani's novels and stories, although not all overtly political, are closely tied to the fate of Palestine, which shaped his own life. In "The Death of Bed Number 12," which was published in *Modern Arabic Short Stories* (1967), dislocation—both existential and social—figures as a central theme. At one level, the hospitalized narrator is undergoing a personal crisis of disorientation, triggered by the death of a fellow patient. At another level, the life story of the patient that the narrator invents focuses on a more literal displacement. In this story within a story, his protagonist moves from a village where life was orderly, tranquil, and undeviating to the city of Kuwait, where life is not so simple, and he longs for the place where balance existed, where life made sense. In view of the narrator's own interpretation of the stories we tell—that we always see others from our own viewpoint—we may assume from his tale that it is the narrator himself, and indeed the author, who feels loss and exile as profound concerns.

Dear Ahmed,

I have chosen you in particular to be the recipient of this letter for a reason which may appear to you commonplace, yet since yesterday my every thought has been centred on it. I chose you in particular because when I saw him yesterday dying on the high white bed I remembered how you used to use the word "die" to express anything extreme. Many is the time I've heard you use such expressions as "I almost died laughing," "I was dead tired," "Death itself couldn't quench my love," and so on. While it is true that we all use such words, you use them more than anybody. Thus it was that I remembered you as I saw him sinking down in the bed and clutching at the coverlet with his long, emaciated fingers, giving a convulsive shiver and then staring out at me with dead eyes.

But why have I not begun at the beginning? You know, no doubt, that I am now in my second month at the hospital. I have been suffering from a stomach ulcer, but no sooner had the surgeon plugged up the hole in my stomach than a new one appeared in my head, about which the surgeon could do nothing. Believe me, Ahmed, that an "ulcer" on the brain is a lot more stubborn than one in the stomach. My room leads on to the main corridor of the Internal Diseases Wing, while the window overlooks the small hospital garden. Thus, propped up by a pillow, I can observe both the continuous flow of patients passing the door as well as the birds which fly past the window incessantly. Amidst this hubbub of people who come here to die in the serene shadow of the scalpel and whom I see, having arrived on their own two feet, leaving after days or hours on the death trolley, wrapped round in a covering of white; in this hubbub I find myself quite unable to make good those holes that have begun to open up in my head, quite incapable of stopping the flow of questions that mercilessly demand an answer of me.

I shall be leaving the hospital in a few days, for they have patched up my insides as best they can. I am now able to walk leaning on the arm of an old and ugly nurse and on my own powers of resistance. The hospital, however, has done little more than transfer the ulcer from my stomach to my head, for in this place, as the ugly old woman remarked, medicine may be able to plug up a hole in the stomach but it can never find the answers required to plug up holes in one's thinking. The day she said this the old woman gave a toothless laugh as she quietly led me off to the scales.

What, though, is such talk to do with us? What I want to talk to you about is death. Death that takes place in front of you, not about that death of which one merely hears. The difference between the two types of death is immeasurable and cannot be appreciated by someone who has not been a witness to a human being clutching at the coverlet of his bed with all the strength of his trembling fingers in order to resist that terrible slipping into extinction, as though the coverlet can pull him back from that colossus who, little by little, wrests from his eyes this life about which we know scarcely anything.

As the doctors waited around him, I examined the card that hung at the foot of his bed. I had slipped out of my room and was standing there , unseen by the doctors, who were engaged in a hopeless attempt to save the dying man. I read: "Name: Mohamed Ali Akbar. Age: 25. Nationality: Omani." I turned the card over and this time read: "Leukemia." Again I stared into the thin brown face, the wide frightened eyes and the lips that trembled like a ripple of purple water. As his eyes turned and came to rest on my face it seemed that he was appealing to me for help. Why? Because I used to give him a casual greeting every morning? Or was it that he saw in my face some understanding of the terror he was undergoing? He went on staring at me and then—quite simply—he died.

It was only then that the doctor discovered me and dragged me off angrily to my room. But he would never be able to banish from my mind the scene that is ever-present there. As I got on to my bed I heard the voice of the male nurse in the corridor alongside my door saying in a matter-of-fact voice:

"Bed number 12 has died!"

I said to myself: "Mohamed Ali Akbar has lost his name, he is Bed number 12." What do I mean now when I talk of a human being whose name was Mohamed Ali Akbar? What does it matter to him whether he still retains his name or whether it has been replaced by a number? Then I remembered how he wouldn't allow anyone to omit any part of his name. Every morning the nurse would ask him, "And how are you, Mohamed Ali?" and he would not reply, for he regarded his name as being Mohamed Ali Akbar—just like that, all in one—and that this Mohamed Ali to whom the nurse was speaking was some other person.

Though the nurses found a subject for mirth in this insistence on his whole name being used, Mohamed Ali Akbar continued to demand it; perhaps he regarded his right to possessing his name in full as being an insistence that he at least owned something, for he was poor, extremely poor, a great deal more so than you with your fertile imagination could conceive as you lounge around in the café; poverty was something engraved in his face, his forearms, his chest, the way he ate, into everything that surrounded him.

When I was able to walk for the first time after they had patched me up, I paid him a visit. The back of his bed was raised and he was sitting up, lost in thought. I sat on the side of the bed for a short while, and we exchanged a few brief, banal words. I noticed that alongside his pillow was an old wooden box with his name carved on it in semi-Persian style writing; it was securely tied with twine. Apart from this he owned nothing except his clothes, which were kept in the hospital cupboard. I remembered that on that day I had asked the nurse:

"What's in the old box?"

"No one knows," she answered, laughing. "He refuses to be parted from the box for a single instant."

Then she bent over me and whispered:

"These people who look so poor are generally hiding some treasure or other—perhaps this is his!"

During my stay here no one visited him at the hospital. As he knew no one I used to send him some of the sweets with which my visitors inundated me. He accepted everything without enthusiasm. He was not good at expressing gratitude and his behaviour over this caused a certain fleeting resentment in me.

I did not concern myself with the mysterious box. Though Mohamed Ali Akbar's condition steadily worsened, his attitude towards the box did not change, which caused the nurse to remark to me that if there had been some treasure in it he would surely have given it away or willed it to someone, seeing that he was heading for death at such speed. Like some petty philosopher I had laughed that day saying to myself that the stupidity of this nurse scarcely knew any bounds, for how did she expect Mohamed Ali Akbar to persuade himself that he was inevitably dying, that there was not a hope of his pulling through? His insistence on keeping the box was tantamount to hanging on to his hope of pulling through and being reunited with his box.

When Mohamed Ali Akbar died I saw the box at his side, where it had always been, and it occurred to me that the box ought to be buried unopened with him. On going to my room that night I was quite unable to sleep. While Mohamed Ali Akbar had been deposited in the autopsy room, wrapped up in a white covering, he was, at the same time, sitting in my room and staring at me, passing through the hospital wards and searching about in his bed; I could almost hear the way he would gasp for breath before going to sleep. When day dawned across the trees of the hospital garden, I had created a complete story about him for myself.

Mohamed Ali Akbar was a poor man from the western quarter of the village of Abkha in Oman; a thin, dark-skinned young man, with aspirations burning in his eyes that could find no release. True he was poor, but what does poverty matter to a man if he has never known anything else? The whole of Abkha suffered from being poor, a poverty identical to Mohamed Ali Akbar's; it was, however, a contented poverty, a poverty that was deep-seated and devoid of anything that prompted one to feel that it was wrong and that there was something called "riches." And so it was that the two water-skins Mohamed Ali Akbar carried across his shoulders as he knocked on people's doors to sell them water, were the two scales which set the balance of his daily round. Mohamed Ali Akbar was aware of a certain dizziness when he laid down the water-skins, but when taking them up again the next morning he would feel that his existence was progressing tranquilly and that he had ensured for himself a balanced, undeviating journey through life.

Mohamed Ali Akbar's life could have continued in this quiet and ordered fashion had fate emulated civilization—in not reaching faraway Oman. But fate was present even in far-off Oman and it was inevitable that Mohamed Ali Akbar should suffer a little from its capricious ways.

It happened on a scorchingly hot morning. Though the sun was not yet at the meridian, the surface of the road was hot and the desert blew gusts of dust-laden wind into his face. He knocked at a door which was answered by a young, brown-skinned girl with wide black eyes, and everything happened with the utmost speed. Like some clumsy oaf who has lost his way, he stood in front of the door, the water-skins swinging to and fro on his lean shoulders. Abstractedly he stared at her, hoping like someone overcome with a mild attack of sunstroke that his eyes would miraculously be capable of clasping her to him. She stared back at him in sheer astonishment, and, unable to utter a word, he turned his back on her and went off home with his water-skins.

Though Mohamed Ali Akbar was exceptionally shy even with his own family, he found himself forced to pour out his heart to his elder sister. As his mother had died of smallpox a long time ago and his father was helplessly bedridden, it was to his sister that he turned for help, for he had unswerving confidence that Sabika possessed the necessary intelligence and judgement for solving a problem of this sort. Seated before him on the rush mat, shrouded in her coarse black dress, she did not break her silence till Mohamed Ali Akbar has gasped out the last of his story.

"I shall seek her hand in marriage," she then said. "Isn't that what you want?"

"Yes, yes, is it possible?"

Removing a straw from the old rush mat, his sister replied:

"Why not? You are now a young man and we are all equal in Abkha."

Mohamed Ali Akbar spent a most disturbed night. When morning came he found that his sister was even more eager than himself to set off on her mission. They agreed to meet up at noon when she would tell him of the results of her efforts, and from there they would both make the necessary arrangements for bringing the matter to completion.

Mohamed Ali Akbar did not know how to pass the time wandering through the lanes with the water-skins on his shoulders. He kept looking at his shadow and beseeching God to make it into a circle round his feet so that he might hurry back home. After what seemed an eternity, he made his way back and was met at the door by his sister.

"It seems that her mother is agreeable. But it must all be put to her father, who will give his answer in five days."

Deep down within him Mohamed Ali Akbar felt that he was going to be successful in making the girl his wife. As far as he was able to imagine he began from henceforth to build up images of his future with this young and beautiful brown-skinned girl. His sister Sabika looked at the matter with a wise and experienced eye, but she too was sure they would be successful, for she was convinced that her brother's name was without blemish among the people of Abkha; she had, in addition, given a lot of attention to gaining the approval of the girl's mother, knowing as she did how a woman was able to put over an idea to her husband and make him believe that it was his own. Sabika, therefore, awaited the outcome of the matter with complete composure.

On the fifth day Sabika went to the girl's house in order to receive the answer. When she returned, however, her disconsolate face showed that she had failed. She stood in a corner of the room, unable to look

Mohamed Ali Akbar in the eye, not knowing how to begin recounting what had happened.

"You must forget her, Mohamed Ali," she said when she had managed to pluck up her courage.

Not knowing what to say, he waited for his sister to finish.

"Her father died two days ago," continued Sabika, finding an opportunity in his silence to continue. "His dying wish to his family was that they should not give her to you in marriage."

Mohamed Ali Akbar heard these words as though they were addressed to someone else.

"But why, Sabika—why?" was all he could ask.

"He was told that you were a scoundrel, that you lived by stealing sheep on the mountain road, trading what you steal with the foreigners."

"I?"

"They think you are Mohamed Ali," said Sabika in a trembling voice she was unable to control. "You know—the scoundrel Mohamed Ali? Her father thought that you were he. . . ."

"But I am not Mohamed Ali," he replied, palms outstretched like a child excusing himself for some misdeed he has not committed. "I'm Mohamed Ali Akbar."

"There's been a mistake—I told them at the beginning that your name was Mohamed Ali. I didn't say Mohamed Ali Akbar because I saw no necessity for doing so."

Mohamed Ali Akbar felt his chest being crushed under the weight of the blow. However, he remained standing where he was, staring at his sister Sabika without fully seeing her. Blinded by anger, he let fly a final arrow:

"Did you tell her mother that I'm not Mohamed Ali but Mohamed Ali Akbar?"

"Yes, but the father's last wish was that they shouldn't marry her to you."

"But I'm Mohamed Ali Akbar the water-seller, aren't I?"

What was the use, though, of being so stricken? Everything had, quite simply, come to an end, a single word had lodged itself in the gullet of his romance and it had died. Mohamed Ali Akbar, however, was unable to forget the girl so easily and spent his time roaming about near her house in the hope of seeing her once again. Why? He did not know. His failure brought in its wake a savage anger which turned to hate; soon he was no

longer able to pass along that road for fear that his fury would overcome
him and he would pelt the window of her house with stones.

From that day onwards he refused to be called by anything but his name
in full: Mohamed Ali Akbar, all in one. He refused to answer to anyone
who called him Mohamed or Mohamed Ali and this soon became a habit
with him. Even his sister Sabika did not dare to use a contracted form
of his name. No longer did he experience his former contentment, and
Abkha gradually changed to a forbidding graveyard in his eyes. Refusing
to give in to his sister's insistence that he should marry, a worm called
"wealth" began to eat its way into his brain. He wanted to take revenge on
everything, to marry a woman with whom he could challenge the whole
of Abkha, all those who did not believe that he was Mohamed Ali Akbar
but Mohamed Ali the scoundrel. Where, though, to find wealth? Thus
he decided to sail away to Kuwait.

The distance between Abkha and Ras al-Khaima is two hours by foot,
and from Ras al-Khaima to Kuwait by sea is a journey of three days, the
fare for which, on an antiquated boat, was seventy rupees. After a year or
two he would be able to return to Oman and strut about proudly in the
alleyways of Abkha wearing a snow-white *aba* trimmed with gold, like
the one he had seen round the shoulders of a notable from Ras al-Khaima
who had come to his village to take the hand of a girl the fame of whose
beauty had reached all the way there.

The journey was a hard one. The boat which took that eager throng
across the south and then made its way northwards to the corner of the
Gulf was continually exposed to a variety of dangers. But ebullient souls
accustomed to life's hardships paid no heed to such matters; all hands
cooperated in the task of delivering safely that small wooden boat floating
on the waves of the great sea. And when the sails of the ships lying in
Kuwait's quiet harbour came into view, Mohamed Ali Akbar experienced
a strange feeling: the dream had now fallen from the coloured world
of fantasy into the realm of reality and he had to search around for a
starting-point, for a beginning to his dream. It seemed to him that the
fantasies nourished by his hate for Abkha and for which he now sought
vengeance were not of sufficient moment. As the frail craft approached,
threading its way among the anchored boats, he was slowly drained of his
feeling and it appeared to him that his long dreams of wealth were merely
a solace for his sudden failure and that they were quite irrational. The
packed streets, the buildings with their massive walls, the grey sky, the
scorching heat, the warm air of the north wind, the roads crammed with

cars, the serious faces, all these things appeared to him as barriers standing between him and his dream. He hurried aimlessly through this ocean of people, conscious of a deep feeling of loss which resembled vertigo, almost convinced that these many faces which did not glance at him were his first enemy, that all these people were the walls obstructing the very beginning of the road to his dream. The story was not as simple as in Abkha. Here it was without beginning, without end, without landmarks. It seemed to him that all the roads along which he walked were endless, that they circuited a rampart that held everything—every single thing—within its embrace. When, at sunset, a road led him to the seashore and he once again saw the sea, he stood staring across at the far horizon that joined up with the water: out there was Abkha, enveloped in tranquillity. It existed, every quarter had its beginning and its end, every wall carried its own particular lineaments; despite everything it was close to his heart. He felt lost in a rush of scalding water and for the first time he had no sense of shame as he lifted his hand to wipe salty tears from his cheeks.

Mohamed Ali Akbar wept without embarrassment, perhaps for the first time since he grew up, involuntarily, he had been overcome by a ferocious yearning for the two water-skins he used to carry across his shoulders. He was still staring out at the horizon while night gradually settled down around him. It made him feel in a way that he was present in a certain place at a certain time and that this night was like night in Abkha: people were sleeping behind their walls, the streets bore the lineaments of fatigue and silence, the sea rumbled heavily under the light of the moon. He felt relief. Wanting to laugh and yet unable to, he wept once again.

Dawn brought him an upsurge of fresh hope. He rose and went running through the streets. He realized that he must find someone from Oman with whom he could talk and that he would, sooner or later, find such a person, and from there he would learn where he was destined to proceed, from where to make a start.

And so Mohamed Ali Akbar attained his position as errand boy at a shop and was provided with a bicycle on which to carry out his duties. It was from this bicycle that the features of the streets, the qualities of the walls, registered themselves in his head. He felt a certain intimacy with them, but it was an intimacy imposed upon a background of a forbidding impression that he was being dogged by the eyes of his sister Sabika, the chinks in the girl's window, and Mohamed Ali the scoundrel who, unwittingly, had caused such dire disaster.

Months passed with the speed of a bicycle's wheels passing over the surface of a road. The wealth he had dreamed of began to come in and Mohamed Ali Akbar clung to this tiny fortune with all his strength, lest some passing whim should sweep it away or some scoundrel lay his hands on it. Thus it was that it occurred to him to make a sturdy wooden box in which to keep his fortune.

But what did Mohamed Ali Akbar's fortune consist of? Something that could not be reckoned in terms of money. When he had collected a certain amount of money he had bought himself a diaphanous white *aba* with gold edging. Every evening, alone with his box, he would take out the carefully folded *aba*, pass his thin brown fingers tenderly over it and spread it before his eyes; on it he would spill out his modest dreams, tracing along its borders all the streets of his village, the low, latticed windows from behind which peeped the eyes of young girls. There, in a corner of the *aba*, reposed the past which he could not bring himself to return to but whose existence was necessary in order to give the *aba* its true value. The thin fingers would fold it gently once again, put it safely back in its wooden box, and tie strong cord round the box. Then, and only then, did sleep taste sweet.

The box also contained a pair of china earrings for his sister Sabika, which he would give her on his return to Abkha, a bottle of pungent perfume, and a white purse holding such money as God in His bounty had given him and which he hoped would increase day by day.

As for the end, it began one evening. He was returning his bicycle to the shop when he felt a burning sensation in his limbs. He was alarmed at the thought that he had grown so weak, and with such speed, but did not take a great deal of notice, having had spells of trembling whenever he felt exceptionally homesick for Sabika and Abkha; he had already experienced just such a sensation of weakness when savagely yearning for all those things he hated and loved and had left behind, those things that made up the whole of his past. And so Mohamed Ali Akbar hastened along the road to his home with these thoughts in mind. But his feeling of weakness and nostalgia stayed with him till the following midday. When he made the effort to get up from bed, he was amazed to find that he had slept right through to noon instead of waking up at his usual early hour. What alarmed him even more was that he was still conscious of the feeling of weakness boring into his bones. Slightly afraid, he thought for a while and imagined himself all at once standing on the seashore with the glaring sun reflected off the water almost blinding him, the two water-skins on his shoulders, conscious of a sensation of intense exhaustion.

The reflection of the sun increased in violence, yet he was unable to shut his eyes—they were aflame. Abruptly he slid back into sleep.

Here time as usually understood came to an end for Mohamed Ali Akbar. From now on everything happened as though he were raised above the ground, as though his legs were dangling in mid-air: like a man on a gallows, he was moving in front of Time's screen, a screen as inert as a rock of basalt. His part as a practising human had been played out; his part as a mere spectator had come. He felt that there was no bond tying him to anything, that he was somewhere far away and that the things that moved before his eyes were no more than fish inside a large glass tumbler; his own eyes, too, were open and staring as though made of glass.

When he woke up again he realized that he was being carried by his arms and legs. Though he felt exhausted, he found the energy to recall that there was something which continued to be necessary to him and called out in a faint voice:

"The box . . . the box!"

No one, however, paid him any attention. With a frenzied movement he rose so as to get back to his box. His chest panting with the effort of getting to his feet, he called out:

"The box!"

But once again no one heard him. As he reached the door he clung to it and again gasped out in a lifeless voice:

"The box. . . ."

Overcome by his exertions, he fell into a trance that was of the seashore itself. This time he felt that the tide was rising little by little over his feet and that the water was intensely cold. His hands were grasping a square-shaped rock with which he plunged downwards. When he awoke again he found himself clasping his old box tied round with cord. While spectres passed to and fro in front of him, a needle was plunged into his arm, and a face bent over him.

Long days passed. But for Mohamed Ali Akbar nothing really happened at all. The mercilessness of the pain continued on its way, and he was not conscious of its passing. He was conscious only of its constant presence. The sea became dissolved into windows behind wooden shutters low against the side of the street, a pair of china earrings, an *aba* wet with salt water, a ship suspended motionless above the waves, and an old wooden box.

Only once was he aware of any contact with the world. This was when he heard a voice beside him say:

"What's in the old box?"

He looked at the source of the voice and saw, as in a dream, the face of a young, clean-shaven man with fair hair who was pointing at the box and looking at something.

The moment of recollection was short. He returned to gazing silently at the sea, though the face of the clean-shaven, blond young man also remained in front of him. After this he felt a sudden upsurge of energy; for no particular reason things had become clear to him. He distinctly saw, for the first time since he had collapsed, the rising of the sun. It seemed to him that he was capable of getting up from his bed and returning to his bicycle. Everything had grown clear to him: the box was alongside him, bound round as it had always been. Feeling at peace, he moved so as to get up, when a crowd of men in white clothes suddenly descended upon him, standing round him and regarding him with curiosity. Mohamed Ali Akbar tried to say something but was unable to. Suddenly he felt that the tide had risen right up to his waist and that the water was unbearably cold. He could feel nothing. He stretched out his arms to seize hold of something lest he should drown, but everything slid away from under his fingers. Suddenly he saw the clean-shaven face of the blond young man again; he stared at him, somewhat frightened of him on account of his box, while the water continued to rise higher and higher until it had screened off that fair, clean-shaven face from his gaze.

"Bed number 12 has died."

As the male nurse called out I was unable to free myself from Mohamed Ali Akbar's eyes staring out at me before he died. I imagined that Mohamed Ali Akbar, who refused to have his name mutilated, would now be satisfied at being merely "Bed number 12" if only he could be assured about the fate of his box.

This, my dear Ahmed, is the story of Mohamed Ali Akbar, Bed number 12, who died yesterday evening and is now lying wrapped round in a white cloth in the autopsy room—the thin brown face that shifted an ulcer from my intestines to my brain and who caused me to write to you, so you don't again repeat your famous phrase "I almost died laughing" in my presence.

Ever yours,

I haven't yet left the hospital. My health is gradually getting back to normal and the method by which I gauge this amuses me. Do you know how I measure my strength? I stand smoking on the balcony and throw the cigarette end with all my strength so that it falls along the strips of green grass in the garden. In past weeks the cigarette would fall just within the fourth strip, but today it was much nearer the sixth.

From your letter I understood you to say that you were in no need of being a witness to Mohamed Ali Akbar's death to know what death is. You wrote saying that the experience of death does not require the tragic prologues with which I described Mohamed Ali Akbar's life and that people die with far greater matter-of-factness: the man who fell down on the pavement and so let off the loaded pistol he had with him, whose bullet ripped open his neck (he was in the company of a strikingly beautiful girl), or the one who had a heart attack in the street one April evening, having become engaged to be married only a week before. Yes, that's all very true, my dear Ahmed, all very true, but the problem doesn't lie here at all, the problem of death is in no way that of the dead man, it is the problem of those who remain, those who bitterly await their turn so that they too may serve as a humble lesson to the eyes of the living. Of all the things I wrote in my last letter what I want to say now is that we must transfer our thinking from the starting-point to the end. All thinking must set forth from the point of death, whether it be, as you say, that of a man who dies contemplating the charms of the body of a wonderfully beautiful girl, or whether he dies staring into a newly shaven face which frightens him because of an old wooden box tied round with string. The unsolved question remains that of the end; the question of nonexistence, of eternal life—or what? Or what, my dear Ahmed?

Anyway, let's stop pouring water into a sack with a hole in it. Do you know what happened after I sent you my last letter? I went to the doctor's room and found them writing a report about Mohamed Ali Akbar. And they were on the point of opening the box. Oh, Ahmed, how imprisoned we are in our bodies and minds! We are always endowing others with our own attributes, always looking at them through a narrow fissure of our own views and way of thinking, wanting them, as far as we can, to become "us." We want to squeeze them into our skins, to give them our eyes to see with, to clothe them in our past and our own way of facing up to life. We place them within a framework outlined by our present understanding of time and place.

Mohamed Ali Akbar was none of the things I imagined. He was the father of three boys and two girls. We have forgotten that over there men marry early. Also, Mohamed Ali Akbar was not a water-seller, water being plentiful in Oman, but had been a sailor on one of the sailing ships that ply between the ports of the south and the Gulf, before settling down here quite a time ago.

It was in fact four years ago that Mohamed Ali Akbar arrived in Kuwait. After unimaginably hard effort he managed—only two months ago—to open what passed for a shop on one of the pavements of New Street. As to how he provided for his children in Oman, we simply don't know.

I read in the doctor's report that the patient had lost his sight six hours before death and so it would seem that Mohamed Ali Akbar had not in fact been staring into my face at the moment of his death as he was then blind. The doctor also wrote that as the address of the patient's family was not known, his burial would be attended solely by the hospital grave diggers.

The doctor read out the report to his colleague. It was concise and extremely condensed, merely dealing in technical terms with the man's illness. The doctor's voice was lugubrious and colourless. When he had finished reading he proceeded to untie the string round the box. At this point I thought of leaving the room, for it was none of my business: the Mohamed Ali Akbar I knew had died and this person they had written about was someone else; this box, too, was some other box. I knew for certain what Mohamed Ali Akbar's box contained. Why should I bother myself about some new problem?

And yet I was unable to go to the door, but stood in the corner, trembling slightly.

The box was soon opened and the doctor quickly ran his fingers through the contents. Then he pushed it to one side.

Fearfully I looked into the box: it was filled with recent invoices for sums owed by the shop to the stores which supplied it; in one corner was an old photo of a bearded face, an old watch strap, some string, a small candle and several rupees among the papers.

I must be truthful and say that I was sadly disappointed. Before leaving the room, though, I saw something that stunned me: the nurse had pushed aside Mohamed Ali Akbar's invoices and revealed a long china earring that glittered. In a daze I went to the box and picked up the earring. I don't know why it was that I looked at the nurse and said:

"He bought this earring for his sister Sabika—I happen to know that."

For a brief instant she stared at me in some surprise—then she laughed uproariously. The doctor, too, laughed at the joke.

You are no doubt aware that nurses are required to humour patients with stomach ulcers in case they should suffer a relapse.

Yours ever—

Born and educated in Chicago, Ray Russell had a wide-ranging literary career as a novelist, story writer, screenwriter, poet, and executive editor of *Playboy Magazine,* a stint he once called "a delightful detour from the main highway of my life, writing." An author who took the comic form seriously, Russell turned to the satiric possibilities of the letter story in "Evil Star," which was first published in *Paris Review* in 1976 and was reprinted in *The Paris Review Anthology* in 1990. In this attorney's letter to an author, a prepublication review of the author's book for potential libel, the understatement of the lawyer's remarks serves to underline the sleaziness of the book itself, a sly juxtaposition of tones that gives the story its comic thrust.

Dear Mr. Bernstein:

At the request of your publisher and our client, my colleagues and I have now read and discussed the typescript of your book. We are pleased to report that, with the exception of some isolated sections which we will specify, the book is not, in our opinion, actionable and should not expose you to litigation when published. It is a work of scholarly analysis, thoroughly documented, and even though much of it is pungently expressed, it lies well within the area of fair comment. You have obviously "done your homework," amassed considerable research, and consistently cited "chapter and verse," so to speak, in tracing the sources of Avery Bream's work. Your extensive parallel excerpts from his writings and the writings of others, from which you demonstrate his were derived, put you on firm legal, as well as literary, ground.

These parallels of style and subject matter are most impressive. Your own cleverness is rivalled only by that of Mr. Bream himself. I refer to his technique of borrowing a plot from one writer and retelling it in the style of another, thus achieving an artful act of camouflage undetected until now. I was astonished to learn, for instance, that his most famous best-seller, *Evil Star*, is practically a carbon copy of Dreiser's *An American Tragedy*, done in the style (or, as you put it, "filtered through the prism") of James Branch Cabell. It was likewise illuminating to discover that his acclaimed *Midnight Mushrooms* is little more than *Othello* with the races switched, told in the manner of early Saroyan, and with no acknowledgment to Shakespeare (unless we count the title, a quotation from *The Tempest*); and that his *Pristine Christine* is none other than the Agatha Christie classic *The Murder of Roger Ackroyd*, as it might have been written by Burroughs (you should clarify as to whether you have reference to William or to Edgar Rice) and with the Christine of the title (a play on Christie?) taking the place of the original victim. We suggest a title change, however, for Chapter III, in which the bulk of these and other parallels are cited. Even though *The Thieving Magpie* is the title of a famous opera, words like "thief" should be avoided.

On p. 97, after you quote Bream's statement, "I am the equal, in my fashion, of Tolstoy, Proust and Joyce" (from an interview in *Newsweek*), you make your point elegantly when you say: "The painter Ingres told those who likened him to Raphael, 'I am very small, just *so high,* next to him.' The composer Rossini made a pilgrimage to kneel before the manuscript score of Mozart's *Don Giovanni,* declaring it a sacred relic." Why not leave it at that? To add, as you do, that Bream is "a conceited pig" not fit to "empty the bedpans" of Tolstoy, et al., is painting the lily, as well as flirting with litigation.

A similar example of gilding refined gold occurs on p. 118, following your sentence, "For over a decade, he has been promising to astound us with a vast confessional tome of Rousseau-like candor in which he will beat his breast and cry *mea culpa* to a host of sins, literary and otherwise; but the years come and go, and the guilt-heavy volume never appears." That is fine, but the short burst that follows ("What's the matter, Bream—*chicken?*") is, from the legal point of view, touchy.

Our Mr. Vieck asks me to say that, speaking now not as attorneys but as impartial readers, we hope we may be forgiven for commenting on the language you employ in Chapter VIII to describe the first Mrs. Bream. It seems inordinately biased in her favor. This is not, I reiterate, a legal point, but for you to call her "an angel whose delicate foot scarce touched the sordid earth when she walked" (p. 130), "too good by far, too radiant for this world" (p. 131), "an anthology of all the virtues" (p. 132), "a fount of undemanding, uncomplaining love" (p. 133), "a golden spirit the like of which no mortal eye will ever see again" (p. 134), etc., strikes us as somewhat excessive. When such phrases are read alongside your less than complimentary remarks about her husband, the contrast tends to cast doubt upon your academic detachment.

In Chapter IX, *Champion of the Overdog,* you walk a tightrope in showing Bream as being a far cry from the fearless anti-Establishment crusader and spokesman for writers' rights he pretends to be. The change or deletion of a few passages should make the chapter safe from litigation. Second paragraph, p. 155, the word "coward" is ill-advised, as is the phrase in the next paragraph, "soul of a weasel." Pp. 157–158 make vivid reading, but in them you are guilty of that with which you charge Bream: lack of substantiation. "His oft-repeated claim to have broken the writing arm of a magazine editor who had 'emasculated' his prose," you say, "is less piquant than it might be if he would, just once, name the offending butcher." Good point, but you spoil it (and skate on thin legal ice) when you add: "In fact, that editor has privately recounted the truth about the famous fray. Bream, it seems, had offered a timorous, whining protest to the emendations, thus provoking the overworked editor to gruffly respond, 'Damn it, I sweated blood to make that unreadable swill fit for human consumption. And this is the thanks I get? You're lucky I publish your shit at *all*! On the stressed word, the angered editor brought his fist down forcibly on his desk, breaking the little finger of his right hand." *You* do not name the editor, either, you see, so the authenticity of both versions is suspect.

The same chapter (p. 159) contains a passage that could be considered defamatory not only to Bream but also to Siegfried Rheinfahrt, the book publisher. I refer to the quoted letter, from and to unidentified sources, which describes an incident at a booksellers' convention: "You should have seen our dearly beloved Aviary buttering up that Nazi goniff, Rheinfahrt. I mean, it's one thing for Aviary to change his name and try to pass for goy, and it's another for him to fawn upon and flatter that lizard who's not only a crook but an anti-Semite. Most of us snubbed Siggie cold, but not ol' Aviary. Oh, no. It was nauseating. He did everything but kiss the s.o.b.'s ass, and maybe in the *privvissy,* as he'd say in that phony accent he's begun to affect, of his hotel suite, he even did that." The passage should be excised.

Are you sure of your facts (p. 201) when you describe Bream "running from bookstore to bookstore, spending his entire advance check buying up copies of his novel to get it on the [bestseller] list . . ."? What proof of this could you provide, if challenged? On the same page, how can you possibly know that he "not only wined and dined" but also "tickled more than the fancy" of the "aging female critic" who, according to you, "bears a startling resemblance to Samuel Johnson"? Moreover, if we understand what you are suggesting in the "tickled" line, does this not contradict the allegation in your p. 492 footnote (see below)? Please think about these points carefully.

I'm afraid we cannot recommend the retention of your allusions to Bream's income in the form they are now presented (p. 299). Nor do we quite understand the precise nature of your charges. Do you mean to imply that he failed to declare a substantial portion of his earnings for that year? That is a serious allegation. Or do you merely mean that he lied to the press, inflating the true figures in order to appear more affluent and successful than he actually was? Do you really plan to reproduce photocopies of his IRS returns? (I refer to such phrases as "See Plate 1," "See Plate 2," and so on.) How were these documents obtained?

Your comments about his mother (p. 307) present no legal problem because she is deceased, although in some quarters these passages may be criticized on grounds of taste.

The telephone conversation between Bream and his psychoanalyst (pp. 349–350) poses a quadruple problem, however. First: it could only have been obtained by wiretap, which is illegal. Second: it puts both patient and doctor in a most unfavorable light. Third: as our forensic medicine expert, Dr. Kenney, reminds us, you are not a licensed psychiatrist, so you are not legally qualified to diagnose Bream's mental condition as displaying evidence of "self-destructive tendencies . . . irreversible paranoia . . . dangerously sociopathic hostilities . . . desire for humiliation and punishment . . . schizoid hallucinations and delusions," etc. Fourth: as you point out by the long parallel quotations in the right-hand columns of these pages, the phone conversation is identical, word for word, to the conversation between the fictitious characters Dr. Proctor and Bernie Amber in Bream's novel, *Negative Feedback*. You claim (but without adequate support) that the real-life conversation took place five months *after* the publication of the book, indicating that "Bream is perhaps the only novelist in history whose own life plagiarized his work. So cowed and mesmerized was his puppet doctor by the fame of the celebrated patient that he responded on cue, Charley McCarthy–like, to Bream's leading questions and insults." Is it not possible, we submit, that you are mistaken about the date of the conversation? Might it not have occurred *prior* to the writing of the book, and been used as grist for the author's mill (a not uncommon practice among fiction writers)? Indeed, is it not an open secret in literary circles that Amber is the most transparently autobiographical character in the entire Bream *oeuvre*? Is not AMBER—as our crossword fanatic, Mr. Fenwick, says—a simple anagram for BREAM? For these several reasons, we counsel you to forego this conversation.

Similarly troublesome is the first of the two footnotes on p. 492 (beginning "Freud, Jung and even Reich all agree . . ."). While it may be perfectly true that certain aspects of his lifestyle are indicators of "impotence or other sexual dysfunction" rather than the "prowess he publicly professes," there is no way you can satisfactorily prove this, even by quoting the anonymous "Ms. X." Besides, here you are venturing into personal attack rather than professional criticism. We realize that you consider this an important insight into the "pathological sex episodes" of his work, which is the theme of this chapter, but we urge you to delete this footnote, as well as the parenthetical reference (in the body of the following page, 493) to what you call his "underendowment." The supportive Polaroid photograph which you indicate will appear on the "facing page" of the published book certainly must not be used. It is irrelevant that you obtained "the standard release form" signed by the photographer, his second ex-wife. What is required is a release from the subject, or model, Mr. Bream himself, and that, in our opinion, will be obtained only with the greatest difficulty. And surely the reference (same page) to his "*vain attempts* at solitary vice" (italics mine) is pure conjecture on your part?

(Before I forget it, allow me to backtrack and cover a couple of small spots I missed. In Chapter VIII, where you picture Bream's miscegenational first marriage, is it necessary to say "murderously jealous rages" and "where the body is buried," even though these expressions have a clearly metaphorical intent? They would not, perhaps, be problems were it not for the tragic sailing accident that took the life of the first Mrs. Bream, plus the fact that her body was never recovered. Some readers might interpret your figures of speech literally, as a monstrous accusation, and you would then be extremely vulnerable to the possibility of a lawsuit. Also inadvisable is the phrase, "Flowers die; rats live." You really must not call Bream a rat. And only this moment Mr. Fenwick calls my attention to the fact that the title of Bream's most famous novel is "rats live" in reverse—isn't that interesting?)

Now for the bad news. We must seriously question the wisdom of your lengthy (95 pages!) Appendix, in which you provide, verbatim and unexpurgated, letters written over the years by various editors, creditors, writers, literary agents, relatives, former fans and friends of Bream's, and so forth. The material, even if provably factual, is extremely damaging to Bream and was not originally intended by the letter writers for publication. In most cases, it seems unlikely that you have even secured proper permission. We strongly advise an appendectomy, that is to say removal of the entire Appendix.

Your revision of the above specified areas should protect you from litigation and, if I may say so, result in a most valuable work of contemporary scholarship which I, for one, found to be brisk reading. May I look forward to receiving a personally inscribed copy of the first edition?

Yours truly,

For

West, Fenwick, Schlusselmann, Kenney, & Vieck

Arthur Lowell West

P.S. Our Mr. Schlusselmann points out the amusing coincidence that your name is the German equivalent of a well-known Bream character. Are you aware of this?

Although most of us know the English writer A. A. Milne for his children's books, such as *Winnie-the-Pooh* (1926) and *When We Were Very Young* (1924), he worked in a variety of literary genres. A storywriter, a playwright, an essayist, and a novelist whose traditional mystery, *The Red House Mystery* (1922), has become a classic, Milne was also a humorist for *Punch*. We see his lively humor at play in "The Rise and Fall of Mortimer Scrivens," a letter tale about borrowing, blemishing, and bidding for books, which appeared in his collection *A Table near the Band* (1950). As messages—and personalities—cross in this epistolary farce, we are always steps ahead of the characters, who know no more than they could and write just the letters they would.

Extract from "Readers' Queries" in "The Literary Weekly":

Q. What is it which determines First Edition values? Is it entirely a question of the author's literary reputation?

A. Not entirely, but obviously to a great extent. An additional factor is the original size of the first edition, which generally means that an established author's earliest books are more valuable than his later ones. Some authors, moreover, are more fashionable than others with bibliophiles, for reasons not always easy to detect; nor does there seem to be any explanation why an author, whose reputation as a writer has never varied, should be highly sought after by collectors at one time, and then suddenly become completely out of fashion. So perhaps all that we can say with confidence is that prices of First Editions, like those of everything else, are determined by the Laws of Supply and Demand.

Mr. Henry Winters to Mr. Brian Haverhill.

Dear Mr. Haverhill,

It may be within your memory that on the occasion of an afternoon visit which you and Mrs. Haverhill were good enough to pay us two years ago I was privileged to lend her Chapman's well-known manual on the Viola, which, somewhat surprisingly, she had never come across; I say surprisingly, for undoubtedly he is our greatest authority on the subject. If by any chance she has now read it, I should be very much obliged by its return at your convenience. I would not trouble you in this matter but for the fact that the book is temporarily out of print, and I have been unable therefore to purchase another copy for myself.

Miss Winters is away for a few days, or she would join me in sending compliments to you and Mrs. Haverhill.

Yours very truly,
Henry Winters.

Mr. Brian Haverhill to Mr. Henry Winters.

Dear Winters,

I was much distressed to get your letter this morning and to discover that Sally and I had been behaving so badly. It is probably as much my fault as hers, but she is away with her people in Somerset just now, and I think must have taken your book with her; so for the moment I can do nothing about it but apologise humbly for both of us. I have of course written to her, and asked her to send it back to you at once, or, if it is here in the house, to let me know where she has hidden it.

Again all my apologies,
Yours sincerely,
Brian Haverhill.

Brian Haverhill to Sally Haverhill.

Darling,

Read the enclosed and tell me how disgraced you feel—and how annoyed you think Winters is. I don't care for that bit about purchasing another copy for himself. He meant it nasty-like, if you ask me. Still, two years is a long time to take over a book, and you ought to have spelt it out to yourself more quickly. I could have helped you with the longer words.

The funny thing is I don't seem to remember anything about this viola book, nor whether it is the sort you play or the sort you grow, but I do seem to remember some other book which he forced on us—essays of some sort, at a guess. Can you help? Because if there were two, we ought to send both back together. I have staved him off for a bit by saying that you were so devoted to Chapman that you had taken the damned book with you. It doesn't sound likely to me, but it may to him. And why haven't we seen Winters and his saintly sister for two years? Not that I mind—on the contrary—but I just wondered. Are we cutting them or are they cutting us? One would like to know the drill in case of an accidental meeting in the village.

My love to everybody, and lots of a very different sort to your darling self. Bless you. Your Brian.

Sally Haverhill to Brian Haverhill.

Darlingest, I did mean to ring you up last night but our line has broken down or the rent hasn't been paid or something, and I couldn't do it in the village, not properly.

How awful about Mr. Winters! It was flowers of course, silly, not musical instruments, because I was talking about violas to him when you were talking about the Litany to Honoria, I remember it perfectly, I was wearing my blue and yellow cotton, and one of her stockings was coming down. But you're quite right about the other one, it was called *Country Filth* and *very* disappointing. It must be somewhere. Do send them both back at once, darling—you'll find Chapman among the garden books— and say how sorry I am. And then I'll write myself. Yes, I think he's really angry, he's not a very nice man.

No, I don't think we've quarrelled. I did ask them both to our cocktail party a few weeks later, but being strict T.T.'s which I only found out afterwards, Honoria was rather stiff about it. Don't you remember? And then I asked them to tea, and they were away, and then I sort of felt that it was their turn to write. I'll try again if you like when I come home . . .

Brian Haverhill to Sally Haverhill.

Darling Sal,

1. Don't try again.

2. I have found Chapman nestling among the detective stories. I deduced that it would be there as soon as you said garden books.

3. Books aren't called *Country Filth,* not in Honoria's house anyway, and if they were, what would you be hoping that they were like? Tell your mother that I'm surprised at you.

4. There are a thousand books in the library, not to mention hundreds all over the place, and I can't possibly look through them all for one whose title, size, colour and contents are completely unknown to me. So pull yourself together, there's a dear, and send me a telegram with all that you remember about it.

5. I adore you.

Brian.

Sally Haverhill to Brian Haverhill.

Something about country by somebody like Morgan or Rivers sort of ordinary size and either biscuit colour or blue all my love Sal.

Country Tilth: The Prose Ramblings of a Rhymester: by Mortimer Scrivens (Street and Co.)

1. A World Washed Clean.

Long ere His Majesty the Sun had risen in His fiery splendour, and while yet the first faint flush of dawn, rosy herald of His coming, still lingered in the east, I was climbing (but how blithely!) the ribbon of road, pale-hued, which spanned the swelling mother-breasts of the downland. At melodic intervals, with a melancholy which little matched my mood, the lone cry of the whimbrel . . .

Brian Haverhill to Sally Haverhill.

O lord, Sally, we're sunk! I've found the damned book—*Country Tilth* by Mortimer Scrivens. It's ghastly enough inside, but outside—darling, there's a large beer-ring such as could never have been there originally, and looking more like the ring made by a large beer-mug than any beer-ring ever did. You can almost smell the beer. I swear *I* didn't do it, I don't treat books like that, not even ghastly books, it was probably Bill when he was last here. Whoever it was, we can't possibly send it back like this.

What shall I do?

1. Send back Chapman and hope that he has forgotten about this one; which seems likely as he didn't mention it in his letter.

2. Send both back, and hope that he's a secret beer-drinker and made the mark himself.

3. Apologise for the mark, and say I think it must be milk.

4. Get another copy and pass it off as the one he lent us. I suppose Warbecks would have it.

What do you advise? I must do something about the viola book soon, I feel. I wish you were here . . .

Sally Haverhill to Brian Haverhill.

One and Four darling writing Sal.

Mr. Brian Haverhill to Messrs. Warbecks Ltd.

Dear Sirs,

I shall be glad if you can find me a first-edition of *Country Tilth* by Mortimer Scrivens. It was published by Street in 1923. If it is a second-hand copy, it is important that it should be fairly clean, particularly the cover. I should doubt if it ever went into a second edition.

Yours faithfully,
Brian Haverhill.

Mr. Brian Haverhill to Mr. Henry Winters.

Dear Winters,

I now return your book with our most profound apologies for keeping it so long. I can only hope that you were not greatly inconvenienced by its absence. It is, as you say, undoubtedly the most authoritative work on the subject, and our own violas have profited greatly by your kindness in introducing us to it.

Please give my kindest regards to Miss Winters if she is now with you. I hope you are both enjoying this beautiful weather.

Yours sincerely,
Brian Haverhill.

Mrs. Brian Haverhill to Mr. Henry Winters.

Dear Mr. Winters,

Can you ever forgive me for my unpardonable carelessness in keeping that delightful book so long? I need hardly say that I absorbed every word of it, and then put it carefully away, meaning to return it next morning, but somehow it slipped my memory in the way things do—well, it's no good trying to explain, I must just hope that you will forgive me, and when I come home—I am staying with my people for three weeks— perhaps you will let us show you and Miss Winters how well our violas are doing now—thanks entirely to you!

A very nice message to Miss Winters, please, and try to forgive,

Yours most sincerely,
Sarah Haverhill.

Sally Haverhill to Brian Haverhill.

Darling,

I hope you have sent the book back because I simply grovelled to the man yesterday, and I had to say I hoped they'd come and see our violas when I got back, but of course it doesn't mean anything. What I meant by my telegram was send the book back, which I expect you've done, and try and get a copy of the other just in *case* he remembers later on. If it's such a very bad book it can't cost much. Bill is here for a few days and says that he never makes beer-rings on books, and it must be one of *your* family, probably Tom, and Mother says that there is a way of removing beer-rings from books if only she could remember what it was, which looks as though she must have got the experience from my family not yours, but it doesn't help much. Anyhow I'm *sure* he's forgotten all about the book, and it *was* clever of you to find it, darling, and I do hope my telegram helped . . .

Messrs. Warbecks Ltd. To Mr. Brian Haverhill.

Dear Sir,

We have received your instructions *re* Country Tilth, and shall do our best to obtain a copy of the first edition for you. If it is not in stock, we propose to advertise for it. We note that it must be a fairly clean copy.

Assuring you of our best attention at all times,

Yours faithfully,
H. and E. Warbecks Ltd.
(p.p. J. W. F.)

Mr. Henry Winters to Mr. Brian Haverhill.

Dear Mr. Haverhill,

I am glad to acknowledge receipt of *The Care of the Viola* by Reynolds Chapman which arrived this morning. My impression was that the copy which I had the pleasure of lending Mrs. Haverhill two years ago was a somewhat newer and cleaner edition, but doubtless the passage of so long a period of time would account for the difference. I am not surprised to hear from Mrs. Haverhill that the book has been of continued value to her. It has been so to me, whenever in my possession, for a good many years.

Yours very truly,
Henry Winters.

Brian Haverhill to Sally Haverhill.

Darling Sally,

Just to get your values right before you come back to me: It is the Haverhills who are cutting the Winterses, and make no mistake about it. I enclose his foul letter. From now on no grovelling. Just a delicate raising of the eyebrows when you meet him, expressing surprise that the authorities have done nothing and he is still about.

Warbecks are trying to get another copy of *Country Tilth*, but I doubt if they will, because I can't see anybody keeping such a damn silly book. Well, I don't mind if they don't. Obviously Winters has forgotten all about it, and after his ill-mannered letter I see no reason for reminding him . . .

Sally Haverhill to Brian Haverhill.

Sweetie Pie,

What a *brute* the man is, he never even acknowledged *my* letter, and I *couldn't* have been nicer. I think you should definitely tell Warbecks that you don't want the book now, and if he *does* ask for it ever, you either say that he never lent it to you or else send back the copy we've got, and say that the beer-mark was always there because you remember wondering at the time, him being *supposed* not to have beer in the house, which was why you hadn't sent it back before, just seeing it from the outside and not thinking it could possibly be *his* copy. Of *course* I shall never speak to him again, horrible man. Mother says there used to be a Dr. Winters in Exeter when she was a girl, and he had to leave the country suddenly, but of course it may not be any relation . . .

Brian Haverhill to Sally Haverhill.

Sally darling, you're ingenious and sweet and I love you dearly, but you must learn to distinguish between the gentlemanly lies you *can* tell and the other sort. Don't ask your mother to explain this to you, ask your father or Bill. Not that it matters as far as Winters is concerned. We've finished with him, thank God . . .

Mr. Henry Winters to Messrs. Warbecks Ltd.

Dear Sirs,

My attention has been fortuitously called to your advertisement enquiring for a copy of the 1st Edition of Mortimer Scrivens' *Country Tilth*. I am the fortunate possessor of a 1st Edition of this much-sought-after item, which I shall be willing to sell if we can come to a suitable financial arrangement. I need hardly remind you that 1st editions of Mortimer Scrivens are a considerable rarity in the market, and I shall await your offer with some interest.

Yours faithfully,
Henry Winters.

Mr. Henry Winters to Miss Honoria Winters.

Dear Honoria,

I trust that your health is profiting by what I still consider to be your unnecessary visit to Harrogate. Do you remember a book of essays by Mortimer Scrivens called *Country Tilth,* which used to be, and had been for upwards of twenty-five years, in the middle shelf on the right-hand side of the fireplace? I have looked for it, not only there but in all the other shelves, without result, and I can only conclude that you have taken it up to your bedroom recently, and that it has since been put away in some hiding place of your own. It is of the *utmost importance* that I should have this book AT ONCE, and I shall be obliged by your immediate assistance in the matter.

The weather remains fine, but I am gravely inconvenienced by your absence, and shall be relieved by your return.

Your affec. brother,
Henry Winters.

Miss Honoria Winters to Mr. Henry Winters.

Dear Henry,

Thank you for your letter. I am much enjoying my stay here, and Frances and I have been making a number of pleasant little "sorties" to places of interest in the neighbourhood, including one or two charming old churches. Our hotel is very quiet, thanks to the fact that it has no licence to provide intoxicating drink, with the result that an extremely nice class of person comes here. Already we are feeling the beneficial effects of the change, and I hope that when I return—on Monday the 24th—I shall be completely restored to health.

Frances sends her kindest remembrances to you, for although you have never met her, she has so often learnt of you in my letters that she feels that she knows you quite well!

Your affectionate sister,
Honoria.

P.S. Don't forget to tell Mrs. Harding in advance if you are *not* going to London next Thursday, as this was the day when we had arranged for the window-cleaner to come. She can then arrange for any other day suitable to you. You lent that book to the Haverhills when they came to tea about two years ago, together with your Viola book. I remember because you told me to fetch it for you. I haven't seen it since, so perhaps you lent it afterwards to somebody else.

Messrs. Warbecks Ltd. to Mr. Brian Haverhill.

Dear Sir,

Country Tilth

We have received notice of a copy of the 1st edition of this book in private possession, but before entering into negotiations with the owner it would be necessary to have some idea of the outside price which you would be prepared to pay. We may say that we have no replies from the trade, and if this copy is not secured, it may be difficult to obtain another. First editions of this author are notoriously scarce, and we should like to feel that, if necessary, we could go as high as £5, while endeavouring, of course, to obtain it for less. Trusting to have your instructions in the matter at your early convenience,

Yours faithfully,
H. & E. Warbecks Ltd.

Mr. Brian Haverhill to Messrs. Warbecks Ltd.

Dear Sirs,

Country Tilth.

I had assumed when I wrote to you that a first edition of this book, being of no literary value, would not have cost more than a few shillings, and in any case £1 would have been my limit, including your own commission. In the circumstances I will ask you to let the matter drop, and to send me your account for any expense to which I have put you.

Yours faithfully,
Brian Haverhill.

Mr. Henry Winters to Mr. Brian Haverhill.

Dear Sir,

I now find, as must always have been known to yourself, that at the time of my lending Mrs. Haverhill *The Care of the Viola* by Reynolds Chapman, I also lent her, or you, a 1st edition of *Country Tilth* by Mortimer Scrivens. In returning the first named book to me two years later, you ignored the fact that you had this extremely rare book in your possession, presumably in the hope that I should not notice its absence from my shelves. I must ask you therefore to return it *immediately,* before I take other steps in the matter.

Yours faithfully,
Henry Winters.

Mr. Brian Haverhill to Messrs. Warbecks Ltd.

Dear Sirs,

This is to confirm my telephone message this morning that I am prepared to pay up to £5 for a 1st edition of *Country Tilth,* provided that it is in reasonably good condition. The matter, I must say again, is of the most urgent importance.

Yours faithfully,
Brian Haverhill.

Brian Haverhill to Sally Haverhill.

O hell, darling, all is discovered. I had a snorter from that devil this morning, demanding the instant return of *Country Tilth,* and this just after I had told Warbecks not to bother any more! They had written to say that they only knew of one copy in existence (I told you nobody would keep the damn thing) and that the man might want £5 for it. So naturally I said "£5 my foot." I have now rung them up to withdraw my foot, which I had so rashly put in it, and say "£5." But £5 for a blasted book which nobody wants to read—and just because of a beer-ring which is its only real contact with life—seems a bit hard. Let this be a lesson to all of us never to borrow books, at least never from T.T.'s. Alternatively, of course, to return them in less than two years—there *is* that . . .

Messrs. Warbecks Ltd. to Mr. Henry Winters.

Dear Sir,

Country Tilth.

If you will forward us your copy of the 1st edn. of this book for our inspection, we shall then be in a position to make what we hope you will consider a very satisfactory offer for it in accordance with its condition.

Awaiting a reply at your earliest convenience, as the matter is of some urgency.

Yours faithfully,
H. and E. Warbecks Ltd.

Mr. Henry Winters to Mr. Brian Haverhill.

Sir,

Country Tilth.

Unless I receive my copy of this book within 24 hours I shall be compelled to consult my solicitors.

Yours faithfully,
Henry Winters.

Mr. Brian Haverhill to Messrs. Warbecks Ltd.

Dear Sirs,

Country Tilth.

In confirmation of my telephone message this morning I authorise you to make a firm offer of £10 for the 1st edn. of this book for which you are negotiating, provided that it is delivered within the next 24 hours.

Yours faithfully,
Brian Haverhill.

Messrs. Warbecks Ltd. to Mr. Henry Winters.

Sir,

Country Tilth.

We are still awaiting a reply to our letter of the 18th asking you to forward your copy of the 1st edn. of this book for our inspection. We are now authorised by our client to say that he is prepared to pay £10 for your copy, provided that its condition is satisfactory to him, and that we receive delivery of it by the 22nd inst. After that date he will not be interested in the matter.

Yours faithfully,
H. & E. Warbecks Ltd.

Mr. Henry Winters to Brian Haverhill.

Sir,

The enclosed copy of a letter from Messrs. Warbecks speaks for itself. You have the alternative of returning my book *immediately* or sending me your cheque for £10. Otherwise I shall take legal action.

H. Winters.

Sally Haverhill to Brian Haverhill.

Darling one, *what* do you think has happened!!! This morning we drove into Taunton just after you rang up, Mother having suddenly remembered it was Jacqueline's birthday to-morrow, and in a little bookshop down by the river I found a copy of *Country Tilth* in the 6d box! Quite clean too and no name inside it, so I sent it off at once to Mr. Winters, with a little letter just saying how sorry I was to have kept it so long, and not telling a single "other sort" except for being a little sarcastic which I'm sure is quite a gentlemanly thing to be. So, darling, you needn't bother any more, and after I come back on Monday (HOORAY!) we'll go up to London for a night and spend the £10 I've saved you. What fun! Only of course you must ring up Warbecks *at once . . .*

Mrs. Brian Haverhill to Mr. Henry Winters.

Dear Mr. Winters,

I am sending back the other book you so kindly lent me. I am so sorry I kept it so long, but it had *completely* disappeared, and poor Brian has been looking everywhere for it, and worrying *terribly,* thinking you would think I was trying to steal it or something! Wasn't it *crazy* of him? As if you would!—and as if the book was worth stealing when I saw a copy of it in the 6d box at Taunton this very morning! I expect you'll be wondering where I found your copy. Well, it was most odd. I happened to be looking in my dressing-case just now, and there is a flap in the lid which I hardly ever use, and I noticed it was rather bulging—and there was the book! I've been trying to remember when I last used this particular dressing-case, because it looks as though I must have taken the book away with me directly after you so kindly lent it to me, and of course I remembered that it *was* just before I came to see my people, which I do every year at this time, that we came to see *you*!

I must now write and tell Brian the good news, because after turning the house upside down looking for it, he was actually *advertising* for a copy to replace it, and offering £10—ten *pounds,* think of it, when its actual value is *sixpence*! Wouldn't it have been awful if some horrible mercenary person who happened to have a copy had taken advantage of his ignorance of book prices and swindled him? But, whatever its value, it doesn't make it any the less kind of you to have lent it to me, or careless of me to have forgotten about it so quickly.

Yours most sincerely,
Sarah Haverhill.

P.S. Isn't this hot weather delightful? Just perfect for sunbathing. I can see you and Miss Winters simply *revelling* in it.

Since the 1970s, Stephen Dixon, a native New Yorker, has been chron-icling urban lives and relationships in his fiction. The author of more than twenty books, Dixon has been especially prolific as a short story writer, publishing thirteen collections of short fiction. "Man of Letters" appeared in *The Stories of Stephen Dixon* (1994) and, earlier, in *Quite Contrary: The Mary and Newt Story* (1979), a set of interrelated tales that tracks a relationship in all its contemporary messiness. In this letter tale, Dixon, with his ear for the vernacular, persuasively conveys Newt's stream of thought. It is significant, though, that these are not simply thoughts but letters; that Newt is typing them suggests some intention—or, at least, some hope—of putting them in the mail. It is that doomed intention and hopeful belief that gives the story both its pathos and its comic edge.

Em—

I don't want to see you anymore. There's a lot else that can be said about this decision of mine, but I don't want to go into it. So that's it then. Don't come by. And I won't be coming up there again. Much love, Newt

Em—

I think we need a nice long rest from each other. You're aware yourself that things haven't been going well with us for a while. Thing that most elicited my decision was that I just didn't like the way you set the relationship for us. The "week" together this summer. On a "beach." Perhaps you have to act like this. What you are, want to become, your history. But it's now too much for me. I won't be coming up. I don't want you coming by. I want no communication between us of any kind. I can't say "Maybe some other time perhaps." I just don't feel like that. I'm sorry. Love, Newt

Dear Em:

I won't be coming to Stonehill anymore. I don't want you to come to my flat again. I just don't want to go on with our relationship anymore. It's not going to change: the relationship or my decision. At least it doesn't seem so to me. Most of all, I'm tired of you setting our pace. That "week" in the summer. On a "beach." It's usually your way. It's a shame you can't just let things happen between us without always analyzing it, trying to control it, putting me to tests, being worried that everything will pass you by and too many things will never be tried out by you if you stay only with one mate.

I do think about you sweetly. Fooling around. Holding you close. Talking. All that. But the other disturbing things that have happened between us, if they're not already embedded in my head, just don't creep in anymore, they rush.

I don't feel responsible for this break. For a little, all right. But it does seem it has to go the way you want it, without any give and take, and I find I can't exist in an atmosphere like that. Especially when it's coupled with your repeatedly turning me on and off and I think your serious remarks about how you look forward to the day when you'll be able to manage two and maybe three successful love affairs at one time, so I just don't want to see you anymore.

I don't say that what you're proposing for yourself is impossible or wrong. Maybe I am "rigid," "superannuated," as you said—whatever, but it just isn't my way. And I do love you very much, but for the first time in my life that doesn't seem to be enough to make me want to stay. So, cheers then—En

Dear Mary—

I won't be coming to Stonehill anymore. I don't want you to come by my place. I just don't want to go on with our relationship anymore. I'm tired of you always setting the pace. The "week" this summer. On a "beach." And I don't think it's because I'm "indecisive" or don't like to make "any decision" that this is the case. You take over because you want to, have to, whatever's the force. If you tell me once more it's partly astrological, I'll have to yell at you again "That's asinine."

I went along like a "dud" because I don't like to direct a relationship based on love. It's a pity you can't let it happen without dashing it to dust every time it goes well. We've gone on for hours about the reasons for all that: the history. But to me there really aren't any explanations.

I also can't get the bad things out of my head. I think about you sweetly. Fooling around. Joking. Holding you close. Talking. Walking. Working. All that. But the other disturbing things just don't creep in, they rush. And a lot else about what's happened between us just hasn't been etched out of my head yet. Your turning me on and off. Blowing me up. Indifferently letting me go. Separating "for the time being" because you thought it was the "wrong time for us" or it was just "bad timing when we met" and soon after that your returning and for a while staying and being open and loving and then re-going when you thought it was the wrong time for us again or just thought that for yourself it was best. I always felt when you returned "Well that's the last time for that, folks," but it never was. Now I think "How in hell could I have thought any of those times after the first few times could have been the last time?" And after the last time I suppose I was just holding on. Like a kite. No, a kite doesn't hold on, it's held, and I was held, though not tight like a kite. Oh, I was held tight like a kite sometimes, but we're talking about my holding, not being held. Maybe the kite holds on to a tree. But you're no tree, though you do have roots. But so do turnips, teeth and attributes that lead to actions and decisions, but as you can see I'm the worst at analogues, metaphors and similes. Yes, you can so be a tree. But no, I wasn't a kite that way except maybe in my becoming entangled in you and not being able to fly freely or sail away or something because of the string. But a kite becomes entangled around something, not in it, except if it maybe got blown into a window or cave. But even there it would probably only get entangled around a table or chair in the window or a rock in the cave, and not entangled around the window or cave it got blown in. Anyway, now I'm letting go.

I don't feel responsible for causing this break. Or, maybe a little. But I'm not going to rationalize it away by saying, as you hinted the last time we drove in, that what we both probably have wanted for the last few weeks is for the relationship to quietly and unemotionally end. Maybe that's the way you want it, but I really don't care. I don't care anymore what you want or what you'll do. Honestly, I'm saying that what we had eventually went the way you wanted it, without any compromising on your part or give and take, and I couldn't tolerate it, so I just don't want to see you anymore.

I still love you, but for the first time in my life the existence or reality or whatever it could be called concerning this love for you just doesn't seem to be enough to make me want to stay. I'm sorry. I hate writing letters like this, like less to get them, but there's no other way I see to express what I must say, short of calling you, and I don't have a phone, it's a trudge through slush and snowdrifts to reach a booth, and you know I'm even more uncommunicative, befuddling and in the end agonizingly battological when I try speaking on one. So, best ever then—Newt

Dear Em—

I won't be coming to Stonehill anymore. I don't want you coming by my place. Simple as I can say it: I don't want to go on with our relationship anymore. It's not going to change. The relationship won't. You talked a lot about "growth," both as individuals and as a couple. But we didn't grow together after the first few months, only repeated the same mistakes and agonies endlessly rather than understanding and correcting them and moving on.

I'm also tired of you always setting the pace, the distance, how high we could climb. That "week" in the summer. On a "beach." Why didn't you also suggest what color bathing suit I could bring along and how many hours in the sun I'd be allowed a day? It's usually been your way, do you agree? I went along like that because I don't like to direct a relationship of any kind—love, business, professional, familial, matrimonial, you name it: none. It's a pity you couldn't have let things sail freely without always dashing and mashing them against rocks every time it went well.

You said you were afraid of getting trapped. Well maybe the reverse is the trap. The trap could be what you think it's not. Maybe. In other words, the trap might not be the one you think you'll get in with me, but the one you go to to avoid getting in a trap with me, which then wouldn't make it a trap. Wouldn't make the anticipated trap with me a trap. The trap would be the trap you divert to to avoid that anticipated trap. No, the trap is trying to establish here what is and isn't a trap.

We've gone on for hours and ruined too many weekends discussing and discovering the reasons for our inability to sustain a preponderatingly smooth relationship—our histories and also the irreconcilabilities built into any more than casual comings together of two people: professional, familial, amorous, etc. (see above). But to me, either a couple make it or they don't. Deep endearing feelings and mutual respect keep them together, and the theories and therapies and the rest of it regarding love are at the most temporarily satisfying but usually stultifying and ultimately desolating and worthless. Even here, the more I think of it, the more I'm giving some theory about it, and the more doltish I am but bombastic I sound and perplexed I get. The hell with it.

I also can't get the bad things out of my head. I think about you sweetly most times. Fooling around. Holding you close. Working. Walking. Talking. Laughing. Jogging. Hogging. Joking. Just dancing to some dumb radio tune together or silently reading different books on the same couch or challenging those boys to a two-on-two basketball game or chasing away those oafs that day who didn't know there were two of us who could bite and bodychop with the best of them to protect old winos and not one. All that. But the other disturbing things just don't creep in, they rush. A lot else about what's happened between us just hasn't been carved out of my head yet. Turning me on and off. Blowing me up. Flying me like a kite or balloon. Popping me when need be or letting me hang or cutting the string whenever you wanted to and letting me go. I always thought "Em won't do that again." I was always so hopeful. Optimistic. See the bright flashing lights in his naive eyes. After that last time—your last break—I suppose I was just holding on. What in the world was your need for always wanting to come back to me after you broke us up "for the benefits of us both" and after I'd finally felt "Good, I found I can live without her again. Took me four days which is a day more than the last three times but two days less than the first, so maybe in my twenty years of developed sexuality or so I've actually grown some." Now I'm letting go. Nothing much to hold on to anyway, so it isn't hard, and I don't mean to sound tough.

I also don't feel that responsible for any of this. Not at all responsible. And I'm not going to rationalize my decision to disband by saying, as you suggested, or more accurately, kidded around about as we drove in last time (and to pinpoint the spot: on the big bridge at the bistate halfway marker which you only then discovered and pointed out after having passed it a few hundred times and my having remarked about the marker to you at least twice), that a quiet uncomplicated indestructible separation is what we've both probably been wanting for the last month. I'm saying that what we had eventually went the way you wanted it, not me, and without any give, take or faint nod toward compromise on your part, and I couldn't tolerate it, though for a while deluded myself that I could because one great day your attitude would change to me and us and my acceptance and sufferance would have been worth it. But now when I think about it I can't stand it and can barely tolerate myself for being such a shortsighted simp and slave.

So I just don't want to see you again—it's important that's clear. I love you very much, that's too damn true, and still do, I'm saying that, no matter how foolish or even gain-making that must now sound, but for the first time in my life the existence or fact of my love just doesn't seem to be enough to make me want to stay. Isn't enough—absolutely—so that's it, I'm afraid. Love, Newt

Dear Emmy—

I won't be coming to Stonehill anymore. I don't want you to come by my place again. I just don't want to go on with our relationship anymore. I'm weary of you always setting the pace. How high we should climb, far we can go. Let's sprint, rest, fall back, on our face, scrape our knees, break our ankles, spurt, zip, lunch, get lost, make it a marathon, two marathons, three. That "week" this coming summer. On a "beach." And "always" is an emotional word you said and I said "It's just a much abused one," but you know what I mean. I went along as I did because I don't like directing a relationship of any kind, personal or professional. What a waste you couldn't let whatever it was between us happen without your customary dashing it to dust every time it went well.

You said you're afraid of getting trapped. But maybe the reverse is the trap. Maybe the trap's what you're moving to now. We've gone on for weekends about this—our histories. That I met you after not being close to a woman for years. That you met me a few months after you left the man you were close to for years. "That the cross-purposes and inconciliabilities of our aims, outlooks and maybe our natures are monumental." I said "What do you mean?" You said "The most ignorant men are those who feign ignorance." I said "What do you mean?" You said "The most ignorant men are those who continue to feign ignorance." I said "What about women?" You said "The most ignorant of the most ignorant men are those who continue to feign the same ignorance that classified them among the most ignorant of men." I said "What do you mean?" You said. I said. You said that being tied down to one man over a period of sixteen years was enough and that instead of pinning into a second you wanted a rest. I said "I won't keep you back or hold you down." You said "Right now just seeing only one man is keeping me back and down." I said. You said "Truthful as the pain must be to you, I want to explore other relationships, lifestyles and professions." I said "I suppose I really couldn't tolerate seeing you if you were at the same time seriously seeing other men or casually allowing them to slip it in." You said "If that arrangement doesn't suit you, Newt, then maybe after a few years, if either of us is still available, which sounds impossible, we can try as a single couple again." I said "That would probably be impossible." You said "We revolve undolved without resolve." I said "What do you mean, what do you mean?" You said "From paddle to pedal to piddle to podel to puddle again." I said "Don't I know. But why'd you always, unpsychotherapized always, come back to me after all those times you told me to go or you picked up and went, and never after more than five or six days?" "You mean I never came back to you after more than five or six days?" "Yes," I said. "Five," you said and I think I said "I think the maximum was six."

Though I do think of you sweetly most times. Holding you close. Joking, jogging, nuding and screwing around. Sleeping, seeping, eyes uttering, nares stuttering, walking, talking, doing ludicrous things. Precious and energetic and hilarious and creative things. Holding you close. Just playing those boys two-on-two basketball that playground day. Fending off that pack of oafs in front of Oscar's with our hoofs, cuffs and butts when our wits didn't work. Quipping, unzipping, being comfortable and rumpled while silently reading side by side on your settee. Holding you close. Nuzzling. Puzzling. All of those. More of these. Unstrapping, while lips lapping—But the other disturbing things that happened just don't flip in, they flush. A lot else just hasn't been excised out of my head yet. Those four to five times you dropped the relationship cold. Wanted to go back to Myles. "Go if you got to go I sometimes say another way about something else," I said, but when he wouldn't do the bee's dance for you you devised some other plan. "Cancel your plane reservation overseas with me as I want to go alone. Timing, poor rhyming, but we're just never going to materialize, Newt." Your loving letters, each one better, till the last one when you said "When you come to the airport for me could you only come to return my keys and cars?" Then after an exhilarating night and day at the terminal and home you gave me the boot again and three days later got into my building somehow and through my peephole said would I be dumb and daft enough to have you back? "Of course—I'll open the door." Well enough, I'm tired of being turned on and off. Hot water today?—okay. Tepid?—you bet. What's that: boiling, hyperborean?—no sweat. Of being your straw man, tin man, wrong man, enough. Blowing me up. Letting me fly. Like a balloon or kite: piping goodbye as you cut me loose. You: "Howdy-do again, you undrownable goose." Each time my feeling that time's the last. Emotional always so hopeful I was—my eternally gyring eyes, or what you twice called "The naively cherished long overromantic view." Well now I'm letting go. Hip, hip, and nothing much to hold on to anyway, so it's not that hard. And I don't mean to be mean with these remarks, and why couldn't I ever resist your returns long enough till I had become fully unglued?

I don't feel responsible for any of this. Maybe a little. And I'm not going to rationalize my decision away by saying as you hinted when we drove in last time that if we both had the courage to say it, a complete break is what we've been wanting for the past two months. You did, I didn't, and now I don't care what you want or do. I'm saying that what we had eventually went the way you wanted it, with little give or take, and I couldn't tolerate it, though for a while blinded myself that I could— deluded myself was what I was thinking of now and wrote in the previous letter to you that I'm typing this from—and now when I think about it I can't stand it. Can't stand the thought of it all. I don't want to see you again. Don't want you ever to come by here again. If you do—so much as ring my vestibule bell or let yourself in some way and come up and rattle your baby tap on my door—I'll drag you downstairs by the hair and throw you into the street. I will. So don't!

I love you very much, which has to sound ridiculous and suspicious and quite peculiar after all I said above, but for the first time in my life the existence or whatever it is of this love for someone just doesn't seem to be enough to make me want to stay. Isn't enough. So that's it then: never again, and there'll be no other word more. Newt

Dear Em:

I've tried writing you about something that's sitting very heavy on my mind. A series of letters so far. They're all in front of me, one on top of the other, till the last long one I just finished and am looking at now. Nothing useful, sensible or insightful came out of any of them, and at their very best they were a lot of drivel, bad gags and rhythmic rot. Even this one, I can see, still trying to rhyme and alliterate to impress instead of saying simply what I want to express, though no matter how wretched it is I'm going to send it off. What I intended saying in each of the previous letters today was that I don't want to see you anymore. I still feel that way. It just isn't going to work. We aren't. So please don't come by, I won't be busing up, and there'll be no further communication between us of any kind from now on. Very best and my love, Newt

Dear Em—

There's only one thing I want to say here. I won't be busing up, I don't want you coming by, and we won't be seeing each other again. So that's it. There'll be no other communications, explanations, letters, calls, nothing else between us from now on. Thanks for understanding that and much love, Newt

Dear Em—

I've decided we shouldn't see one another anymore and that there'll also be no explanations or communications about it either. Love, Newt

Dear Mary—

No more, and no explanations either. Thanks. Newt

Dear Em—

No more and no explanations. Newt

Dear Em—

No more and no explanations. En

Dear Em—

No more.

Em: No more. En

Em: no more

Dear Mary—

This weekend, instead of my busing up, why don't you drive in and stay here? I think we've some things to discuss, and just for a change let's spend an entire weekend in the city. The snow's supposed to be gone and the sky clear and weather relatively mild.

I wanted to write you about what's been on my mind lately concerning our relationship, but decided against even trying to put it down in words, as I thought it best to just talk things out. We always did that pretty well and I'm sure that this problem too will be resolved. If you can't come in, could you call Harriet? I'll be dropping by her place Thursday night and will get your message and then take the bus up Friday afternoon—probably the 4:55, as that one skips several towns and takes the upper route rather than the river and is less crowded, and as long as I have the choice I prefer shorter more comfortable trips and climbing down to crawling up. If you do come in I've already selected the perfect restaurant for our undutch dinner Friday night and "beeg talk." We haven't had dinner alone together in a quiet good place for a long time and that was always a nice experience for us and lots of fun. As a dining celebration excuse we'll make it your teaching snow day this week, all right by you?

So, if I don't hear from you I'll know you'll be driving in. If for any reason you want to phone me, tell Harriet. Otherwise: my love, drive carefully, have a pleasant end of week and no matter what I'll be seeing you Friday night. Newt

In her fiction, Gail Godwin has often dealt with women's lives and with the difficulties of relationships. In "False Lights," she turns to the awkward ties between first and second wives. Although the story consists mainly of a young wife's fantastic torrent of words to her abandoned predecessor—an instance of the letter story as an embarrassing piece of self-revelation—it is the older woman's correspondence bracketing the sprawling discourse that pins it firmly in place. The clearest character in the tale, though he is silent, may be the man who links the two women. Like other works by Godwin, this *Esquire* story, which appeared in her 1976 collection, *Dream Children*, has a southern setting; Godwin was born in Birmingham, Alabama. The story takes its title from an Outer Banks legend, recounted within the story, about land pirates who hung lanterns on mules at night, luring captains to wreck their ships upon the shoals and spill their cargo. More than one set of false lights flicker in this satirical comment on relations between women and men.

Then reckon your course on shadows

Mrs. Karl Bandema
Box 59
Ocracoke, N.C. 27960   June 16

Dear Violet,

Please forgive the familiar address when I don't even know you, but the more formal would still feel strange. I hope you'll understand. Along with this note, there should arrive a small parcel containing Karl's pills. I don't know if you have a doctor on the island, so I took the liberty of having Karl's old prescription refilled. The moment his weight goes over 185, he should take one of these every morning *after breakfast.* Also, no fat or salt in food preparation, less beef, more chicken and fish, more vegetables and salads, but no dressing on the salad, unless a little lemon. (Starting the meal with the salad helps cut the appetite.) And no cheese, except cottage cheese, and no alcohol.

Sincerely,
Annette Bandema

Mrs. Karl Bandema
231 E. 48th St.
New York, N.Y. 10017   June 18

Dear Annette,

The parcel arrived today, with your note. I will do as you say. K. is in pretty good shape at the moment. He goes for a long swim before breakfast, takes several walks by himself during the course of his working day, and then we swim and walk in the evenings. The vegetables are easy because I planted a garden. (Peas, beans, squash, cucumber, spinach, tomatoes, carrots, radishes, and three kinds of lettuce.) As for fish, no shortage of that here. I do bluefish stuffed with spinach sometimes three nights a week. There is a local doctor, but so far only I have had to go to him. I tend to get ear infections. There is no liquor store on the island. I appreciated your note and wish you all the best.

Violet

June 18—maybe June 19 by now

Dear Annette, dear Annette Bandema,

The most natural way for me to think of you is dear Mrs. Bandema, but how can there be two of us? And yet here we both are. I feel I cheated myself by mailing that letter off so quickly. I couldn't wait to write it, to hurry back to the post office and mail it, even though the mail had already gone out for the day. It said nothing, absolutely nothing. Spinach and beans, walks and swims, all wrapped up in a cautious parcel of triumphant politeness. "I will do as you say," etc. And yet I told you more about me than you told about yourself. You know, or will know when you get my letter, that I get ear infections and that I have a garden, and—if you read between the lines—that I am alone a good deal of the day. I have no knowledge about you, except what I manage to compile from my husband's novels, steering uncertainly between fiction and fact. I shouldn't probably say *my husband*. It hurts and bewilders you. It would me. It's all so strange. I think it would feel less so to me if we could meet, just the two of us, in some neutral place, the way generals of opposing sides meet to sign a truce. Not that we need sign a truce, exactly. We are not on opposite sides.

I'm going to tell you something very peculiar: I feel close to you. I think about you all the time. When I am walking around the island, or sitting on the beach by myself, or even—I hope you won't think this perverse—when I am lying in his arms. I hold imaginary dialogues with you (somewhat similar to the tone of our brief exchange, all about food and recipes and such), and sometimes I ask your advice about things I'm sure you know better than I. I often imagine you watching me, us, as I used to imagine God watching me when I was a child, and sometimes when I am swimming I find myself showing off to you in the sea, taking extra care with my strokes, or persisting a little longer than I ordinarily would if nobody were watching. And often I see little things I'd like to send to you. A tiny painting in oil, done by a local artist, of fishing boats or the lighthouse. I watch this artist work down on the beach. He is a strange, bitter sort of fellow who has lived here many years. He told me about the land pirates who used to work this stretch of shore. At night, they hung lanterns around the necks of mules and walked the animals back and forth across the sand, until some unfortunate ship captain, mistaking the swaying lanterns for lights at sea, would crash upon the shoals and spill his cargo right into their hands.

This artist has his easel rigged so he can paint six small pictures at once. He does all six seas, then all six lighthouses, or all six boats. He says there will always be pirates wherever there are fools. He sells his work to a gallery in Nags Head, which hangs one at a time till that one is sold then puts up another in its place, and so on . . . I have often had the urge to send you one, just as I had to restrain myself the other day from buying you a shipwreck map from the Visitor's Center when I bought myself one, a map of the Ghost Fleet, all the ships that have gone down on the Outer Banks (more than five hundred ships, all along this treacherous coast): they call this "the Graveyard of the Atlantic," and I thought you would be touched and haunted, as I was, for the whole thing is rather mysterious and puts one in the frame of mind where individual lives and who is whose wife in a particular segment of time seem suddenly so fleeting and insignificant, mere events in an infinite process of events that will all be washed away, as the sea has washed away the faces of all those drowned men. I don't understand time. The more I think about it, the less I understand it. Sometimes I am quite certain it is only a way to console ourselves about the inevitability of change, merely a word containing no real thing, anymore than the shipwreck map can contain bodies or salt water—or "Mrs. Bandema" can be anything more than a legal and social convenience. There is no real Mrs. Bandema.

On such a level, I think we could meet.

On such a level, I think you could be with us now, on this island. I have so much time to myself. I would enjoy your company.

It occurs to me that as recently as a hundred years ago this letter would have been considered highly irregular, perhaps impossible. And what of a hundred years from now? Karl says the novel of 2075 would be unrecognizable to us today, that it will be a pure and better thing, tuned in to more important signals, no longer obsessed with gossip and personal petty detail. If we had lived in 2075, would marriage also be a new thing, where we could all survive together, nobody's happiness depleting anybody else's, all of us sailing through change as effortlessly as gulls through air, time no more enemy than water as seen from above? Will there be marriage, will there be wives, in 2075?

That young woman crawling through the mud, carrying medical

supplies in her teeth, through two miles of mud in enemy territory: I
don't know how many times I have reread that passage in Karl's book.
That was you. What love, what danger, what a love story! I am sure there
will be nothing in my life to compare to that. No such challenge, no
such heroism. I did not have to crawl, or even walk outside my father's
house, to get Karl. Karl entered my father's house, and I went straight
from my father's love to Karl's, no alien land, no great test, between. I
earned nothing. Heroics are not easily had for the young in our times.
Perhaps that is why they go to such extremes to create their own dangers.
Karl says he will never put me in a book; he says he wants me to stay
where I am, on this island with him. He says that you only put people
into books to improve their lives, or when they are gone, or when you
are no longer able to see them. It is a kind of memorial, he says—as the
shipwreck map is a memorial, I guess, and a keepsake for tourists who
can never know what it is like to feel oneself dashed to pieces on rocks.
And yet, though he has put you away so memorably in his books (I weep
every time I read of your death, so young, at only nineteen, completed as
a heroine at nineteen, before you ever had a chance to live, to marry, to
have that little boy who died, but who in Karl's books has been allowed
to grow up and live), you are very present to me. The real you, a woman
in her fifties, goes on existing for me.

I imagine your days, tracking them alongside my own. I sometimes feel
we are interchangeable, except for the accident of time. It might have been
the other way around, me first, then you, a woman's face that changes
through one long event of a man's, an artist's, life. It could have been me on
all fours with the medicine that saved his life, and you, young and untried,
years later, placing a pink tablet beside his breakfast plate with no danger
to yourself, completing the journey, all danger over, all the interesting
wars and legendary shipwrecks over. (" . . . *With swift communications,
advances in safety-at-sea techniques, and sophistication of tools for rescue,
tragic incidents along the coast occur only rarely now.*") Perhaps I will send
you one of these maps, after all.

I hear the ocean pounding. What are you hearing now? This is the
time of night, or morning, when everything rushes through my brain. I
can't stop or even control its course, so I just ride the torrent. Sometimes
I don't fall asleep until I hear the birds singing. Not that I mind, it's just
that insomnia seems such a waste on me. He would make so much better
use of it. He salvages from everything—his anger, his disappointments,
his mistakes, his boredom. He makes it all reappear in meaningful, lasting

shapes. At the moment I am seeing my garden, the sea breeze ruffling the Bibb lettuces that glow faintly in the dark, delicate and phosphorescent-looking, and the weighted curves of the tomato plants, their first fruit emerging through the bluish, fringy foliage, and the straight dirt spaces between, glinting with diamond flakes of sand.

It appalled me at first when I had to "thin out." I knelt above those inch-high plants, thinking, Who am I to do this, what right have I to choose? But the book said you had to be ruthless, you weren't doing any of them a favor if you allowed them to steal from and stunt one another. So I taught myself to pull things up by the roots. Choosing between the weak and the strong, and sometimes between the strong and the stronger, is supposed to make you philosophical.

I remember a famous philosopher who once came to my father's house for dinner. He told us how, after the war, he had been taken on a tour of a concentration camp, and how he went back to his hotel seething with such impotent anger that he got a violent headache and could not eat or sleep. While still in this state, he picked up a book on Einstein and suddenly understood for the first time the world-shaking boldness of "Energy equals Mass multiplied by the square of the Velocity of Light," and was filled with a great tranquility and acceptance, could now view the thousands of charred and tortured bodies with the same meditative, detached eye one would view the death of stars or the decay of huge primeval forests into coal. As a small girl, I thought him a very cold, strange man, for whom $E=MC^2$ could balance the shredding and burning of people. Yet, in my garden, my fingers hover, choose, pluck. I hear the old killer sea behind me murmuring in my ear, and I accept the history of doomed sailors, the inexorability of evolution, and you, crawling through enemy mud, risking your life, in a Europe of thirty-three years ago, so that I could have a husband on Ocracoke today.

Something is always plucking, thinning out. The philosopher lost his headache and went down and had a huge meal. And I, in my garden, feel less guilty about you.

Yesterday I was walking on the beach, looking for unusual shells, along that particular stretch where the *Charmer,* the *Lizzie James,* the *Lydia Willis* went down. I was thinking about the women after whom these ships were named, wondering what kind of women they had been, and what they had meant to the men who honored their names—and of course I thought then of Karl's novel, the one he calls *Yolande* (which is you) and, though he has assured me I'll never be in any book, I couldn't help wondering what he would call me, the name he would think fittest to memorialize me.

I was walking along with my head down, not paying much attention to where I was going, and walked right into the fishing line of an elderly woman standing near the surf, wearing a pair of men's trousers cut off at the knees, her skin burned crisp as a potato chip. She said not to worry, she had caught nothing but two crabs all morning and was getting ready to quit anyway. She had sharp eyes and kept staring at my face, my legs, my wedding ring, and before I knew what was happening, I had told her all about myself. She hadn't heard of Karl, but she said she didn't read much since her husband died, she was too busy traveling, making up for lost time. She and another widow had bought a camper together and had so far camped, she said, in thirty-nine states, not counting Canada and Mexico. She asked me Karl's age, and my age, and then laughed dryly and said, "Well, dear, you'd better start making your list." I asked what list and she said, "The list of all the things you want to do, only he won't let you do, but you can do after he's gone." When I said there was nothing I wanted to do without Karl, she narrowed her old eyes and asked how long we had been married. "Oh, no wonder," she said when I told her. "You wait a couple of years."

I went back to the cottage and made lunch. Gazpacho, tuna-fish salad with only enough mayonnaise to hold it together, even though your letter had not yet arrived. I watch his calories where they provide the least enjoyment, but I doubt I will ever interfere with his lunchtime wine and soda, which he refills frequently if his morning has been especially good or bad. Yesterday it was bad. Over his second glass, he told me that he had been tricked by the dream of Art into throwing away his life, as my pirates had tricked all those captains. Nothing he had written was of any value to the future, he said; he had wasted his past producing quaint relics, and he was missing his present, imprisoning himself in a roomful of ghosts, while Life, and me in it, flowed by outside. He refilled his glass again, saying he hadn't even looked at the garden this week, and appeared to be on the verge of tears. I cleared the table and came and stood behind him and folded my hands upon his breast. I suggested we take a nap. He said I was the first person in many years to cause him to suspect real life was as interesting as fiction, but it was too late for him to change. I did something selfish: poured him more wine and we had the nap.

Was it you, many years ago, who also interested him in real life?

Today his work went so splendidly that at lunch he announced if the wind stayed behind him like this, he'd have "all those ghosts" out of his head by summer's end. He ate too fast and sloshed innumerable refills of Chablis to the brim of his glass. His eyes looked through me toward, I suppose, ecstatic horizons.

"But what will you do then?" I asked.

"I will write about whatever lies on the other side of deaths and births and ego, whatever lies on the other side of settling scores and erecting monuments." His face was angrily spiritual as he explained how the artists of the future would be impersonal receivers and transmitters of the messages of the universe. It was neither the time for mentioning your letter nor for uttering dietetic precautions. He had abandoned us for 2075.

I sat across from him, nostalgic for yesterday's nap, and imagining you and me, years from now, traveling together in our camper, both of us burned a deep earthly brown, each of us wearing an old pair of his trousers, cut off at the knees, bumping sagely up and down the roads of America's scenic landscapes, taking equal turns at the wheel, comparing our experiences as the wives of Karl Bandema.

Last Saturday, Karl and I went to a party in Nags Head. We had gone over on the ferry to buy supplies, and Karl ran into a newspaper columnist he knew while we were (I'm sorry to report) in the liquor store.

"You have got to come to this party, Karl. They'll be flattered to have you, and you wouldn't believe these people. They'll furnish you with material enough to last the winter," the columnist said.

Karl frowned. "Poor old Violet here would probably like it," he said at last. "She's stuck on the island with only my boring company all week."

And I said it might be fun—because I saw that he wanted to go.

The house, large and rambling in a Victorian style of architecture, was set high on stilts, and two cabin cruisers were docked underneath. A freshly painted sign over the garage said: "HAPPY SHACK, The Hon. Terence Mulvaney, Dunn, N.C."

The columnist introduced us to the host, Judge Mulvaney, a fastidious man in his sixties, with a birdlike profile and elegant manners.

"I have the greatest respect for literature," he said, shaking Karl's hand warmly. "It ranks second only to my admiration of youth and beauty," he said, shaking my hand.

"The judge is also a new bridegroom," the columnist told Karl, sending him a secret look that said, "See? I told you!"

"I don't normally wear shirts full of white ruffles," explained Mulvaney to me, "but my bride made me buy this on our honeymoon in Mexico, and her wish is my law."

Everyone around him laughed. Mulvaney looked delighted with himself. Karl took a long, deep sip of his julep, and I made my first public début as Mrs. Karl Bandema.

I looked around the gracious stretches of the room, with its comfortable faded furniture, its nautical touches. "I love your house," I said.

"Thank you, it's been in the family for a long time," the judge said. "Nancy Jean will show you the rest of it." He reached an arm sideways and fluttered his suntanned fingers, and within seconds a very pretty dark-haired girl ducked up at us from under his armpit. "Nancy, honey, show Mrs. Bandema the cottage. You girls run along and have a good time," he said.

Nancy put her arm around my waist. "I think you and I have got a lot in common," she whispered. Off we went, children, Karl and the judge watching us benevolently.

She led me upstairs to an enormous old bedroom. "All in white, that's me, the all-in-white girl!" She laughed and flung herself down in a swoosh of white silk trousers on a king-size bed covered in white organdy, with at least a dozen white lace and organdy pillows. The old casement windows were open, and you could see the ocean, peaceful and pink with sunset.

Nancy patted the collection of pillows. "Come lie down and let's talk! You don't want to be dragged around somebody else's old house. I'll tell you the interesting things about it later. I haven't talked to a soul my age in months. Did he divorce his old wife for you? So did mine! Does she bother you-all constantly? No? You're lucky, let me tell you! It's gotten to where I simply will not put a soufflé in the oven anymore, because as sure as I do the phone rings just as I'm taking it out and it's her, with one of her ladylike suicide threats. And then at the most *inopportune* times—I'm sure you know what I mean—she calls to say she's sure a burglar has broken into their old house, or the water pipes have frozen and she can't do a thing by herself, so I have to call up the plumbers or the police—the whole thing upsets Terence so—and then I have to deal with his bad mood and his guilt . . . Oh, the *guilt*, I get so sick of the guilt—they hadn't slept in the same room for centuries and she was the one who wanted out first . . . Listen, make yourself comfortable, let me pour you a little more. I keep a pitcher up here for myself when I get bored with the company downstairs. Don't you love this room! It was *meant* to be all in white. When his daughter—she's just a year older than me—saw the wallpaper samples and swatches of fabric I had when we were still engaged, she said, 'But Nancy Jean, you can't be meaning to put that in my father's bedroom; that's the kind of thing that's more suitable for a virgin's bower.' 'But that's just what I am, honey,' I told her. And I was, you know. The judge is a nut on chastity. You wait, when he gets into high gear tonight, he'll tell you how chastity and ambition are the lost virtues of today's young. What does your husband start preaching when he gets high?"

"How artists won't be obsessed with personal things in the future, how they will have left their egos behind in order to be transmitters for the universe."

"Honey, men will always have egos. You take my word for it."

It was dark when we went downstairs, laughing. I was tipsy. "You have got to come visit me this winter in Dunn," Nancy said. Then she got serious and muttered off a grave recitation. "The Mulvaneys were the third family to build . . . house built over the water so sailing boats could unload luggage and parties on the porch . . ." etc., etc.

Downstairs, Judge Mulvaney was saying, "The girls have lost their maidenhood and the boys their desire to succeed. That's why this country has gone to hell. I had a reputable gynecologist sign an affidavit that Nancy Jean was chaste before I married her . . ."

"See," whispered Nancy happily, pinching me.

Later, sitting in the circle of Karl's arm, I listened to him tell his audience how, for the artist, personal concerns will be obsolete in 2075, no more hunger for fame or recognition, no preoccupation with pettiness. "We will only be interested in our anonymous role as messengers for the universe."

I caught Nancy's eye and winked.

On the last ferry back to Ocracoke, Karl put his head down into my hair. He stood behind me at the rail. The wind was cold, but he said it cleared his head. "God, what terrible people, what a wasted evening," he moaned. He had to hold on to me to keep his balance. "Why did we go? I wish we had just gone back to our own little island and had a quiet evening. I'm going to give up drinking. I'm going to give up people—all except you. I feel set back a hundred years! As if I didn't have enough people swarming around in my head, waiting to be disposed of, waiting to be explained! Why were you gone so long? What could you have possibly found to talk about with a girl like that? An *affidavit* for chastity, for Christ's sake! What on earth could have happened in that man's life to make him do a ridiculous thing like that? Listen, do you know what I'm thinking? We could stay on the island all winter. The hell with hurricanes! Are you afraid of hurricanes? Will you stay with me, Violet? Will you stay on with me while I endure my everlasting penance? What are you thinking? Tell me the exact flow of your thoughts, everything, leaving nothing out."

I was thinking of you, Annette, wondering if you were lying in the dark imagining burglars. I did not think so. When the thing you dreaded most has already come true, what further dangers are there to imagine? I was also thinking of pirates, and ripening tomato plants, and whether Karl would mind if I visited Nancy on the mainland if we stayed for the winter in Ocracoke. And whether I should even want such a thing in the first months of married life. And I was thinking about that night at my father's. Everybody was dancing, people of all ages, my father with the student who later became his wife—all these young brides—everybody was dancing except the famous novelist who had come to speak at our college's spring symposium ("What Are Our Next Frontiers?"). Earlier that evening, he and a famous biologist had agreed onstage that a new dawn was on its way, and our next evolutionary assignment would be to carry information around the universe. "All the old concerns will be sloughed off like dead cells," the novelist had exclaimed excitedly, "all those personal, selfish concerns we believe have to be the stuff of novels." He kept wiping the perspiration from his forehead, nervous and elated; he looked like an ill man inspired by a vision of perfect health. "Then will you stop writing novels?" demanded a student in the audience. "I would hope . . . yes . . . I would hope to have the courage and intelligence to do just that," the novelist replied quickly, his voice harsh. "I mean, if I could not get a clear reception, if I couldn't hear my assignment, yes, I would certainly stop writing novels." Then Karl laughed. "Luckily, I probably won't be around long enough to greet the new world. I can indulge myself in the fancies of the old one a while longer."

Then he was watching the dancers and I was watching him. He gulped his drink in compulsive sips, his tired, slightly wild eyes skimming us from beneath bristling eyebrows. I believed I could see him rapidly picking up, sometimes putting down in the same instant, our potential mysteries. Then his gaze came to rest on me, and I asked him if he would like to dance. "I have a piece of metal in my leg," he said, "but please stay and talk to me. I am lucky to be alive." Touching his damp forehead to mine, he shouted over the music, "A very courageous French girl saved my life—just about your age."

"I wish you wouldn't abandon the old world just yet," I said to him later that night. I was just beginning to discover that world, and so far he had been the best thing in it, the most compelling figure.

And you were part of it.

"What are you thinking?" this man asked now, my husband now, in a world fast growing extinct but not yet dead. Oh, no, not quite. For weren't we on a ferry crossing to an island that was ours alone?

"Perhaps we'll see a shipwreck if we stay the winter. They are rare these days, but not entirely impossible," I replied.

Now he is asleep, dreaming onward the mysteries of all those people who keep him from becoming a perfect messenger, who keep him here with me. You, in an infinite number of forms, but never older than nineteen, and that little boy who has led so many interesting lives, and maybe now the judge and Nancy Jean. I wonder what this man will make of them. Perhaps one night, in spite of himself, he'll experiment with a better form of me, and then I will join you. We will meet at last. That is a chance I made up my mind I would take. Do you think, for yourself, it's been worth it?

I am here for the time being near the dark cool of my garden, helplessly thinking of so many things, drowned captains in their watery slumbers, Nancy deep in white organdy with her judge, a million other things, all in the space of a single wink. I could no more transfer it to paper than I could have told him everything I was thinking. I do not understand time. I do not understand marriage. If they prove, like the sentimental demands of the ego, to be outdated fancies, is it that you, Annette, drowned in the same archaic sea in whose dangers I furtively rejoice?

Affectionately,
Violet

Mrs. Karl Bandema
Box 59
Ocracoke, N.C. 27960   June 25

Dear Violet,

Since there is a doctor on your island, he should be able to prescribe Karl's pills when needed from now on.

I am afraid I cannot abet you in your extensive fancies concerning other centuries. The future I leave to those who must live in it; the past, insofar as it involves my own life, is my own affair. It is very much this year and this century for me. I assure you, time is more than just a word for me.

Nor can I encourage you in your hopes for a meeting. Outside your imagination, we have nothing to offer each other. I prefer to remain

Sincerely,

Annette Bandema

(or Mrs. Bandema, if you like, but not a defeated general, not a shipwrecked or drowned swimmer, and certainly not a potential camping companion).

A family's untidy story is laid bare by what is said and left unsaid in the letters of "Simple Arithmetic," by Virginia Moriconi, a novelist and story writer who was born in New York City and lived abroad for many years. Originally published in the *Transatlantic Review* and selected for *The Best American Short Stories 1964,* this sharp-humored tale revolves around a broken family—divorced parents and adolescent son—who are separated by both miles and emotions. As letters go back and forth, we find the boy, who is in school in Switzerland, unable either to reach his mother or to penetrate the facade of his newly remarried father, who nags him to stop overspending, to do his eye exercises, and to improve his spelling, unaware—or at least unwilling to acknowledge—that, like his son, he has failed to bring his balance "foreward" and so has rendered his (familial) accounts "a little bizerk."

Geneva, January 15

Dear Father:

Well, I am back in School, as you can see, and the place is just as miserable as ever. My only friend, the one I talked to you about, Ronald Fletcher, is not coming back any more because someone persuaded his mother that she was letting him go to waste, since he was extremely photogenic, so now he is going to become a child actor. I was very surprised to hear this, as the one thing Ronnie liked to do was play basketball. He was very shy.

The flight wasn't too bad. I mean nobody had to be carried off the plane. The only thing was, we were six hours late and they forgot to give us anything to eat, so for fourteen hours we had a chance to get quite hungry but, as you say, for the money you save going tourist class, you should be prepared to make a few little sacrifices.

I did what you told me, and when we got to Idlewild I paid the taxi driver his fare and gave him a fifty-cent tip. He was very dissatisfied. In fact he wouldn't give me my suitcase. In fact I don't know what would have happened if a man hadn't come up just while the argument was going on and when he heard what it was all about he gave the taxi driver a dollar and I took my suitcase and got to the plane on time.

During the trip I thought the whole thing over. I did not come to any conclusion. I know I have been very extravagant and unreasonable about money and you have done the best you can to explain this to me. Still, while I was thinking about it, it seemed to me that there were only three possibilities. I could just have given up and let the taxi driver have the suitcase, but when you realize that if we had to buy everything over again that was in the suitcase we would probably have had to spend at least five hundred dollars, it does not seem very economical. Or I could have gone on arguing with him and missed the plane, but then we would have had to pay something like three hundred dollars for another ticket. Or else I could have given him an extra twenty-five cents which, as you say, is just throwing money around to create an impression. What would you have done?

Anyway I got here, with the suitcase, which was the main thing. They took two week-end privileges away from me because I was late for the opening of School. I tried to explain to M. Frisch that it had nothing to do with me if the weather was so bad that the plane was delayed for six hours, but he said that prudent persons allow for continjensies of this kind and make earlier reservations. I don't care about this because the next two week-ends are skiing week-ends and I have never seen any point in waking up at six o'clock in the morning just to get frozen stiff and endure terrible pain even if sports are a part of growing up, as you say. Besides, we will save twenty-seven dollars by having me stay in my room.

In closing I want to say that I had a very nice Christmas and I apreciate everything you tried to do for me and I hope I wasn't too much of a bother. (Martha explained to me that you had had to take time off from your honeymoon in order to make Christmas for me and I am very sorry even though I do not think I am to blame if Christmas falls on the twenty-fifth of December, especially since everybody knows that it does. What I mean is, if you had wanted to have a long honeymoon you and Martha could have gotten married earlier, or you could have waited until Christmas was over, or you could just have told me not to come and I would have understood.)

I will try not to spend so much money in the future and I will keep accounts and send them to you. I will also try to remember to do the eye exercises and the exercises for fallen arches that the doctors in New York prescribed.

Love,
Stephen

New York, January 19

Dear Stephen:

Thank you very much for the long letter of January fifteenth. I was very glad to know that you had gotten back safely, even though the flight was late. (I do not agree with M. Frisch that prudent persons allow for "continjensies" of this kind, now that air travel is as standard as it is, and the service usually so good, but we must remember that Swiss people are, by and large, the most meticulous in the world and nothing offends them more than other people who are not punctual.)

In the affair of the suitcase, I'm afraid that we were both at fault. I had forgotten that there would be an extra charge for luggage when I suggested that you should tip the driver fifty cents. You, on the other hand, might have inferred from his argument that he was simply asking that the tariff—i.e. the fare, plus the overcharge for the suitcase—should be paid in full, and regulated yourself accordingly. In any event you arrived, and I am only sorry that obviously you had no time to learn the name and address of your benefactor so that we might have paid him back for his kindness.

I will look forward to going over your accounting and I am sure you will find that in keeping a clear record of what you spend you will be able to cut your cloth according to the bolt and that, in turn, will help you to develop a real regard for yourself. It is a common failing, as I told you, to spend too much money in order to compensate oneself for a lack of inner security, but you can easily see that a foolish purchase does not insure stability, and if you are chronically insolvent you can hardly hope for peace of mind. Your allowance is more than adequate and when you learn to make both ends meet you will have taken a decisive step ahead. I have great faith in you and I know you will find your anchor to windward in your studies, in your sports, and in your companions.

As to what you say about Christmas, you are not obliged to "apreciate" what we did for you. The important thing was that you should have had a good time, and I think we had some wonderful fun together, the three of us, don't you? Until your mother decides where she wants to live and settles down, this is your home and you must always think of it that way. Even though I have remarried, I am still your father, first and last, and Martha is very fond of you too, and very understanding about your problems. You may not be aware of it but in fact she is one of the best friends you have. New ideas and new stepmothers take a little getting used to, of course.

Please write me as regularly as you can, since your letters mean a great deal to me. Please try too, at all times, to keep your marks up to scratch, as college entrance is getting harder and harder in this country, and there are thousands of candidates each year for the good universities. Concentrate particularly on spelling. "Contingency" is difficult, I know, but there is no excuse for only one "p" in "appreciate"! And do the exercises.

Love,
Father

Geneva, January 22

Dear Mummy:

Last Sunday I had to write to Father to thank him for my Christmas vacation and to tell him that I got back all right. This Sunday I thought I would write to you even though you are on a cruze so perhaps you will never get my letter. I must say that if they didn't make us write home once a week I don't believe that I would ever write any letters at all. What I mean is that once you get to a point like this, in a place like this, you see that you are supposed to have your life and your parents are supposed to have their lives, and you have lost the connection.

Anyway I have to tell you that Father was wonderful to me and Martha was very nice too. They had thought it all out, what a child of my age might like to do in his vacation, and sometimes it was pretty strenuous, as you can imagine. At the end the School sent the bill for the first term, where they charge you for the extras which they let you have here and it seems that I had gone way over my allowance and besides I had signed for a whole lot of things I did not deserve. So there was a terrible scene and Father was very angry and Martha cried and said that if Father always made such an effort to consider me as a person I should make an effort to consider him as a person too and wake up to the fact that he was not Rockefeller and that even if he was sacrificing himself so that I could go to one of the most expensive schools in the world it did not mean that I should drag everybody down in the mud by my reckless spending. So now I have to turn over a new leaf and keep accounts of every penny and not buy anything which is out of proportion to our scale of living.

Except for that one time they were very affectionate to me and did everything they could for my happiness. Of course it was awful without you. It was the first time we hadn't been together and I couldn't really believe it was Christmas.

I hope you are having a wonderful time and getting the rest you need and please write me when you can.

All my love,
Stephen

Geneva, January 29

Dear Father:

Well it is your turn for a letter this week because I wrote to Mummy last Sunday. (I am sure I can say this to you without hurting your feelings because you always said that the one thing you and Mummy wanted was a civilized divorce so we could all be friends.) Anyway Mummy hasn't answered my letter so probably she doesn't aprove of my spelling any more than you do. I am beginning to wonder if maybe it wouldn't be much simpler and much cheaper too if I didn't go to college after all. I really don't know what this education is for in the first place.

There is a terrible scandal here at School which has been very interesting for the rest of us. One of the girls, who is only sixteen, has gotten pregnant and everyone knows that it is all on account of the science instructer, who is a drip. We are waiting to see if he will marry her, but in the meantime she is terrifically upset and she has been expelled from the School. She is going away on Friday.

I always liked her very much and I had a long talk with her last night. I wanted to tell her that maybe it was not the end of the world, that my stepmother was going to have a baby in May, although she never got married until December, and the sky didn't fall in or anything. I thought it might have comforted her to think that grownups make the same mistakes that children do (if you can call her a child) but then I was afraid that it might be disloyal to drag you and Martha into the conversation, so I just let it go.

I'm fine and things are just the same.

Love,
Stephen

New York, February 2

Dear Stephen:

It would be a great relief to think that your mother did not "aprove" of your spelling either, but I'm sure that it's not for that reason that you haven't heard from her. She was never any good as a correspondent, and now it is probably more difficult for her than ever. We did indeed try for what you call a "civilized divorce" for all our sakes, but divorce is not any easy thing for any of the persons involved, as you well know, and if you try to put yourself in your mother's place for a moment, you will see that she is in need of time and solitude to work things out for herself. She will certainly write to you as soon as she has found herself again, and meanwhile you must continue to believe in her affection for you and not let impatience get the better of you.

Again, in case you are really in doubt about it, the purpose of your education is to enable you to stand on your own feet when you are a man and make something of yourself. Inaccuracies in spelling will not simplify anything.

I can easily see how you might have made a parallel between your friend who has gotten into trouble, and Martha who is expecting the baby in May, but there is only a superficial similarity in the two cases.

Your friend is, or was, still a child, and would have done better to have accepted the limitations of the world of childhood—as you can clearly see for yourself, now that she is in this predicament. Martha, on the other hand, was hardly a child. She was a mature human being, responsible for her own actions and prepared to be responsible for the baby when it came. Moreover I, unlike the science "instructer," am not a drip, I too am responsible for my actions, and so Martha and I are married and I will do my best to live up to her and the baby.

Speaking of which, we have just found a new apartment because this one will be too small for us in May. It is right across the street from your old school and we have a kitchen, a dining alcove, a living room, two bedrooms—one for me and Martha, and one for the new baby—and another room which will be for you. Martha felt that it was very important for you to feel that you had a place of your own when you came home to us, and so it is largely thanks to her that we have taken such a big place. The room will double as a study for me when you are not with us, but we will move all my books and papers and paraphernalia whenever you come, and Martha is planning to hang the Japanese silk screen you liked at the foot of the bed.

Please keep in touch, and please don't forget the exercises.

Love,
Father

Geneva, February 5

Dear Father:

There is one thing which I would like to say to you which is that if it hadn't been for you I would never have heard of a "civilized divorce," but that is the way you explained it to me. I always thought it was crazy. What I mean is, wouldn't it have been better if you had said, "I don't like your mother any more and I would rather live with Martha," instead of insisting that you and Mummy were always going to be the greatest friends? Because the way things are now Mummy probably thinks that you still like her very much, and it must be hard for Martha to believe that she was chosen, and I'm pretty much confused myself, although it is really none of my business.

You will be sorry to hear that I am not able to do any of the exercises any longer. I cannot do the eye exercises because my roommate got so fassinated by the stereo gadget that he broke it. (But the School Nurse says she thinks it may be just as well to let the whole thing go since in her opinion there was a good chance that I might have gotten more cross-eyed than ever, fidgeting with the viewer.) And I cannot do the exercises for fallen arches, at least for one foot, because when I was decorating the Assembly Hall for the dance last Saturday, I fell off the stepladder and broke my ankle. So now I am in the Infirmary and the School wants to know whether to send the doctor's bill to you or to Mummy, because they had to call in a specialist from outside, since the regular School Doctor only knows how to do a very limited number of things. So I have cost a lot of money again and I am very very sorry, but if they were half-way decent in this School they would pay to have proper equipment and not let the students risk their lives on broken stepladders, which is something you could write to the Bookkeeping Department, if you felt like it, because I can't, but you could, and it might do some good in the end.

The girl who got into so much trouble took too many sleeping pills and died. I felt terrible about it, in fact I cried when I heard it. Life is very crewel, isn't it?

I agree with what you said, that she was a child, but I think she knew that, from her point of view. I think she did what she did because she thought of the science instructer as a grownup, so she imagined that she was perfectly safe with him. You may think she was just bad, because she was a child and should have known better, but I think that it was not entirely her fault since here at School we are all encouraged to take the teachers seriously.

I am very glad you have found a new apartment and I hope you won't move all your books and papers when I come home, because that would only make me feel that I was more of a nuisance than ever.

Love,
Stephen

New York, February 8

Dear Stephen:

This will have to be a very short letter because we are to move into the new apartment tomorrow and Martha needs my help with the packing.

We were exceedingly shocked by the tragic death of your friend, and very sorry that you should have had such a sad experience. Life can be "crewel" indeed to the people who do not learn how to live it.

When I was exactly your age I broke my ankle too—I wasn't on a defective stepladder, I was playing hockey—and it hurt like the devil. I still remember it and you have all my sympathy. (I have written to the School Physician to ask how long you will have to be immobilized, and to urge him to get you back into the athletic program as fast as possible. The specialist's bill should be sent to me.)

I have also ordered another stereo viewer because, in spite of the opinion of the School Nurse, the exercises are most important and you are to do them religiously. Please be more careful with this one no matter how much it may "fassinate" your roommate.

Martha sends love and wants to know what you would like for your birthday. Let us know how the ankle is mending.

Love,
Father

Geneva, February 12

Dear Father:

I was very surprised by your letter. I was surprised that you said you were helping Martha to pack because when you and Mummy were married I do not ever remember you packing or anything like that so I guess Martha is reforming your charactor. I was also surprised by what you said about the girl who died. What I mean is, if anyone had told me a story like that I think I would have just let myself get a little worked up about the science instructer because it seems to me that he was a villan too. Of course you are much more riserved than I am.

I am out of the Infirmary and they have given me a pair of crutches, but I'm afraid it will be a long time before I can do sports again.

I hope the new apartment is nice and I do not want anything for my birthday because it will seem very funny having a birthday in School so I would rather not be reminded of it.

Love,
Stephen

New York, February 15

Dear Stephen:

This is not an answer to your letter of February twelfth, but an attempt to have a serious discussion with you, as if we were face to face.

You are almost fifteen years old. Shortly you will be up against the stiffest competition of your life when you apply for college entrance. No examiner is going to find himself favorably impressed by "charactor" or "instructer" or "villan" or "riserved" or similar errors. You will have to face the fact that in this world we succeed on our merits, and if we are unsuccessful, on account of sloppy habits of mind, we suffer for it. You are still too young to understand me entirely, but you are not too young to recognize the importance of effort. People who do not make the grade are desperately unhappy all their lives because they have no place in society. If you do not pass the college entrance examinations simply because you are unable to spell, it will be nobody's fault but your own, and you will be gravely handicapped for the rest of your life.

Every time you are in doubt about a word you are to look it up in the dictionary and memorize the spelling. This is the least you can do to help yourself.

We are still at sixes and sevens in the new apartment but when Martha accomplishes all she has planned it should be very nice indeed and I think you will like it.

Love,
Father

Geneva, February 19

Dear Father:

I guess we do not understand each other at all. If you immagine for one minute that just by making a little effort I could imaggine how to spell immaggine without looking it up and finding that actually it is "imagine," then you are all wrong. In other words, if you get a letter from me and there are only two or three mistakes well you just have to take my word for it that I have had to look up practically every single word in the dictionary and that is one reason I hate having to write you these letters because they take so long and in the end they are not at all spontainious, no, just wait a second, here it is, "spontaneous," and believe me only two or three mistakes in a letter from me is one of the seven wonders of the world. What I'm saying is that I am doing the best I can as you would aggree if you could see my dictionary which is falling apart and when you say I should memmorize the spelling I can't because it doesn't make any sence to me and never did.

Love,
Stephen

New York, February 23

Dear Stephen:

It is probably just as well that you have gotten everything off your chest. We all need to blow up once in a while. It clears the air.

Please don't ever forget that I am aware that spelling is difficult for you. I know you are making a great effort and I am very proud of you. I just want to be sure that you keep trying.

I am enclosing a small check for your birthday because even if you do not want to be reminded of it I wouldn't want to forget it and you must know that we are thinking of you.

Love,
Father

Geneva, February 26

Dear Father:

We are not allowed to cash personal checks here in the School, but thank you anyway for the money.

I am not able to write any more because we are going to have the exams and I have to study.

Love,
Stephen

New York, March 2

NIGHT LETTER
BEST OF LUCK STOP KEEP ME POSTED EXAM RESULTS LOVE

FATHER.

Geneva, March 12

Dear Father:

Well, the exams are over. I got a C in English because aparently I do not know how to spell, which should not come as too much of a surprise to you. In Science, Mathematics, and Latin I got A, and in French and History I got a B plus. This makes me first in the class, which doesn't mean very much since none of the children here have any life of the mind, as you would say. I mean they are all jerks, more or less. What am I supposed to do in the Easter vacation? Do you want me to come to New York, or shall I just stay here and get a rest, which I could use?

Love, Stephen

New York, March 16

Dear Stephen:

I am *immensely* pleased with the examination results. Congratulations. Pull up the spelling and our worries are over.

Just yesterday I had a letter from your mother. She has taken a little house in Majorca, which is an island off the Spanish coast, as you probably know, and she suggests that you should come to her for the Easter holidays. Of course you are always welcome here—and you could rest as much as you wanted—but Majorca is very beautiful and would certainly appeal to the artistic side of your nature. I have written to your mother, urging her to write to you immediately, and I enclose her address in case you should want to write yourself. Let me know what you would like to do.

Love,
Father

Geneva, March 19

Dear Mummy:

Father says that you have invited me to come to you in Majorca for the Easter vacation. Is that true? I would be very very happy if it were. It has been very hard to be away from you for all this time and if you wanted to see me it would mean a great deal to me. I mean if you are feeling well enough. I could do a lot of things for you so you would not get too tired.

I wonder if you will think that I have changed when you see me. As a matter of fact I have changed a lot because I have become quite bitter. I have become bitter on account of this School.

I know that you and Father wanted me to have some expearience of what the world was like outside of America but what you didn't know is that Geneva is not the world at all. I mean, if you were born here, then perhaps you would have a real life, but I do not know anyone who was born here so all the people I see are just like myself, we are just waiting not to be lost any more. I think it would have been better to have left me in some place where I belonged even if Americans are getting very loud and money conscious. Because actually most of the children here are Americans, if you come right down to it, only it seems their parents didn't know what to do with them any longer.

Mummy I have written all this because I'm afraid that I have spent too much money all over again, and M. Frisch says that Father will have a crise des nerfs when he sees what I have done, and I thought that maybe you would understand that I only bought these things because there didn't seem to be anything else to do and that you could help me some how or other. Anyway, according to the School, we will have to pay for all these things.

Concert, Segovia	(Worth it)	16.00	(Swiss Francs)
School Dance		5.00	
English Drama	(What do they mean?)	10.00	
Controle de l'habitant	(?)	9.10	
Co-op purchases		65.90	
Ballets Russes	(Disappointing)	47.00	
Librairie Prior		59.30	
Concert piano	(For practicing)	61.00	
Teinturie	(They ruined everything)	56.50	
Toilet and Medicine		35.00	
Escalade Ball		7.00	
Pocket Money		160.00	
77 Yoghurts	(Doctor's advice)	42.40	
Book account		295.70	
Total		869.90	(Swiss Francs)

Now you see the trouble is that Father told me I was to spend about fifty dollars a month, because that was my allowance, and that I was not to spend anything more. Anyway, fifty dollars a month would be about two hundred and ten Swiss Francs, and then I had fifteen dollars for Christmas from Granny, and when I got back to School I found four Francs in the pocket of my leather jacket and then I had seventy-nine cents left over from New York, but that doesn't help much, and then Father sent me twenty-five dollars for my birthday but I couldn't cash the check because they do not allow that here in School, so what shall I do?

It is a serious situation as you can see, and it is going to get a lot more serious when Father sees the bill. But whatever you do, I implor you not to write to Father because the trouble seems to be that I never had a balance foreward and I am afraid that it is impossible to keep accounts without a balance foreward, and even more afraid that by this time the accounts have gone a little bizerk.

Do you want me to take a plane when I come to Majorca? Who shall I say is going to pay for the ticket?

Please do write me as soon as you can, because the holidays begin on March 30 and if you don't tell me what to do I will be way out on a lim.

Lots and lots of love,
Stephen

Geneva, March 26

Dear Father:

I wrote to Mummy a week ago to say that I would like very much to spend my Easter vacation in Majorca. So far she has not answered my letter, but I guess she will pretty soon. I hope she will because the holidays begin on Thursday.

I am afraid you are going to be upset about the bill all over again, but in the Spring term I will start anew and keep you in touch with what is going on.

Love,
Stephen

P.S. If Mummy doesn't write what shall I do?

Reginald McKnight is the author of a novel, *I Get on the Bus* (1990), and three collections of stories, including *Moustapha's Eclipse* (1988), which won the Drue Heinz Literature Prize, and *The Kind of Light That Shines on Texas* (1991), in which "Quitting Smoking" appears. In this, as in other of his stories, McKnight explores the experience of being a middle-class African American in our society, where racial (and racist) stereotypes are insidious. His protagonist, a young African American in crisis after a heart-wrenching breakup with his white lover, writes to the only person he feels will understand: an African American who not only shared a relevant traumatic experience in the past, but who shares his background, as someone who is "tall and black, but can't play hoops worth a damn" and who "hung around maybe too many white people growing up." McKnight uses the letter format to create a confidential, personal narrative that moves conversationally toward its powerful and unexpected conclusion. This is a personal letter that is, of course, addressed to us all.

Jan. 16, 1978   Manitou Spgs., CO

Dear B___,

Happy New Year and all that. Man, are you ever hard to get ahold of. I wrote your ex-ol' lady first, and she said, and I quote, "As to his whereabouts, well, your guess is as good as mine. The last I heard he was still with TWA, but based in London. I do know that he was suspended for six weeks for giving free tickets to London to that girlfriend of his. I'm surprised they didn't flat out fire him." She mainly ranted about how you only write and send money on your boy's birthday. She's still pretty pissed off at you, my man. Anyway, she said that your folks might know and she gave me their new address and phone # in Texas. I didn't even know they moved. Anyway, money's been a little tight lately, and I don't even have a phone at the moment, so I wrote a card. Didn't here anything for a long time, but then your kid sister, Mayra, wrote me, and this is what she said: "We got your letter a long time ago, but we don't know excatly where B___ is My brother has moved alot in the last couple of years because of his job. The reason I'm writing you instead of my mother is because my mother is discusted with B___. But she won't tel anybody why. And she says she doesn't know his adress. I know she does but I can't find it any where. But I will look for it and if I find it I will send it to you. My big sister Letonya said if she gets the adress she will send the letter to B___ but I don't think so because she is getting married and is always forgetting to do things. Mamma is discusted with Letonya because she says shes too young to get married. Right now your letter is on the fridge with a magnit on it."

I thought you'd like that, B___.

Then I called TWA. They were kind of nasty, and no help at all. They did tell me you were on leave, though, but wouldn't say where. So, how did I get your address? Letonya came through. She said you were living it up in Madrid for six months, and then you'd be going back to London. I guess she'd be married by now.

I guess you're probably surprised to hear from me after all these years, homes, and I bet you're surprised at how long this letter is, or for me right at this second, how long it's gonna be. This'll be the longest thing I'll ever have written by the time I'm done. I know that already, B___, 'cause the stuff I got on my mind is complicated and confusing. I've been sleeping pretty bad lately, 'cause I've been thinking about that thing that happened when you, me, Stick, and Camel saw that guy snatch that woman into his car in front of Griff's, just after hoops practice. I'm sure you remember. It bothered me a lot back then, of course, but you know it's been nine years now and you get over things like that after a while. And for a long time I didn't really think about it all that much. But something happened a few weeks ago between me and my girlfriend, Anna, that brought all that stuff up again and has pretty much messed up things between me and her. The stuff I'm gonna tell you, speaking of "between," is just between you and me. Period. OK? But I've gotta tell you the whole thing so you'll understand where I'm coming from and understand why I've done what I've done. I feel bad that I've gotta talk about Anna behind her back like this, but goddamnit, you're the only guy who'd understand what I'm trying to work out in my mind. You and me are pretty much cut from the same tree, you could say. We both grew up in this town. Well, I'm in Manitou now and not Colo. Spgs., but I'll get to that later. We both hung around maybe too many white people growing up. We're both tall and black, but can't play hoops worth a damn. We both have had very weird relationships with redheaded, green-eyed women, only you actually married yours. Anna and I just lived together. Yeah, "live" in the past tense. Looks like it might be over between me and Anna. Over, unless, after you've read all this, you think what I've done is wrong, and you say that I should give Anna another chance, or she should give me one. You know, I was gonna try to get in touch with the other "fellas" about this, too. I know where the Stick is. I think I do, anyway. I ran into Coach Ortiz at José Muldoon's and he told me the Stick is teaching poli sci at some college in Athens, Georgia. I'd tried his folks' place first, but the old phone # don't work and they're not in the book. The last I heard about Camel is that he joined the service. The army or the air force, I'm not sure. Can you imagine that big buck-tooth hippie in the service? But anyway, I decided not to write or call those guys 'cause, to be honest, they're white and I don't think they'd understand.

Right now, I'm living in Manitou Springs, like I said, in a place called Banana Manor. A big stone monster painted bright yellow and trimmed in brown. It used to be a hotel, I guess. It's kind of a hippie flophouse. Lots of drugs, sex, rock 'n' roll, long hair, and cheap rent. I got a room here and pay only $65 a month for it. Most of my stuff's still at the place me and Anna shared, and I still go by there and pick up my mail and stuff, but I only go there when she's not around, mainly 'cause it'd hurt too much to see her. I leave her notes and still pay my share of the rent. Don't know how long I'll do that though.

Before I get to my point (sorry it's taking me so long) I guess I oughta catch you up on me. After all, B——, we ain't seen each other in about six years, or written or called since you split with Kari. How's your boy, by the way? Good, I hope. Well now, I finally got my certificate in cabinetry at Pikes Peak Comm. Col. Actually, I copped an A.A. in general studies, too. I had the money and the time, so I figured, what the fuck. Besides, Anna kept ragging on me till I did. Graduated third in my cabinetry class, quit this stockBOY gig I'd had at Alco's and got a part-timer at Chess King. I sold shake yo' booty clothes to mostly army clowns from Fort Cartoon. (That's what my Anna calls Fort Carson.) Well, I got fired for "studying at work" and "ignoring customers," which all I have to say about is if you remember my study habits in high school, you'll know it was all bullshit. They fired me 'cause I wouldn't wear their silly-ass clothes on the job. My mom always used to tell me, "You ain't got to dress like a nigro to look like a nigro, boy."

So I was out of work for about two months and moved in with Anna, which had its ups and downs (no pun). Anna's got a couple of years on me. Actually five, but she looks about 20. She has a kid, though, and to tell you the truth, I could do without the instant family stuff. But Max, her kid is all right for a rug rat. I mean, he wets the bed sometimes, and he's about as interested in sports as I'm interested in *Sesame Street,* but he's smart, funny, and likes me, so I could hang with it. To tell you the truth, I miss him a lot.

But like I'm saying, there were some good things about living with Anna, and some things that weren't so good. Good and not so good. The usual. She's divorced, and 31, like I said. We met at the community college about a year and a half ago. It was in the Spring Quarter, and the weather was perfect, in the 80's, sky like a blank blue page. I was sitting on a bench outside the cafeteria, talking to this friend of mine, when she walked by in a pink Danskin top and a pink and white flowered skirt. My asshole friend yells out, "Hey! You got the most beautiful breasts I've ever seen." And she blushed and kept walking. I told Steve that was no way to talk to a woman and he told me that broads like that kind of talk, and besides, he didn't say "tits." I told him to screw off and ran after her. I apologized to her and told her I had nothing to do with what Steve'd said. She kind of nodded real quick, mumbled something, and kept walking. Then I walked away, and didn't figure I'd ever see her again. I felt like an idiot. Didn't even wanna think about it.

Well, about two weeks later I was in the parking lot and just about to my car when I hear this little voice say, "You have the most beautiful ass I've ever seen." It was Anna, and as they say, da rest is history. She's 5'2" and has a body that would make your teeth sweat. Steve was right about her bust, but he missed the rest. Like I say, she's got red hair, green eyes, but the weird thing is she tans real good. Not like most redheads who sit out in the sun for two seconds and end up looking like blisters with feet, or get so many freckles that you wanna hand 'em a brown Magic Marker and tell 'em to go finish the job. So anyway, she's also about a hundred times smarter than I am, which is no big deal, 'cause she never jams it down my throat. Besides, since I started at the cabinet mill I make more scratch than she does. (She's on welfare.) Anna's a sociology major at Colorado College now, and she'd been trying to talk me into going there to get a degree in something, but for one thing I don't have the money, and for another thing, you don't exactly see legions of folks our color over there so I doubt they'd want me. Anyhow, I'm not exactly a genius. I might have done good in cabinet school, but I couldn't pull higher than six or seven B's in general studies. Screw 'em. Plus, I know the kind of bullshit you had to put up with at Graceland College, amongst all that wheat and corn and cow squat. I still have that letter where you told me about the "joke" (ha-ha) Klan party your friends threw for you on your birthday. That kind of thing ain't for the kid here.

Anyway, let me get to my point before I bore you to death. OK, so like one night, about a month ago, Anna and I were in the sack and she wouldn't even kiss me good night. This is strange, I was thinking, 'cause usually she's more interested in sex than I am, which means she likes it more than a woodpecker likes balsa. So I asked her what the hell was wrong. (Actually, I said, "Hey, babes, you OK?") And she started crying, real slow and silent. So I got up and burned a doobie. (Yes. I smoke now. Actually, I smoke cigarettes, too, but I'd pretty much quit while I was with Anna. More about that later.) I passed it to her and she took a couple hits. So like I asked her again what was up and she said she got upset 'cause that day in class they were talking about social deviants (sp?) and her prof said that all of society makes it easy for men to commit rape and that there was no real way to completely eradicate it. So Anna said back to the guy that castration would sure the hell stop it. And then nobody said much of anything for like a minute. Then the prof came back with all that talk show crap that rape isn't sexual, but violent, etc., etc. And Anna just sat there for a while, while the guy kept talking, and she told me that she'd made up her mind not to say anything else. But then, before she knew what hit her, she just sort of blared out, "Then give them the fucking death penalty!" That's exactly what she said. And that started a huge argument in the class.

Well, Anna crushed out the joint in the ashtray. She did it real hard and all I could think about was somebody crushing out a smoking hard-on, which I'm sure she wanted me to think. She's really into symbols and shit. In fact, I think she wanted me to get my A.A. just so I'd get all the symbols she dumps on me. All right, so I was kind of surprised, 'cause even though Anna's kind of a women's libber, she's always been pretty mellow about things, and she's always been real anti–death penalty. So I asked her why she'd said that stuff in class. She didn't say anything for about a minute. She was just staring up at the passion plant that we have hanging over our bed. So I asked her if she was ever raped. I asked her flat out, and I was sorry I had. She still didn't say anything. And then she just sort of curled up on the bed. She curled up as tight as a fist and goddamn did she ever cry. Jesus, Jesus, Jesus, B___, I was scared, kind of. I've never seen nothing like that. She didn't make any kind of sound hardly. It was like she was pulling up a rope that was tied to something heavy as the moon. Goddamn, those tears were coming from way, way down. I touched her and every muscle in her was like bowed oak. She was just kind of going uh, uh, uh, her whole body jerking like a heart. Then she threw her arms around me so fast, I thought for a second she wanted to slug me. I couldn't swallow, and I could feel my veins pounding where the inner part of my arm touched her back and shoulders. We held each other so tight, we were like socks rolled up and tucked away in a drawer. I guess I never loved or cared so much about anybody as then.

About, I don't know how long later, she told me about it. We'd went into the kitchen 'cause I was hungry, and she wanted some wine. Her eyes were all puffy and red. Her voice croaked. And every once in a while she'd shiver, and get this scared look in her eye and look all around the room. She was whispering 'cause she didn't want to wake up Max, who's room is right next to the kitchen. But the whispering sort of made it weirder or scarier or something. I kept gulping like some cartoon character, and my feet and hands were like ice. I couldn't look at her.

It was this friend of her ex's who'd did it. She says they were sitting in her and her old man's living room. Her old man was at work. He was a medic at Fort Cartoon. I met him once when he came from Texas, where he lives now, to see Max. Guy's an extreme redneck. So anyway, she says she and this guy were getting high on hash, and just talking about stuff. Anyway, they were just sitting there, getting high, when just like that, this guy pulls a knife and tells her to strip and he rapes her. It made me kind of nervous and sick to hear all that. She told me she'd never told anyone else. I guess it sounds kind of dumb, but I felt honored that I was the only person she'd ever told that to. It sort of made me love her even more. Then just like on some cop show or something, she started telling me that she felt all dirty because of what that guy did. It kind of surprised me that a real woman would talk that way. I pretty much thought that kind of stuff was just made up. But she doesn't even watch t.v., except for the news and tennis matches, so I'm sure she wasn't saying it because she'd heard someone else say it. But I hugged her real tight, after she said that, and I told her that she was the sweetest, most beautiful woman I'd ever known. I meant it, too. I didn't stop telling her till she smiled a little.

We went back to the bedroom and got back in bed. I never did get anything to eat. Pretty soon she was asleep, but I couldn't sleep at all. It was partly because of what she'd told me, and partly because of what she'd made me remember. That's why I'm writing you, B___. I couldn't and I still can't sleep because of what you and me and Stick and Camel saw that one night when we were standing outside the gym. It was the only time the four of us ever just hung out together like that. I don't even know why we were all there together. Do you? I mean, the Stickmeister never hung with the three of us, 'cause we weren't real popular. And Camel could have walked home. Usually it was just you and me who'd be out there, waiting for the activity bus. It was colder than Jennifer Lash's underdrawers out there. Remember? You didn't have a jacket, and you offered five bucks to Camel if he'd let you wear his. I remember we all cracked up when you did that.

So, laying there next to Anna it's like I was reliving that night. I kept seeing the blue car, and how the woman kept saying please, please, please, please, and how she tried to crawl under the car, and how you and me were starting across the street, but Stick grabbed your arm and said, he might have a gun, he might kill her—and then how you just stood there saying Hey! Hey! Hey! And then they were gone. Everything was just taillights all of a sudden. I can't believe we just stood there. And I was so goddamn embarrassed when the cop asked what year the car was, and we didn't know, what the license plate read, and we didn't know. And I think we were all embarrassed when we told the cop our stories. I remember you said she was dressed like a nurse and you saw her on the sidewalk, just walking, and then the car pulled up and the guy pulled her in. Then I told them that, no, no, no, first she tried to crawl under the car, then he pulled her in. Then Camel said no, no, no, there were two guys, and the guy in the passenger seat had a gun. Then Stick said no, no, no, no, I think she was in the car first and tried to get out, and the guy pulled her back in. Come on, guys, Stick said, don't you remember when the guy kept asking her for the keys? And no, Camel, there wasn't a gun. I just thought the guy might have a gun. And I remember, you said, B___, God! What's wrong with you, Stick, that was the woman saying *please, please, please;* nobody said a damn thing about no keys! She was crawling under the car and screaming please!

Jesus. Please, keys, tease, ease, bees, knees, cheese. Jeez, what a buncha idiots we must've looked like. But the thing that got me the most, the thing that fucked me up the most that night was when the cop asked the big money, bonus question, what color was the guy? Couldn't tell, you and me said. Too dark. Camel and Stick said, at the same time, black. Then we started arguing. No, no, no, too dark to tell. No, no, no, Afro, he had an Afro. No, butthole, how could you tell? Do you remember if the woman was black? No? Then what makes you think the guy was black? The woman was white, you chump. Yeah? Well what color was her hair? How long was it? How tall was she? Heavyset, was she, or thin? Old or young? Too dark to tell. Too dark to tell. And what makes you think she was in the car first, Stick?

God, what idiots we were. And I sat up in bed that night, after Anna'd told me what she told me, and I couldn't get it out of my head. But I thought about other things, too, B___. I thought about how I used to fantasize when I was a kid, after I'd seen *To Kill a Mockingbird.* I used to fantasize about how I was on trial for raping a white woman, and how I knew I was innocent, and I'd be up on the witness stand with the prosecuting attorney's hot, tomato-faced mug right up in mine. He'd be spitting crap like, Didn'cha, boy? Didn'cha? You lusted afta those white arms, and those pink lips and those pale blue, innocent eyes, didn'cha, nigger boy?

Objection!

Sustained. Mr. Hendershot, I have warned you about—

Forgive me yo honor—and then he dabs his tomato face down with a crumpled hanky—but when ah think of the way these . . . these animals lust afta our sweet belles, why, sir, it makes mah blood boil. No more questions. Yo witness, Mistah Wimply.

And my defender would get up there and sputter and mumble. The prosecutor'd be laughing into his cuffs, dabbing his face, winking and blinking at the jury. Wimply'd look like a fool, but somehow I'd be able to say the right things, and I'd speak as powerfully as Martin Luther King Jr. himself. And while I talked I'd be looking at my accuser with my big puppy eyes and I'd talk about love and justice and peace, equality, never taking my eyes off her beautiful face. She'd start to sweat and tremble, then she'd pass out. The crowd'd go huzzah, hummah, huzzah. The judge would bang away with his gavel. But soon enough the testimony would end, the jury would come back and basically say, hang the black bastud. Then we'd come back the next day, and the judge would say, Scott Winters, you have been found guilty by a jury of your peers. You have committed a vile and foul crime, my boy, and this court has decided to make you pay the ultimate penalty . . . But all of a sudden, B——, my accuser would pop up from her seat and say, No! He's innocent! Innocent, I tell you. I accused him of the crime because I love him, but all he did was ignore me every time I tried to talk to him or smile at him. He ignored me. Then she'd cry like a son of a bitch, and the crowd'd start up with the huzzah, hummah, huzzah. And the judge would be hammering away with his gavel, the prosecutor'd be patting his fat face with his hanky, and the woman would run into my arms. And that'd be that.

Don't ask me why I'd fantasize about that, and I'm not sure if "fantasy" is even the right word. I just played that, whatever it is, in my head, night after night, and I don't know why, exactly, but I think it's because when somebody says rapist, what picture comes to mind? I know I don't have to tell you, B——, it's me and you and your brother and your dad, and my dad, and all our uncles and cousins, and so on. It's like how Anna said at breakfast last year when she was preaching to me like she always does about women's lib stuff. She said, "Scott, if I were to come back from the doctor's today, came home with tears in my eyes because of what the doctor had told me, what would you say?" Well, I didn't know what she was driving at, and I shrugged and said, "Well, first thing I'd ask is, what'd he tell you?" And she jumped up from her chair and spilled her coffee and mine in the process and said, "Bingo! See! See! 'What did He say'—that's my point. Do you understand me now? We've got these images embedded in our heads and they're based on stereotypes!" I'll tell you what, man, I did get her point, but if I hadn't I woulda said I'd got it just the same. Cripes.

Anyway, there I was in bed with her, listening to her breathing, thinking about those old fantasies, and about that day we saw the woman being snatched off the street, and how this beautiful woman laying next to me had to suffer so hard over something she could never, ever forget. I couldn't sleep. I wanted a cigarette bad, the first time I'd really even thought about squares since her and I moved in together. I slipped out of bed and dressed. I was gonna walk up to the 7-Eleven and buy a pack of Winstons, my old brand. I was gonna walk back home, smoking one after another and think about things like why guys are such dogs, and how in hell Anna could love or trust any guy after what'd happened to her. It was cold that night, and snow was falling, but not too hard or thick. They were big flakes, and the sky was pinkish gray. You could see as far as a block or two. Real beautiful. It was dead quiet, no traffic, no voices, no dogs barking. You know how Colorado Springs can be on a winter night at two in the morning. It's funny, but I kept expecting the night to be split in two by screams, and I imagined myself running to wherever the screams'd come from, and I'd find some bastard pinning a woman down on the sidewalk, holding a blade to her throat, and hissing, shut the fuck up you goddamn cunt. And I'd see his big red balls hanging over her. I'd plow my ol' two-ton mountain boots so hard into them sacks it take a team of surgeons to pull 'em out his stomach. I could see myself taking the knife out his weak hands, and making one clean, quiet slice on his throat, and that'd be that. I'd walk the woman home and call the cops, and split before they got there. I was thinking so deep about this stuff, B___, it took me a while to notice that my fists were clenched, and so were my teeth. And it took me just as long to notice that I was walking, then, in the same goddamn neighborhood where the four of us had seen the woman, the guy, and the blue car.

It really kind of freaked me out. I didn't recognize it right away, because in '69, of course, there'd been a Griff's Burger Bar(f) on that lot. Then they made it into a Taco John's. Now it's some kind of church, but there I was probably standing exactly on the spot where nine years ago that woman'd stood. Man, I just stood there for maybe five minutes. And then I went and sat on the steps of the church. All them things were going through my mind, all the stuff I was fantasizing about, all the stuff I could and couldn't quite remember. Then I started feeling guilty about being there, on my way to get a pack of squares. I hadn't had a cigarette in eight months. Like I said, it was Anna who'd helped me quit them things. It was, in a way, the basis of our relationship. Anna's into health like you wouldn't believe. She used to smoke cigarettes, but quit them and coffee when Max was born. She took up swimming and running to get back in shape after he was six months or so. Then when he was like two or three, she quit eating meat. The first couple times we went out we ate at a pizza place, and it was the first time in my life I'd ever had a pizza with no meat on it. It wasn't bad, but I was still hungry. I told her too, but she said, "It's psychological. You're meat hungry." I paused for a minute and grinned real big. Then she laughed and said, "God, you've got a dirty mind." Well, we went to her place. I'd never even been inside before. It was different, really hippyish. There were plants at every window, and it smelled like incense. There was all this beautiful art on the walls, paintings and prints and lithos. Her bedroom was a loft. It sure didn't look like a welfare house, not what I thought one would look like, anyway. Well, I paid the baby-sitter, even though she didn't want me to. Then we got high. Then we made love.

I'd never felt so good with a woman. It was all so quiet and natural, but still intense. But when I say quiet, I don't mean she was silent. She made so much noise I thought she'd wake her kid. When I say quiet, though, I mean peaceful, sort of spiritual. She went to sleep, but I stayed awake, and then I went outside and lit up a square. When I went back inside, I noticed how bad I stunk. Tobacco'd never smelled so strong or so bad to me. I went to the bathroom and washed my hands and face, tried to brush my teeth with toothpaste and my finger. Next morning, we got up and she fixed me a fritata. (Don't know if I spelled that right or not.) It's this thing with eggs and veggies. We had apple juice and Morning Thunder tea. At first I thought something was wrong with the juice because it was brown, but Anna told me it was natural, and was supposed to look like that. It tasted great. And after breakfast I didn't have a cigarette, which is what I usually do. It wasn't hard. I just didn't want one. We went to school, and met each other during the day as much as we could. I didn't have a cigarette all day. After classes, I picked her up and then we got Max from school, and I took them home. Anna wanted me to stay for dinner, but I was dying for a smoke. When I got home I smoked like a fiend. But the more time I spent with her, the less I cared about cigarettes. It was easy. I quit eating meat, too. I wasn't whipped, man. It just didn't feel right anymore.

So, anyway, B___, there I was on the steps of the church feeling guilty about getting cigarettes. I sat there for a long time, but then got up and walked back home. When I got back into bed with Anna, she woke up, and told me how cold I was. "I went for a walk," I said, which was true, but it felt like a lie. I felt guilty about a whole lot of things that night—for wanting a cigarette, for being a man, and for not telling her about that night and what we saw. It was a work night, too, even though it felt like a Friday. I knew there'd be hell to pay if I showed up late for work. Old man Van Vordt is a prick-and-a-½. You show up more than thirty seconds late and he fires you. You cut a piece of lumber as much as a sixteenth of an inch too short and he fires you. You take more than the twenty minutes he gives us for lunch and you might as well pack your trash and ride out of Dodge. In the six months I've worked with him, he's fired about thirty guys. He only wants to tell you something once. Fuck it up, and you die. He pays good money, though, and that's why I keep going back to that freckle-headed ol' fart. Besides, I love the smell of wood, and the precision and beauty of what we do. He's the best cabinetmaker I've ever run into, and for some reason, he likes me. I'm the only black guy he's ever had working for him. Maybe he believes in affirmative action. But anyway, my point is that I decided to stay up that night, 'cause I couldn't sleep, and I didn't want to be late to work. That made me want a cigarette all the more.

I started smoking about five years ago. To tell you the truth I like smoking a lot. Cigarettes, I mean. Pot's OK, but I like the cigarette buzz more, for some reason. And I like the way my lungs fill up. It makes me feel warm inside, makes me dreamy, sort of. I like making smoke rings, french-inhaling, shotguns. And even though it stinks like hell, I like it when my room fills up with smoke. It's like having indoor clouds. I do go through about a can of air freshener a week, and I gotta run fans and keep windows open to kill the smell, but when the sun's shining through my windows in the afternoons, I'll shut 'em, fire up square after square, lay in my bed, and blow cloud after cloud of blue and yellow smoke. And I hate it when a friend busts into my room on those days and says, "Jeezuz, it stinks in here." Hell, I know it stinks, but you can't smell worth a damn if you're inhaling and blowing. And it's my room.

I started smoking in '73, like I say, when I was still living at my folks' place and you were in college at Graceland. I'd went down to Alamosa to visit with Gary T___ and Dale P___. They were juniors, I think, and were living off campus. Let me tell you, if you think those guys were partiers in high school, you shoulda seen 'em then. Their whole place was set up for partying. No rugs, black lights, strobe lights, lava lamps. They had a refrigerator in the basement that was filled with beer, maybe twelve cases. They had a wet bar upstairs, and this big-ass cabinet filled with every type of booze you could name. Then there was this fishbowl in the kitchen that was full of joints, pills, and blotter acid. It was unreal. Serious to God, I wasn't into any of that stuff at the time, and most of it I'm still not. I've never done acid, speed, coke, downers, dust, and I can't stand most booze. I might have a beer every so often, but I just nurse the hell out of 'em. Man, I can make a can of beer last for a whole party. Actually, I did speed once in high school, and once again a couple months ago when I was working twelve-hour days at the mill. Anyway, I went up to check out Gary and Dale 'cause I hadn't seen them in a year or more. I was really surprised at what they looked like. Both of 'em had hair down to the middle of their backs. Dale was wearing this big honkin Fu Manchu and Gary had a full beard. It was incredible. Neither of them was playing hoop anymore. Gary'd quit and Dale'd wrecked his knees.

So anyway, they weren't having any party that night, but people kept coming by all afternoon and all night to buy drugs. They had quite a nice business. They were each pulling down about 20 thou a year. It's how they paid their tuition. Far as I know they're still dealing.

So like, we shake hands and bullshit, etc., etc., and they show me around their place, etc., etc., and then Gary's fiancée comes by, and we go down to the basement and sit on beanbags and then Gary brings out a gas mask and a bag of Panama Red. Oh, Lord, I started thinking. What if the cops bust down the door and start blazing away? What if it's bad stuff and we O.D. or something? (Yeah, I was pretty naive.) Then Dale said, "You get high, Scott?" And I said, "Oh sure." So when the mask came my way, I huffed and pulled and sucked, but didn't feel a thing. I took about fifteen hits in all, but still didn't feel a thing. Except I did feel paranoid (or as Gary would say, "noid.") I told 'em I still lived with my folks and they'd kill me if I came home reeking. So Dale reached into his T-shirt pocket and took out a pack of Marlboros, and said, "Smoke these on the way back. You'll smell like cigarettes, and that might make 'em mad, but you won't smell like weed, which'll make 'em toss you out." I put 'em in my pocket, and we hung out for a while longer and talked, etc., etc. Then we ordered a couple pizzas, ate, and then I split back home.

I got back to the Springs about one in the morning and I'd forgot all about the cigarettes till I was almost home, so I pulled off at this junior high parking lot, lit one up. After about five minutes I felt like I was floating. I felt calm. It was weird. I mean, I'd spent the entire evening smoking dope, and hadn't felt a thing, but I was getting ripped on a damn cigarette. Well, that was it, man, I was hooked. Into it big time. My mom was pissed off at me when she found out I was smoking, but what could she say really? I mean, both my folks'd started smoking when they were in their teens, and they smoke maybe a pack a day apiece. Things got a little tense around the house, though, so I moved out.

Like I say, I wanted a cigarette, but I didn't smoke. Anna went to school and I went to work. Things seemed pretty normal. I was dragging ass at work, though, and ol' Van de Man was a demon. "Scott! Where's those rabbit cuts I asked you for?" "Scott! I thought I asked you ta clean that planer." "Scott! You building a goddamn ark or what? Thought I asked you for them chester drawer legs a half hour ago!" I saw my career flash before my eyes a half dozen times. It wasn't only 'cause I was tired, and it wasn't only 'cause I would have given my left nut for a cigarette, and it wasn't just that I walked around all with my guts feeling like Jell-O 'cause I was afraid every second of what might happen to Anna when I wasn't home. It was because I thought that since she'd told me about the worst thing that'd ever happened to her, that I should tell her about the worst thing that I ever let happen to someone else. But when I got home that afternoon, I made dinner, we ate, she did the dishes, we went to bed and made love for a long, long time. And that was it. It took me four hours to get to sleep that night.

Days went by and days went by and still I didn't say anything. But all I could think about was how that woman was trying to dig her nails into the pavement while she was under that car. And all I could think about was some bastard holding a knife to my woman's throat and breaking into her like a bullet. And I started getting weird and jealous in funny ways, like once when I drove by campus to pick her up from the library, and she was out front talking to this dude. She was standing out on the lawn, holding her books up over her breasts, and this tall blond bearded dude was craning over her, smiling, talking, moving his hands like he was conducting a goddamn band. I could tell they were looking deep in each other's eyes. I thought I could tell she was into this dude. B___, I know this'll sound stupid, but I was sitting there in my car, thinking, you idiot, don't you know what he's got on his mind? Don't you know what he could do to you? I acted like a prick all night long. To her anyway. With Max, I was like Santa Claus. I rode him on my back like a horse, I played checkers with him. I read him a couple stories. Then after everybody was in bed, I slipped out the house, walked to the 7-Eleven, and bought a pack of cigarettes and a bottle of mouthwash. I went to Monument Valley Park and smoked half a pack, washed my mouth, over and over till the bottle was empty, and then I split back home. Soon as I got back I smoked a joint to mask the smell.

I thought we should be getting closer. I thought she should mistrust every man but me. But then I got to thinking that maybe she could sense something about me, knew I was holding something back, which I was. I was holding two things back. I thought she was sensing something, 'cause her attitude was changing at home. She'd gotten pretty rough with Max. Didn't hit him or anything, but she'd go pyro on him if he spilled milk or messed up his clothes. And she only seemed interested in talking to me about stuff she was doing at school. And when all I could say back was something like, " . . . . . . ?" she started giving me all this women's lib stuff to read. Gyno-this and eco-gyno-poly-that. And when I still didn't get it, she'd just click her tongue at me and roll her eyes, sigh real loud, and stomp off. She started correcting my English, which is something she'd never done, and she started having long phone conversations with people and she'd never tell me who she was calling. And every time I thought maybe I'd better tell her about what you and me and the fellas saw that night, she'd do something else to piss me off, and I'd keep my mouth shut. I think from the time I lit that first square, the base of our relationship started to crumble. But then she was keeping something from me, too. I didn't know for sure, but I could feel it. I couldn't keep my mind off that tall blond son of a bitch.

I started picking up a pack of smokes on the way to work every day. And I started keeping mouthwash, gum, soap, air freshener, a toothbrush, and deodorant in a day sack in my trunk. Sometimes she'd say to me, "Geez, have you been at work or at a disco?" I'd tell her I just thought she'd like it if I didn't come home smelling like a bear. "You smelled like sawdust," she said, "and I like sawdust." But I couldn't stop smoking. And I started up eating meat again, too. On the way to work, I'd toss my cheese and sprout sandwiches and grab a hoagie, a chilli dog, didn't matter. So I'd play Mr. Tofu Head at home and go to work and let myself get scuzzy as hell. It never occurred to me once to look into other women, but I felt just as guilty. I couldn't sleep for shit, and I was getting kinda soft in bed, if you know what I mean. I couldn't stand myself. And I couldn't stand her. After we'd screw—and it was screwing by then, not love—I couldn't stand the touch of her. It was like every damn day I felt like I was gonna explode. I could see myself dropping to the floor at Anna's feet and begging her to forgive me for all the stuff I was doing, and all the stuff I'd failed to do. I'd beg her to forget that tall motherfucker and come back to me.

B___, I tried and tried and tried to tell her, but I couldn't, and I knew I was smoking a wall between us. I knew that, man, so I'd try every day to quit. I'd crush my cigarettes before leaving work, and flush 'em down the toilet. I'd spray, wash, brush, rinse my ass till I was clean as a pimp. I'd do this every day, and every day I saw them squares, spinning round and round that white water, and going down, I thought that'd be it, that I wouldn't smoke any more. I bought a book on self-hypnosis, and a self-hypnosis tape at this health food place where we used to shop. I tried herbal teas and hot showers, gum, candy, jogging, prayer. And I'd go home every day with a new idea, or a new way of picking up the subject of rape. I figured that of all the reasons I'd gone back to smoking, that was it. One day, I said, "Hey, babe, why don't we start giving money to one of them women's shelter things." She was cooking dinner at the time. It was her day to do it. I was kicking back at the kitchen table, drinking some juice. She didn't say anything for like 30 seconds, enough time for me to get nervous and start looking around. I watched Max tumbling around in the backyard. He looked cute as hell, his hair looked like pure white light the way the sun hit it. Then I looked back at Anna. She just picked up a handful of veggie peelings and flung 'em in the trash. "I think that'd be a good idea," she said, but she was looking really tight, really serious when she said it. I knew something wasn't "organic," as she would say, so I asked her what was up. Well, she flung that red hair out of her face, wiped away some sweat from her forehead with the back of her hand, dried her hands on a towel, and left the room. She came back in a minute with a little stash box, and I was relieved for a second 'cause I thought she was gonna twist up a joint and haul me off to bed. I was smiling, I think. She opened the box, reached in, and tossed a cigarette, my brand, on the table. "I found it in your pocket when I did laundry yesterday," she said. She just stood there. I just sat there. "Busted," I said.

Yeah, we fought about it, but I didn't have too much fight in me, really. What could I say? It was mine. "I trusted you," she said. "You told me that when you met me, quitting smoking was the easiest thing in the world," she said. Scott Winters, I was thinking, a jury of your peers has found you guilty . . . It really surprised me when she started crying. I didn't think she'd took it that serious. I mean, she never'd asked me to quit smoking. Never said a word about it. And it was easy. When we moved in together, I just didn't buy anymore squares. That was it.

From that day on, the day I was busted, is when I started thinking about getting in touch with you, B___. I wanted to ask you how you felt when Kari found out about you and that chick you were seeing. How you felt when you got busted. Kari called me up one day, after you and she'd split, and she was so angry I could hear the phone lines sizzling. She said, "I just wanna ask you one thing, Scott. Will you be honest with me? And I said sure I would. And she asked me, "Did B___ really tell you he'd dreamt about me six weeks before he and I actually met? Was that true, Scott?" Well, B___, I'm sorry, bud, but I felt bad for her, and I figured that it wouldn't make any difference since you two'd already split. I told her the truth. I told her, no, you hadn't told me that. Then she asked me if it was true what your girlfriend had told her, that you'd been picked up for flashing back in '72 when you lived in San Francisco, and I told Kari that's what you told me. Then—and her voice got higher and I could tell she was gonna cry—she said, "And then that bitch told me that B___ had gotten a woman pregnant when he was in college. Do you know if that's true?" I told her that I'd heard about it from a very unreliable source. That's all I knew. But it was good enough for her. She started crying, and God did I feel bad. She kept saying, "Thank you, Scott, thank you, thank you. I'm sorry to bother you, but I just wanted the truth for once. All of it. I just wanted to hear someone tell me the truth." She hung up without even saying good-bye.

That's why you haven't heard from me, B___. I was confused and felt ashamed. In fact, that last letter I got from you a few years back is still unopened. I just figured that Kari had called you up to bust your chops, 'cause of what I'd told her, and you were writing to bust mine. I couldn't take that. And if you don't write back now, I'll understand. Anyway, that time, there at the kitchen table, staring at that cigarette, is when I started thinking about you.

I tried to quit, but I couldn't. Sure, I told her I'd quit again, but I never did. I just got smarter about hiding things. I'd quit smoking close to the end of the workday, always kept my squares in my locker at work. That kind of thing. On weekends, I never even thought about cigarettes. I'd take Max to the playground. I'd go grocery shopping. I'd go down to

Pueblo to fish with my folks, with Anna and Max, or by myself, and I'd
never even think about them. But I just couldn't do it this time. Anna
was OK after a few days, but I could tell things were kind of slipping.
And I got to feeling that she didn't care about whether I smoked or not.
I knew I had to tell her about that night. I just never could. It's like she
could sense what I was gonna say, and she'd say something, or give me a
look, and I'd freeze up. Like this one time when she and I took Max to
the "Y" for a swim. She and I got out after a few laps and I asked her what
that guy might have done if she cried out for help. I'd just kind of blurted
it out. I don't think she was ready to talk about this thing at a place like
that, at a time like that. She just hugged Max's towel to her chest, and
looked at the water. She was quiet so long I didn't think she was gonna say
anything. "Well," she said, finally, and her answer was pretty much what
I thought it'd be except she didn't say, *You stupid asshole idiot fuck,* but I
could feel it—"Scott, he said he would kill me. He probably would have."
Then she was quiet for a while, and just slicked her hair back with her
hand. Then she said, "There're times I wish he would have." She walked
away from me, and dove back into the water. That was it. Right then, I
knew I was losing her, and I had to tell her. But you know, sometimes I
think if I hadn't tried, I wouldn't be sitting up here on the third floor of
Banana Manor, listening to the people next door screw their insides out,
and hearing some butthead teenager slamming Fleetwood Mac out his
speakers for the world to hear. I wouldn't be sitting inside this stinking
little cloud of mine at two, now three, now four in the morning, with
a terminal case of writer's cramp, trying to lay down something I wish
never'd happened.

I was gonna tell her, B___, about everything, the way we all just stood
there and watched a huge piece of that woman's life get sucked away into
a car, the make, model, and year of which I guess we'll never know. Man,
we watched that piece of her life shrink down to a pair of taillights, and
we went on with our own. Yeah, I was gonna tell Anna. I was finally
gonna do it, and I was hoping both that she would and wouldn't tell me
about that tall blond dude.

I called in sick to work, and ol' Van de Man was pissed because we
were behind schedule on a contract we'd had with Pueblo 1st Federal.
I'd never took a day off before, though, and I told him that. He pretty
much let me slide then, but he did it in Van Vordt style. "You screw me
one more time like this, Winters, and ya might as well not come back!
Just might as well not come back!" I'm sure that freckled head was hot

enough to cook rice. So, anyway, I picked out a great recipe from *Diet for a Small Planet,* and whipped that up. I ran to Weber Street Liquors and bought her a bottle of Mateus rosé. It's her favorite. I was nervous as hell, and couldn't sit down all day. I went to the Safeway twice and bought a pack of Winstons each time. The first one, I opened the pack, drew one, and lit up, but put it out. The next one I opened as soon as I got home, but I crushed 'em into the toilet and flushed. I cleaned up the house and bought flowers. I was so nervous, I was twitching. I paced around the house all afternoon, trying to think up ways I could tell her, but it all sounded so stupid—*"More wine, dear? Oh, by the way, I witnessed an abduction of a woman when I was a sophomore in high school, didn't do a damned thing about it, though. It probably led to her rape. Maybe even a murder. Just say when!"* I was thinking, Scott, you dork. What good is a clean house and rosé wine gonna do? I felt like a bozo.

So, I went to pick up Max from school, since I knew it was Anna's day to do the laundry. I took the kid into the backyard and I threw him the football for a while, but I was throwing so hard I just about cracked his ribs. He was OK, though. Didn't even cry all that much, but I hugged him and took him inside, fixed him a snack, and let him watch the tube. I really love that kid, I guess. In a way, I guess. At first I was embarrassed at all the stares him and I used to get when I'd take him places. I'm sure some people thought I'd kidnapped him or something, but after a while I didn't even think about it. I think I know how you must feel about being away from your boy.

Anna came home about a quarter to five. Her eyes were all big and she kept asking what the occasion was, and I kept saying, " 'Cause I love you, that's all." We had dinner, put Max to bed, and broke out the wine. Anna didn't know what was bugging me, but she knew I wasn't very together for some reason or another, and it was like she got nervous, too. She got up after a while and started putting laundry away. I looked at her—from her little pink feet to her bush of red hair—and I was thinking, " 'Cause I love you, that's all." She looked gorgeous, and I just knew that what I was gonna tell her'd bring us closer, even if it started off with some hurt. She started to change the sheets on the bed, but I'd already handled that. I swear, the house never looked cleaner, and she kept asking me why this, and why that, but there wasn't, like, excitement in her voice, but like kind of an almost irritated tone, like she felt bad that she hadn't helped, or that I was trying to tell her how to *really* clean house. She kept getting more and more nervous. I think she was figuring I was gonna propose to her, and she's real nervous about marriage. She says she doesn't even wanna think about marriage till she graduates and gets financially together. You know, just in case the next guy dumps her like the first one did.

So she went back to putting laundry away, and I was following her around the house, just yacking about nothing. Then I just sort of started talking real casual about this essay she'd asked me to read. It was by this woman named Sue Brownmiller. I can't remember the title, and it was pretty tough reading, but it's about how women are better at cooperation and being sensitive than guys, and that's what we need in this world. Maybe that's not all she was saying, but that's basically what I got out of it. Took me forever to read it.

Anyway, I started talking to Anna about the article and she started talking about something we argue about all the time—that if women ran the world, it might be a little bit less organized than it is now, but it would definitely be more peaceful. Instead of saying what I usually say, which is, look, as long as there're men on the planet, there'd still be violence, etc., etc., I figured that here was my chance to get to my point. So I just kind of blurted out, "You know, babe, considering all that's happened to you, I wouldn't be surprised if you hated men." And at first I didn't think she knew what I meant, 'cause she just kept opening up drawers and putting stuff away and closing them back up. I figured she'd just click her tongue at me, and roll her eyes and say, "You missed the point, Scott." But then she kind of turned in my direction, but didn't look at me. She pulled her hair away from her face and flung it back. Then she said, "I'm surprised I don't hate black men. The guy who raped me was black." Then she walked out the room with a stack of laundry in her arms. Then she closed the goddamn door. She closed it soft.

I just stood there, staring at the door, B___. It was like she'd stabbed me in the chest and kicked me in the balls at the same time. I'm not exaggerating, man. My nuts were hurting so bad I had to squat for a minute and take some deep breaths. That ever happen to you, where your blood and adrenaline get pumping so bad it hurts your nuts? It took the wind out of me. It was unreal. I never, ever thought she'd say anything like that to me. It was from Mars, man. Why didn't she tell me that night? I was thinking. Why now, this way, like a weapon? What the fuck did I do to deserve that? I just sat there, and my hands were shaking and I thought for sure I was gonna throw up. I felt sick and dead and I couldn't breathe right. It was like my veins'd been tapped and were leaking out all over the floor.

Then, after my blood slowed a bit, I opened up the drawers she'd just shut and I grabbed 3 or 4 of everything, plus a bunch of shit from the closet. Shoes and things. I packed a couple of bags, and I walked into the living room, and to the front door. I looked around the place. It was damned clean, that's for sure. She saw me from the kitchen and she said, "Where do you think you're going?" I just looked at her and shook my head. I wanted to tell her to stick it, but I just shook my head and stepped out. She was on my heels, though, right dead on my heels. She kept pulling on my shoulder and arm, trying to get me to turn around. She kept saying, "What are you doing? Where are you going? What's going on?" Shit like that. I could see her long blue skirt sweeping around and I could see her pink feet. It was cold out there. I felt bad, B___, bad for all kinds of reasons, but I kept moving, jerking my arm or shoulder away from her, you know? My throat was all clutched up tight, and even if I'd wanted to say something to her I couldn't have. I couldn't look at her either. I stuck my car key into the lock, but before I could twist the lock open she grabbed the key ring, and she was flipping by now, practically screaming, ripping at my wrists and hands with her fingernails. She said, "What's going on? What're you doing? Talk to me, Scott, please," and all that. I grabbed her wrist, forced open her hand, took the keys, got in, cranked it up. I never looked back at her face. If I had, I probably wouldn't've split. I mean she was acting completely innocent, like she didn't have any idea of what she'd said. And for a second there, I wasn't sure I was doing the right thing, or if she'd even understood what she'd said or the way she'd said it. By then I was goddamn crying, too. And as I was backing out, she kept saying please, please, please, Scott, please. That's basically why I'm writing you, brother. Do you think she knew what she'd done? I mean, here's kind of the reason why, what I'm gonna tell you now.

I tried not to listen, OK, and I was pulling away. I couldn't see good, because of the tears, but I could see her in the rearview mirror. She was standing in the street with her hands in her hair, pulling it back like she does when it's wet. She kept saying please, please, please, Scott, please, but the farther away I got, it started sounding more like keys, keys, keys, Scott, keys.

Right now I don't know, B___. Sometimes you just don't know. Sometimes you just can't tell what you see or hear or feel. Or remember.

Take care, man,

Love, Scott

In "Correspondence," which was first published in the winter 1992/1993 edition of *Bostonia,* Houston attorney Donna Kline exploits the comic possibilities of epistolary revelation (and self-revelation) to create a shrewd and funny take on American politics, mores, and citizens. The tale revolves, fittingly, around a postal incident, an apparently simple good deed, that gives rise to a series of events and a flurry of epistolary activity. Through the letters and memoranda fired off, which reveal an entertaining cast of characters, we piece together a story that is at once satirical and endearing.

Adeline (Mrs. Joseph P.) Macomber-Smith
c/o Mrs. Peter (Adele) Singleton
34 Garden Valley Drive
East Peach, TX
August 15, 19—

Mr. Phillip Pargeter
P.O. Box 179
Department of Mislaid Mail
United States Post Office, Main Branch
Houston, TX 77002

Dear Mr. Pargeter,

I am writing to thank you for forwarding to me the letter from my son, Cpl. Joseph P. Macomber-Smith, Jr., USMC, and to confirm for you that it was indeed from him. I cannot tell you how much it meant to me to receive that letter. My niece, Adele, had to read it to me because my eyes are not so good anymore, and as you know, the ink was very faded. I have not cried so much since Joe Senior passed away in 1974.

Perhaps you might have some interest in the circumstances. I suppose that many people would be angry to find out that a letter had been lying around some dusty post office for more than 15 years. So many people criticize the Post Office, and stamps *are* very expensive now. For me, however, the delay was a blessing in disguise. I do not know if it was in the Houston papers, but we had a bad brush fire here in East Peach at the beginning of the summer, when the drought was so bad. Joe Senior and I ranched here for over 40 years, both of us having been raised here in Dumas County, and the fire spread to our house before the firemen could contain it because the first cutting of hay was still in the field and was very dry. I was in town visiting my niece and her husband at the time, and people said I was lucky not to be out there all by myself. But, Mr. Pargeter, you will think that I am just a foolish old woman, but I think I minded losing my scrapbooks more than I minded losing the house or the furniture. I had all of Joe Junior's high school yearbooks and clippings from the East Peach Courier when he got his Eagle Scout and All State in track and things like that. I had kept all his letters home too, from when he went into the Marine Corps, just like I kept his father's letters from WW II. Joe Junior wrote to me almost every week, from Parris Island and San Diego and Hawaii when he was on R and R. I'm sure you couldn't know this, but Joe Junior never came home from Viet Nam. He was killed at the place that they call Hamburger Hill.

So you see, the letter that you sent me is the only one that I can have now from my Joe. I do not know how you could possibly have found me after so many years since the envelope had been almost destroyed and the bottom half of the page with my boy's signature had been ripped off. I'm sure it must have been a great deal of trouble and work for you, and I wanted you to know that I appreciated it very much.

If you are ever up here in our part of Texas, I'd like to thank you personally.

Yours truly,
Adeline B. (Mrs. Joseph P.) Macomber-Smith

cc. Congressman John Wingham and Howard S. Margolis, Postmaster, Houston, TX

MEMORANDUM

TO: Hon. John Wingham
FROM: Miss Doris Bird, Chief Administrative Assistant
RE: Mrs. Adeline Macomber-Smith
DATE: August 18, 19_

Attached is a letter from Mrs. Adeline Macomber-Smith, which has considerable human interest potential. Shall I send the usual reply or do you want to do something with this?

MEMORANDUM

TO: Doris
FROM: Congressman Jack
ATTACHMENT: constituent letter
DATE: August 20, 19_

Gives new meaning to the term "dead letter."

Please get me the scoop on this guy Pargeter and write a letter for me to the old lady re: many good workers at postal service, problem is bloated

Democratic bureaucracy. Usual stuff. Also, if Pargeter is OK, letter to Pargeter and local postmaster re: pat on back.

Is East Peach on my itinerary for the speech tour in October? If no, talk to County Chairman re: visit there, photo with Mrs. Adeline, etc. Check was son decorated? If not, find out from Pentagon if too late now.

Also what is status of drought relief program for Dumas County? Cattlemen's Association raising hell.

Phillip Pargeter
Department of Mislaid Mail
United States Postal Service, Downtown Station
Houston, TX 77002
August 20, 19_

Adeline (Mrs. Joseph P.) Macomber-Smith
c/o Mrs. Peter (Adele) Singleton
34 Garden Valley Drive
East Peach, TX

Dear Mrs. Macomber-Smith:

Thank you for your lovely letter of the 15th instant.

I like to think that we at the Postal Service do our best for the citizens of America. I am not far from retirement myself, even now that the age limit is 70.

There have been many frustrations in my job here, because there is so much automation that I think we are in danger of losing sight of the real purpose of the mails which, for me, is to keep the citizens of America in touch with those they love. Nowadays, it seems like all the emphasis is on bulk mail and automation and overnight express and corporate accounts and things like that.

Down here in the delayed correspondence department, though, they kind of let me work away at my own speed. It is very satisfying when I am able to find the recipient of a long lost letter. People call it the "dead letter" office, but I like to think that none of my letters are really dead, they're just a little late getting home.

You may be surprised to learn that there was an article here in the *Chronicle* about the fire in Dumas County. In fact, that's how I finally found you. I'm sending you a copy of the clipping because the reporter mentioned the loss of your house and what a hero Joe Jr. was. I'm sure you are very proud of him.

I'd like to come to East Peach sometime. I'm thinking of retiring somewhere in that part of Texas.

Sincerely,
Phillip Pargeter, Postal Clerk

MEMORANDUM

TO: Hon. John Wingham
FROM: Doris Bird
RE: Mrs. Adeline Macomber-Smith
DATE: August 22, 19__

Mrs. Adeline Macomber-Smith is a major peach blossom in East Peach—still President of the Ladies Auxiliary of the East Peach Cattlemen's Association. Husband Joe was president of the association for years. Niece Adele chairs the speaker's committee of the League of Women Voters for Dumas County.

Joe Jr. received the Silver Star and Army Air Medal, one oak leaf cluster, posthumously.

Your itinerary for September includes Harrisonville, county seat for Dumas County, about 30 miles from East Peach.

Checked with Margolis, acting postmaster for Houston. Pargeter is no one. He has an undistinguished (either way) record at the Postal Service. He has been there 43 years, ever since he got out of the Army after WW II. He is not politically active. Margolis wishes he would go ahead and retire, because he won't learn the automated sorting machine.

Draft letters attached for your signature.

Hon. John (Jack) Wingham
U.S. Congress
Washington, D.C.

August 22, 19__
Adeline (Mrs. Joseph P.) Macomber-Smith
c/o Mrs. Peter (Adele) Singleton
34 Garden Valley Drive
East Peach, TX

Dear Mrs. Macomber-Smith:

Thank you for your letter of August 15. Very few Americans take the time and energy to express their appreciation for the things our government does right. It is letters like yours that remind me of why

I have this job up here in Washington. You can be sure that I will see that the right people learn what a good job workers like Phillip Pargeter can do when the bureaucrats finally get out of their way.

It is my firm opinion, based on the economic studies that were furnished to those of us on the House Interior Committee, that American industry would be at least seven times more efficient, to say nothing of a more effective competitor in the world market place, if a Democratic Congress hadn't hog-tied them with a mile of red tape. The average businessman in American spends 38.3% of his time dealing with federal regulations, like OSHA, and ERISA, and the EPA. The Japanese and Koreans don't have to contend with this sort of burden.

On a more personal note, permit me to express my condolences on the loss of your son. Every time I am reminded of the brave boys who died over there, I feel again my keen regret that I was not called upon to join them in the service of our country.

I will be visiting East Peach in October. May I have the pleasure of calling on you personally at that time? My chief administrative assistant, Miss Doris Bird, will be contacting you directly in that regard.

Sincerely,
Congressman John ("Jack") Wingham
Hon. John (Jack) Wingham
U.S. Congress
Washington, D.C.

August 22, 19_
Mr. Phillip Pargeter
P.O. Box 179
Department of Mislaid Mail
United States Post Office, Main Branch
Houston, TX

Dear Mr. Pargeter:

It gave me great satisfaction to receive a copy of the touching letter from Mrs. Macomber-Smith to yourself regarding your forwarding to her a letter from her late son.

Permit me to say that the extra effort which you obviously put into this humanitarian effort does you and your co-workers great credit.

Sincerely,
Congressman John ("Jack") Wingham

MEMORANDUM

August 23, 19_
TO: Doris
FROM: Congressman Jack

Good letters. Is that 38% stuff for real? If so, be sure it's in my speech on the economy for September.

Let Margolis know on the QT that this kind of thing might help me get him confirmed as postmaster. See if there's anything more we can make out of this fellow Pargeter.

Adeline (Mrs. Joseph P.) Macomber-Smith
c/o Mrs. Peter (Adele) Singleton
34 Garden Valley Drive
East Peach, TX
August 22, 19_

Mr. Phillip Pargeter
P.O. Box 179
Department of Mislaid Mail
United States Post Office, Main Branch
Houston, TX 77002

Dear Mr. Pargeter,

Thank you for your kind letter and the clipping, which I put in my new scrapbook.

I agree with you completely that all of these computers and things can make us forget the important things in life. Thank goodness they can't computerize my garden! That's where I go to think. If I'm happy, I sit down and admire the flowers, but if I'm mad, I pull weeds like crazy.

I think that you would find East Peach a nice place to live, but of course, I would think that since I've lived here my whole life. One of the good things about life in a small town is nobody makes you retire from life. If you would like to come for a visit, Adele and I would be happy to put you up for a couple of days and show you the area.

Warmest regards,
Adeline B. (Mrs. Joseph P.) Macomber-Smith

MEMORANDUM
TO: ALL POSTAL EMPLOYEES
FROM: Howard Margolis, Acting Postmaster
Downtown Station
DATE: August 27, 19_
SUBJECT: GOOD WORK!

I recently received a very pleasant call from Congressman Wingham's Administrative Assistant, relating to a satisfied Postal Service Patron. Our own Phillip Pargeter apparently forwarded a 30 year old letter successfully. "Neither rain nor sleet nor snow nor rush of time etc."

We can all improve both our public image and our own job satisfaction if we strive for such accomplishments.

GOOD WORK, PHIL!

MEMORANDUM
Confidential and Written Pursuant to Public Law No. 1344, 25 United States Code Annotated Section 41.008

TO: Mr. Howard Margolis, *Acting* Postmaster
FROM: Jonas Tripwhistle, Postal Clerk, Grade 7
Downtown Station, Houston, TX
DATE: August 28, 19_
SUBJECT: possible irregularities in the handling of delayed correspondence
COPY: file

Certain facts have come to my attention regarding the processing of delayed correspondence in the Main Station. In light of your recent memorandum relating to Mr. Pargeter's performance, which was, as you no doubt intended, posted prominently on the employee bulletin board in the lunchroom, I felt that it was my duty to report these irregularities promptly as they may indicate a potential for instances of more serious misconduct and possible criminal and/or civil liability. Unlike some people I could name, I take our fiduciary trust to the American public seriously.

As you know, pursuant to Mail Regulations Bulletin No. 9011Z-A988, "Delayed, Lost, and Misaddressed Mail Service Items" (Not including special delivery, express mail, and other special service items), undeliverable mail is to be handled as follows:

1. The item in question is sent *unopened* to the Atlanta Main Branch,

2. Qualified and *authorized* personnel in *Atlanta* open the item in question, ascertain the addressee or sender, if possible, and either

a. forward the item in an approved Postal Service Office envelope to the addressee, or,

b. return the item to the sender if possible.

Phillip Pargeter, the supervising clerk of 8 P.M. to 4 A.M. shift (who was promoted to this position instead of me even though we had almost identical scores on the supervisor's examination), recently received a personal letter from a postal service patron. He has received several such letters in the past, and recently, the occurrence of such correspondence attracted the attention of the undersigned.

While Mr. Pargeter was at lunch on Wednesday, I had occasion to be in his office and since one of the file drawers happened to be open, in violation of mail handling procedures, I went over to close it. I observed, however, in my brief perusal of the files, that Mr. Pargeter has apparently been following a filing system of his own devising, which does not correspond with that set out in the Postal Service Regulation Handbook, chapter 13, paragraph 9, subparagraph a (ix). To whit, Mr. Pargeter has deviated from the standardized system of filing lost and delayed mail and/or postal materials by date, originating zip code, if known, type of material etc. Instead, I observed that the older mail (that more than twenty years old) had been cross-indexed by headings such as "Dear John," "Dear Jane," and "Mom." Such idiosyncratic behavior has the potential to cause serious disruption to the efficient and prompt handling of postal materials.

Phillip Pargeter
Department of Mislaid Mail
United States Postal Service, Downtown Section
Houston, TX 77002
September 2, 19_

Adeline (Mrs. Joseph P.) Macomber-Smith
c/o Mrs. Peter (Adele) Singleton
34 Garden Valley Drive
East Peach, TX

Dear Mrs. Macomber-Smith:

Thank you for another lovely letter and thank you for sending your first letter to the brass. I received a very nice memo from Mr. Margolis, who is the acting postmaster here, and a letter from Congressman Wingham(!). It is the first time I have received such recognition, and since they will probably make me retire in a couple of years, I enjoyed it very much. People who just do their job as best they can don't get a lot of recognition, I've found, especially now when it seems that only people with some kind of complaint get any attention at all.

It was funny you would mention your garden. I've always wanted to have a regular garden again, like my mother had, with beans and tomatoes and things, but there never seems to be enough time. I do find time for my roses, though. Like you, when I'm annoyed, I go out and find some chore to do. Usually, I prune the roses or clip dead blossoms when I'm steamed, but with roses that just means getting stuck by a thorn which makes me even madder.

I'd love to visit East Peach, although I hesitate to intrude on you and your niece.

Also, please don't think I'm being forward but it seems more like we "correspond" on a lot of things, so if you'd like to write to me again, I'd be very pleased. With that in mind, let me give you my home address which is 5412 Garden Valley Drive, Bellaire, Texas.

Sincerely,
Phillip Pargeter
Postal Clerk

MEMORANDUM

TO: Phillip Pargeter
FROM: Howard Margolis, Acting Postmaster
DATE: September 3, 19_
SUBJECT: METHODS AND PROCEDURES RE: DELAYED
POSTAL MATERIALS

Phil, I would appreciate it if you could drop by my office in the next day or so. It's been suggested that you have developed some new ways of handling old delayed mail.

Also, it has come to my attention that you have received several letters from past postal patrons. Such matters are to be referred to Postal Patrons Relations Department; we usually think of that department as being for complaints only, but it's important to remember that they deal with our satisfied customers as well.

5412 Garden Valley Drive
Bellaire, Texas
September 7, 19_

Mr. Howard Margolis, Acting Postmaster
Houston Station
Houston, TX 77002

Dear Mr. Margolis:

I enjoyed our visit yesterday and regret that I have no magical methods that could be implemented generally to speed the resolution of lost and delayed mail. As I explained to you, of course I forward all of our present day undeliverable mail on to Atlanta, per regulations. I found the letters that I work with in a storage closet behind the late shift supervisor's office when I became supervisor for that shift. Naturally, I assumed that because they were so old, that they were intended to stay here in Houston.

The filing system that you mentioned was just an idea that I had that maybe when all the zip codes and address tracings and so on had failed, maybe the human element might help me link up a person and a letter. I am sorry if it violated any regulations.

The only thing that I can suggest to explain my modest successes with these old materials is that I was a route carrier here in Houston and in some small towns for many years. Maybe I developed a feel for the people who live here. Maybe I am just a broken down old postal clerk who has had some good luck matching up letters and people.

Reluctantly, I attach copies of the letters I have received from people. As you can see, some of them weren't successes at all, but most of them were pretty nice about it.

Yours truly,
Phillip Pargeter

Pauline Campbell
3845 Riverside Drive
Riverside, California

Mr. Phillip Pargeter
P.O. Box 179

Department of Mislaid Mail
United States Post Office, Main Branch
Houston, TX 77002

Dear Mr. Pargeter:

I am returning to you the letter of November 14, 1956 which you recently forwarded to me. Regrettably, I do not think that it was from my mother because she was left-handed and her writing sloped backward. It would certainly be easy to make a mistake since most of the address was gone. Besides, I haven't lived in Texas for many years, since I moved to Southern California.

However, I wanted you to know that getting the letter meant a lot to me in a funny kind of way. My mother recently passed away at a nursing home in Stafford, TX. The last few years Mother was ill and you know how cranky old people get. We didn't visit very much and I regretted that my children only remembered their grandmother as a crotchety old lady. That lovely kind letter about the garden and the squirrels at the bird feeder reminded me of the good years my mother had before her stroke and brought back lots of memories for me to pass on to my children. So, thanks for trying.

Sincerely,
Pauline Campbell

Sam Peterson
4515 Azalea Lane
San Antonio, TX

Mr. Phillip Pargeter, Clerk
P.O. Box 179
Delayed Mail Office
Downtown Station
Houston, TX

Dear Mr. Pargeter:

I'm writing to thank you for forwarding the letter to me, dated February 14, 1953. It turned out to be from a girl named Jane Howard that I used to date. Even without the return address and just with the "SWAK" for a signature, I guessed who it was. I don't know if you saw the story in the Houston paper or not, but we had a big reunion of all the guys in my unit that were in Korea together. Well, it was kind of stupid but the reporter put in that story that I had been dating my buddy Fred Howard's sister and that she had wrote me a Dear John when I was still in the service.

Well, as soon as I got the letter you sent me, which I won't repeat to you as it was kind of personal, I called up my buddy and he gave me his sister's address. She's a widow now and I'm divorced so we're going to give it another chance.

Yours truly,
Samuel Peterson, US Army (ret'd).

MEMORANDUM

TO: Mr. Jonas Tripwhistle
FROM: Howard Margolis, Acting Postmaster
DATE: September 7, 19_
SUBJECT: Lost Letter Department

We all appreciate your vigilance in keeping us all toeing the line of the Postal Code. I'm sure you will be pleased to know that I have checked into the matter to which you refer and have found no basis to believe that any misconduct has occurred.

MEMORANDUM

Confidential and Written Pursuant to Public Law No. 1344, 25 United States Code Annotated Section 41.008
TO: Mr. Howard Margolis, Acting Postmaster
FROM: Jonas Tripwhistle, Postal Clerk, Grade 7, Downtown Station, Houston, TX
DATE: September 9, 19_
SUBJECT: RE: continuing investigation of possible irregularities in the handling of delayed correspondence
COPY: file

Over the last few weeks, on my own time after my tour was over, I have taken the opportunity of investigating the situation further. Although superficially Mr. Pargeter's office appeared to be in good order and the file cabinets are being kept more securely locked, I noticed that certain small scraps of letter paper were laying about, all of which appeared to have been torn from larger sheets of writing paper. They had signatures on them. Copies of these scraps are attached to this memo. As you can see, these items contain fragments of signatures, addresses, etc.

I regret to conclude that the above referenced evidence strongly suggests that the aforementioned postal employee has been tampering with the mails, which is, among other things, a violation of the Code of Postal Regulation, Section 43, Subsection 14, paragraph 6, subparagraph b (ii).

Further, I noticed that once again postal materials were not being kept under proper security in that the desk drawer was open. In that drawer, I happened to observe an unlabeled Postal Service Issue file. I took it with me to examine and forward copies of the contents herewith. As you will see, it did not contain postal materials at all but a series of newspaper clippings, having to do with deaths and fires and other morbid events. In my judgment, this raises some issue as to the fitness of Mr. Pargeter for his position.

I have retained the originals of the evidence for my files, since I have learned the hard way that vigilance is not rewarded in the civil service, but I will make them available to you upon reasonable notice.

MEMORANDUM

TO: Mr. Jonas Tripwhistle
FROM: Howard Margolis, Acting Postmaster
DATE: September 11, 19—
SUBJECT: Delayed Mail Office

While we all appreciate your diligence, Mr. Tripwhistle, I hardly see what significance a few scraps of old note paper and some news clippings have. I admit that it is perhaps somewhat strange for Mr. Pargeter to keep a file of obituaries and sentimental human interest stories but I do not see what bearing this hobby of his has on his work.

It is my duty to warn you as well that your zeal could get you into serious trouble if such a file should turn out to be the private property of Mr. Pargeter. I am returning it to him personally.

Jonas Tripwhistle
P.O. Box 707
Your Secret Mailit Service
1755 Elm Street
Bellaire, TX

September 13, 19—
Adeline (Mrs. Joseph P.) Macomber-Smith

c/o Mrs. Peter (Adele) Singleton
34 Garden Valley Drive
East Peach, TX

Dear Mrs. Macomber-Smith:

I regret to inform you that certain facts have arisen in regard to the handling of Delayed and Misaddressed Mail Items, to whit, items such as the letter, purportedly from your son, which you received a few weeks ago.

I would greatly appreciate your sending me a copy of said Mail Service Item.

Sincerely,
Jonas Tripwhistle
Postal Clerk, Grade 7

Jonas Tripwhistle
P.O. Box 707
Your Secret Mailit Service
1755 Elm Street
Bellaire, TX

September 13, 19—
Hon. John (Jack) Wingham
U.S. Congress
Washington, D.C.

Dear Mr. Wingham:

I am bringing this matter to your attention only after having tried and failed to get appropriate attention paid to it here in the Houston Downtown Station. I am a postal clerk, grade 7, in the downtown station.

While we in the Postal Service are accustomed to criticism from all quarters, much of it unfair and unfounded, we still must be vigilant to prevent the occurrence of events in our own ranks from which we may justly be condemned, particularly when your own name is connected with such events. I refer to the Matter of Phillip Pargeter. Enclosed are my two investigative memoranda which are, I trust, self-explanatory. I also enclose copies of the clippings and paper scraps. Perhaps you may wish to have a forensic laboratory, such as that of the Federal Bureau of Investigation, to which I believe that you, as a Member of Congress, have authorized access, examine them.

I need not add that this letter is written under the protection and pursuant to the terms of 25 UNITED STATES CODE ANNOTATED SECTION 41.008. Although I work at the downtown station, sad experience has taught me to observe precautions; if you reply to this letter, please write to me at my private post office box on the address above.

Your sincere admirer,
Jonas Tripwhistle
Postal Clerk, Grade 7

MEMORANDUM

TO: Hon. John Wingham
FROM: Doris Bird
RE: Macomber-Smith matter
DATE: September 15, 19_

I talked to Adele Singleton again re: your East Peach speech. The League of Women Voters is hosting a luncheon for you and Miss Adeline, who is a very sweet lady. She is no one to trifle with—one of those stiff necked ranch women who won the West. I mentioned that you were aware that the Cattlemen's Association was concerned about drought relief and she said "You know they keep trying to raise hell, as if they hadn't figured out that it would likely make it even hotter."

You may wish to look at the enclosed letter, however, from some guy in the Houston postal office. For your information, 25 UNITED STATES CODE ANNOTATED SECTION 41.008 is the so-called "Whistle Blower" Act.

MEMORANDUM

September 16, 19_
TO: Doris
FROM: Congressman Jack

What the hell is this guy Tripwhistle talking about?

Thanks for the crack about the Cattlemen's Association. Remind me to use it when I meet with the extension service down there.

What ever happens, don't let this lunatic trip us up or my speech to the League of Women Voters is likely to be a dead letter. Check into it. What kind of a nut sends people other people's clippings of obituaries?

Mrs. Peter (Adele) Singleton
34 Garden Valley Drive
East Peach, TX
September 15, 19__

Miss Doris Bird, Chief Assistant
Hon. John (Jack) Wingham
U.S. Congress
Washington, D.C.

Dear Miss Bird:

Congressman Wingham probably doesn't remember me but we met when he spoke to the League of Women Voters in Harrisonville.

Anyway, I am writing about two things. First about the Congressman possibly giving a speech in East Peach, I've talked to a couple of people and on behalf of my aunt, myself, and the local Chapter of the League of Women Voters, I can now confirm that we would be delighted if he could find the time to come out here. The Cattlemen's Association will be having its annual barbecue about the time you mention, so perhaps the two events could be coordinated.

Second, however, enclosed is a rather odd letter which causes me some concern. You may have noticed that recently my aunt, Mrs. Macomber-Smith, wrote to you about a letter being forwarded to her from my cousin Joe, who was killed in Viet Nam. Mr. Tripwhistle seems to be hinting that there was something funny about the letter. It would upset my aunt terribly if that letter turned out to be fake or anything. I would be very grateful if you could check into this for us.

Yours truly,
Adele Singleton

cc. Congressman John Wingham and Howard S. Margolis, Postmaster, Houston, TX

MEMORANDUM

TO: Hon. John Wingham
FROM: Doris Bird
RE: Macomber-Smith matter
DATE: September 17, 19__

Things are getting sticky.

Tripwhistle wrote to Adeline as well and Adele wrote me in a panic. See enclosed.

Have put one of the interns to work straightening things out.

MEMORANDUM
TO: Hon. John Wingham
FROM: Doris Bird
RE: Macomber-Smith matter
DATE: September 19, 19_

I called down to the main post office in Houston and got told that there is no Department of Delayed Mail and that all official mail is routed direct to a department, not to a post office box, contrary to Pargeter's return address on his letter to Mrs. Macomber-Smith.

As for dead letters, if something can't be delivered, it's supposed to be routed directly to an office in Atlanta for processing. Pargeter is the supervisor on the 8 P.M. to 4 A.M. shift and it is his job to send things like that to Atlanta.

I talked to Margolis. He says Tripwhistle is a crank, but an energetic crank always spouting off about his rights under the civil service laws.

Margolis has spoken to Pargeter. Apparently Pargeter is just one of those old time clerk types who plug away at their job until they get it done. I asked Margolis about this business of there not being an "Office of Delayed Mail." He said he'd have to check.

Margolis sent me the file that Tripwhistle had given him and some more customer letters that Pargeter had. Pargeter's really made some amazing match-ups. He found a letter taking back a "Dear John" letter and forwarded it to some guy who was overseas in Korea. Even when he screws up, people don't seem to get mad. Samples attached.

Speech for East Peach all set. Local UPI stringer may cover.

MEMORANDUM
TO: Hon. John Wingham
FROM: Doris Bird
RE: Macomber-Smith matter
DATE: September 21, 19_

There's something funny about this guy Pargeter. I told one of the interns to look through all that stuff and see if there was anything more we could use for your speech to the Postal Worker's Union. She sorted the stuff into piles and started matching up the letters and the clippings and the scraps of signatures. It's the damndest thing. First, it looks like none of the letters Pargeter forwarded had a complete name or address on it. Second, there's a clipping of some kind for each of the letters. That is, there was a story in the paper about the people that Pargeter sent the letters on to, an obituary or some human interest piece. But, third, the signature scraps that Tripwhistle sent us don't match up with any of the people who got the long lost letters. Pargeter didn't keep copies of the original letters but you can draw your own conclusions.

I talked to Margolis again. He said Tripwhistle is right that there is no Department of Delayed Mail. He went down to Pargeter's office and found the files just like Tripwhistle says. I don't think Margolis even knew Pargeter had an office. He made it sound like he had to go to the North Pole. Anyway, Margolis told me that Pargeter says all the mail he was working with is stuff that was left over from when the Dead Letter function was moved to Atlanta. Pargeter did mention that sometimes he could identify the recipient of a letter from something in the news or whatever.

Margolis doesn't have a clue what the old system for lost mail was; remember he was the Senator's fund raiser for Harris County and didn't have anything to do with the Post Office until last year. So, for all we know, Pargeter may be telling the truth.

MEMORANDUM

September 23, 19—
TO: Doris
FROM: Congressman Jack
   Do something! ASAP!
   If you think that I'm going to go to East Peach Blossom, or wherever, Texas and give a speech about the kinder, gentler Republican government with the concerns of everyday people at heart and then tell some little old lady that her precious letter was from God knows who because some nut named Pargeter was loose in the postal system, clipping the names off letters and shipping them to whoever he thought might like to get them, you have another think coming. I'm not the only one who can "draw my own conclusions"—that guy from the UPI would be all over us. He's probably been waiting his whole life for a story like this to get him out of the boonies.

MEMORANDUM

TO: Hon. John Wingham
FROM: Doris Bird
RE: Macomber-Smith matter
DATE: September 25, 19—

Margolis says that there's an opening for a regulations compliance officer in Guam.

You do something.

MEMORANDUM

September 26, 19—
TO: Doris
FROM: Congressman Jack

1. God help the postal clerks of Guam. That creep will probably end up as King Tripwhistle the First, if the regulations don't forbid it.

2. I discovered (on my own!) that the postmastership of East Peach was open. I may retire there myself some day. Meanwhile, don't ever schedule me there again, not for a speech or the Democratic Party Chairman's funeral or a rally for me for president or a $10,000 a plate fund-raiser.

MEMORANDUM

TO: Jonas Tripwhistle
FROM: Howard Margolis, Postmaster
DATE: October 8, 19—
SUBJECT: Promotion

Thank you for your recent kind note congratulating me on my confirmation as Postmaster.

I am pleased to tell you that your diligence and devotion to duty have not gone unnoticed in the highest places. Effective October 1, 19—, you have been tendered the position of Regulations Compliance Officer, Grade 9, Guam Station.

Apparently, they have a serious problem there. Please prepare to leave at once.

CONGRATULATIONS.

CC. EMPLOYEES LUNCHROOM BULLETIN BOARD

Adeline (Mrs. Joseph P.) Macomber-Smith
c/o Mrs. Peter (Adele) Singleton
34 Garden Valley Drive
East Peach, TX
October 19, 19—

Mr. Phillip Pargeter
Department of Mislaid Mail
United States Post Office, Main Branch
Houston, TX 77002

Dear Mr. Pargeter,

This is my last "official" letter to you, so I'm writing to you at the Post Office. Congressman Wingham was here yesterday and he gave the nicest speech. A lot of it was about you and how America needs more dedicated workers like yourself, people in government who put caring for people first and still get the work done. Who would have thought that the Republicans would ever get around to it. Well, needless to say, I couldn't agree more. Especially about you!

But, the best part of the speech was the news that you will be coming to East Peach as the postmaster of our little post office here. I'm sure it won't be as exciting as working in the big city because we just have a corner of Hoeffer's Grocery as the post office, but we are all looking forward to your arrival here.

Yours truly,
Adeline B. (Mrs. Joseph P.) Macomber-Smith

P.S. Phil—Mrs. Hoeffer's just told me that you're for sure coming to East Peach to look over the post office on November 15. Would you think me terribly pushy if I invited you to join my niece and her husband and me for dinner?

Your friend,
Adeline

Torgny Lindgren's "Water" appeared in *Merab's Beauty and Other Stories,* a collection of twelve tales and a novella that was published in the United States in 1990. This collection was the second of the Swedish writer's works to arrive in this country, and like the first—a novel, *Bathsheba* (1989)—it draws upon the scriptures for both its themes and its melodic prose. Set in rural Sweden at various times past, these stories are inhabited by characters grappling with a harsh terrain, with their neighbors, and with the inscrutability of God's judgments. Moving deftly from religious debate to broad humor, many of these stories revolve around the power of words and of the Word. "Water," one of two letter stories in the collection, is itself a playfully irregular act of communication that uses the letter format to create both narrative and conceptual surprise as it leads us to the story's unanticipated and moving conclusion.

WATER

To the County Council at Umeå.

There is water that is cold and dense as stone, you cannot drink it, and there is water which is so thin and weak that it does not help if you drink it, and there is water that shudders when you drink it so that you get the shivers; and there is water that is bitter and tastes of sweat; and some water is, as it were, dead, water spiders sink down through it as if it were air. Indeed water is like the sand on the shores of the sea, its numbers are countless.

So that the form which you, the County Council, have sent us to enable us to tell you what our water situation is, that is useless, there isn't room for water in two lines. If you have lived for seventy years as I have done, then you will know so much about water that the whole County Council could drown in that knowledge.

So I cannot say everything.

When we moved up here to Kläppmyrliden we bought the place from Isaac Grundström; they had six children and thought it was too cramped. Theresa and I had of course no children, we had been married more than five years. Isaac Grundström was going to move to Bjurträsk and begin work at the sawmill—that was when we were cheated over water.

We were here in March and viewed the house, and we asked: "What about water?"

"Yes," Isaac Grundström said, "we have always had water."

And they went with us out to the well—the path was covered with snow—it was behind the cowshed; and he sent the bucket down, it was pretty deep, twenty-five feet he said, and we could hear the bucket hitting water, and at that he jerked the chain so that the bucket filled and then he wound it up, and there was clear water, though perhaps a trifle yellow. And I took the scoop and tasted it.

"Yes," I said, "though it has a smoky smell. And tastes of air. It can't be denied that it reminds one of water from melted snow."

And then he took the scoop and drank.

"It tastes of rock," he said. "You can tell that it is water from a well."

"Yes," I said. "Or water that has pushed up through the ice."

"No," he said. "Water from a well."

Though why should we quarrel about water, there was after all water, so I said:

"Water never tastes the same to two people,"

"No one has ever complained about the water here in Kläppmyrliden," he said.

"This thing about water is a sort of habit," I said. "When you have drunk a certain water for a time, then your body is full of that water. And after that you can no longer tell its taste."

So we bought Kläppmyrliden.

But the first winter we lived here, about Candlemas it was, the well was dry.

And we asked people, the neighbors: "How can it be that the well is empty? When we were here last year to look at the place, then there was water. And Isaac Grundström said that it never ran dry."

"That well, that runs dry every winter," said the neighbors. "And some dry summers."

And into the bargain they said: "That was why Isaac Grundström moved. It was because of the water."

"Though last year there was water," I said.

"Never," they then said. "But Isaac Grundström knew that you would ask: 'What about water?' So they filled up the well ready for when you came; they melted snow in the washtub, they worked for three days with the water, they carried it in buckets out to the well, Isaac and Agela and all the six children."

"So they filled the well with melted snow?" I said.

"Yes."

"That's how we were cheated."

Though in fact I understood him, Isaac Grundström, he would not have been able to sell Kläppmyrliden if he had said: "The only trouble is that the well runs dry every February"; and of course he had to get the place sold.

But things went well for us; we were only two, me and Theresa.

I tried at first with the cold well at Kläpp, it was only a few kilometers up in the forest, and I thought, We can very well carry the water, and I hacked and bored down through the ice, but the ice ended in moraine earth, it was frozen solid to the bottom.

After that there was nothing for it but to carry snow and melt it in the washtub. It was a trifle yellow and had a sort of smoky smell and tasted of air.

And I said: "Come the summer I shall dig that well a few feet deeper."

And that's what I did. In May we got our water back, before midsummer we bailed the well dry and I nailed together a twenty-five-foot ladder so that I could get down and then I dug, I dug down two feet for sure and Theresa helped me by winding up what I dug loose, it was hard-packed earth consisting of sand, clay, and gravel, and water came, so much so that it was nearly impossible to dig. And I said: "Now we shall never need to be without water again."

And that year we managed right up to the first Sunday in Lent. But then it dried up. After that we had to melt snow until Holy Week when the water came up through the ice.

Otherwise it was good water, the water that was in the well, smooth and clear, though a trifle sweet.

And when summer came again I dug once more.

It wasn't particularly hard to dig, an iron bar and a spade was all I needed. And things were just the same now as in the previous summer, it ran so that I was standing in water the whole time, though Theresa bailed me out bit by bit.

But after that I came down to rock, real primitive rock; I'd only dug down a foot. And I thought, That's the end now. But I might as well dig it clean, I'll clear the rock so that the bottom of the well is like a sitting-room floor, and I dug with my hands so that not a fistful of sand or clay should remain, but as I did it the rock felt like ice to my hands. So there must be a hole somewhere, just like the cracks you find in sea ice. I had the bad luck to open that crack so that the water I had around my feet ran away, the well was dry in a moment, it even sounded as if the rock was sucking up the water, the noise it made was the same as you make when you pull a cork from a bottle, and not even as much as dew was left.

But Theresa said: "It's not your fault. When it's a matter of depth no one can know what it is just right to dig."

After that we were entirely without. And I had not time to dig anymore that summer.

Summer is as short as a shooting star.

That winter we took water from the cold spring at Kläpp, and when the frost got into the ground then we melted snow in the cauldron that was used for the big wash.

I made a yoke for Theresa so that she could carry two buckets. I formed it to fit her shoulders and neck so that it should not cause her unnecessary pain and produce sores, and Theresa said it was a blessing, that yoke.

If only we had had children they could have carried water.

But neither of us said anything about that. We were unable to have children; the yoke of barrenness is hard to bear. It was hardest for Theresa.

When summer came again I dug over by the woodshed. Theresa stood and pulled up the buckets of earth; I dug down eighteen feet, when I was down to the rock, but there was not a drop of water, the moraine earth was not even damp.

And I said to Theresa: "This damned hump. This dry heap of gravel, this is like the Desert of Sin."

"Though the Scriptures speak of the 'springs of great depth,'" said Theresa.

"Yes," I said. "But how to find them."

"Yes," she said. "'The springs of great depth, they are hidden,' it also says that in the Scriptures."

"It will be the death of me, this water," I said.

"It isn't the water," Theresa then said, "it is quite the other way around."

"But when summer comes I shall dig again," I said, "then I shall dig a bit below the old well, there must be water there."

"Yes," said Theresa. "For water is sure to be somewhere. It's only hidden like the good wine at the wedding in Cana."

And there was water, an absurd amount of water. I began to dig the first week in June and by the third day we could not bail any longer. Theresa was quite done in, I had got straight down to a vein of water, it was in sand and we said: "Now we shall have water for at least as long as we live, this well will never dry up. So at least there'll be water."

And it was only ten feet deep.

But water must be given time to clear, there is always sediment when it is newly dug, sludge and mud and earth. "The well must be given a couple of days, but then we shall never be without water," we said. "And we will thank Our Lord for this single thing that we have at last been given water."

Though of course we had a trial tasting.

And we said: "No, it still has too much of an earthy taste."

But after a week had gone by it was still not clear, it was yellowish brown and on the surface it shimmered like a rainbow, and we were obliged to say: "No, it doesn't taste of earth, it tastes of iron . . . though it will do for the animals," we said.

But not even the cows could bring themselves to drink it, they seemed to be alarmed and bellowed loudly and flung their heads about when we put it out for them, so there was nothing for it but to fill in the new well and I had not time to dig anymore that summer; and I remember that we had got a stillborn calf, and I put him in the bottom and then filled it in; what good has a man for all his toil, it was nothing but a sort of grave mound over the calf.

That winter we thought, At last! Theresa was certain in October; she was sick and couldn't bear any food but salt pork, and I said it was like a miracle—it was like when Moses struck the rock with his staff. We were anxious, and we rejoiced, it was even so that I helped her to carry water, though the neighbors said: "Oh indeed, since when has it been a man's job to carry water?"

But in December she had a miscarriage, she was carrying snow down to the washtub and it seemed as if something burst behind in her back.

She recovered quickly, though; she has always been strong, has Theresa, if I hadn't had Theresa I don't know. And it wasn't anyone's fault, how could anything be anyone's fault?

Then in the winter, in February, I heard someone mention a well digger in Strycksele who was called Johan Lidström, he usually went about with his rod and he never made a mistake, and when he had pointed out the place, he dug, and if there wasn't water he would never take any money.

So I sent a sort of message with Andreas Lundmark—he was going to Strycksele in any case when he went to Vindel—and I sent my greetings to that man Lidström and told him that we were not quite satisfied with the water up at Kläppmyrliden, and that we certainly should not say no to his help if he thought he had time.

On the Monday after Whitsun he came. He was tall and thin and had a bit of a hump—perhaps it was the digging—and he was deplorably cocksure and pretty nearly arrogant, he seemed to be a sort of water doctor.

I told him what had happened to us in the matter of water.

"Now we've been living here for seven years," I said. "Without water. And I really have dug. I've dug so that I've more or less got a hump on my back."

I wanted us to understand each other.

"You have only dug haphazardly," he said. "You've fumbled like a blind man in the dark."

"Not so," I said. "I've dug as wisely as any man. You can see for yourself all the places where I've tried to dig."

"Water is strange," he said. "It is inscrutable. It is a sort of science."

"True," I said. "And one can't live without it."

"Ordinary people should never have a go like this with water," he said. "Those who haven't got the right insight."

"When one is without water then one digs in desperation," I said.

"It's never worthwhile to dig in desperation," he said. "Water does not bother itself about people who cry and complain. You can't take water by surprise."

"But you may come right to a vein of water. Like a trick of fate."

"Yes," he said. "And that's almost the worst of it. Veins of water are as touchy as a child's eye. Veins of water are as fragile as a mirage. People simply destroy veins of water when they dig."

"But you, you never make a mistake," I said. "For you things never go wrong over water."

"Never," he said. "I've learned to take water seriously. Streams of water in the earth, they are like the veins of blood in the human body."

And he added: "The King and Parliament should write a law about water. To prevent people digging just anyhow. And they say the world goes forward! I am convinced," he said, "I am convinced that sooner or later they will be obliged to write such a law. Digging a well, that is like putting a child into the world. Life and water, they are one and the same thing."

And he really took pains, he spent a lot of time, for two days he walked about first spying out the land. He examined the grass, he lifted up the turf and smelled the earth, he went about with his rod—it was of fresh birch—and he crept about on all fours and felt his way with his fingers and he lay down on his stomach and kept quite still, he said he could sometimes hear the water bubbling in the ground, he jabbed with his iron pole and pushed pieces of wood down into the holes. He wanted us to see how remarkable it was, this business with water, that it was knowledge and art.

At last, on the morning of the third day, he said:

"This is the place, it is here I shall dig."

It was behind the woodshed, where the raspberries are, it is mostly only gravel there.

"Twenty feet," he said. "Twenty feet, but then you will have water for the whole of your life, and the children and descendants you have unto the third and fourth generation."

"I will do the roughest digging," I said. "Just the top bit. Before we get down to the water itself. I don't want to injure the vein," I said.

"No," he said, "I shall dig all of it. It is the beginning of a thing that decides the end."

And indeed he was a capable well digger. He did not move fast but all the same he was clever. I sat myself down in the barn doorway and mended the rakes, and in between whiles I took a turn and stood beside him, it was as if he sank into the ground, a foot an hour.

And when he got down so far that only his head was visible I took the pail and helped him to heave up the earth, little by little; he was very careful about the corners and he dug square, not round.

And I said to him: "I have always dug round wells. Not square."

"Yes," he said. "I know. People dig round wells. They believe that you must dig them round."

We had to get up a couple of stones with the stump grubber. And I said to him that it was a lucky thing they were not firmly stuck in the soil.

"I knew that," he said. "I never dig where there are stones stuck fast in the soil."

When Saturday evening came, he had dug seventeen feet. He had a thing like a plummet to measure the depth.

"By Monday," he said, "by Monday then we shall come to water. Then you will see a stream."

He was there over the whole of Sunday, he kept close to the well, but he did not dig, he walked about half kicking the earth, and now and then he sat on the mound of earth, he sat and thought.

But Theresa, she said to me on Sunday evening: "Do you think he'll find water?"

"Yes," I said. "He seems so sure."

"I don't believe he'll ever find a vein," said Theresa. "He is too insolent. He's nothing but arrogance."

"If you've hunted up as much water as he has done, you have the right to be arrogant," I said.

"I believe that the man who can find water, he must be humble," said Theresa. "He must have something like love."

And I remembered how I had dug for all those years and found not a drop.

"You mustn't be superstitious," I said. "Either there is water or there isn't. And I believe in him."

At dinnertime on Monday, he had dug twenty feet and I called and asked: "Do you see any water, Lidström?"

"Not quite yet," he answered. "It may be I am short by a few inches."

But when we had eaten and came out again and he climbed down, why it was just as dry at the bottom as when we went in.

And he called to me. "I'll take out a few spits more."

And he continued to dig.

If by chance the County Council really want to know what has happened to us in the matter of water.

When he had dug twenty-five feet—that was on Tuesday, I wrote it down in the calendar—then I called down to him for the first time: "I don't believe there's water in this place."

But he called back: "I'm quite sure there's water. And I won't give up."

So there was nothing for it but to stand there and take the buckets he filled down in the well; and I felt it with my hand and there was only dry gravel in them. And Theresa came out and stood beside me and I said to her: "It's dry gravel, nothing else."

And then she said: "It's almost worse for this man Lidström. You and I can manage, we are not spoiled in the matter of water. But I don't think he can endure this disgrace."

"So you believe him," I said. "You believe that he has never in his life been mistaken in the matter of water?"

"Yes," she said. "I believe him. Poor man."

"He need not have been so dead sure and so big for his boots," I said. "Even if he usually has luck about water."

"We must think of some way to comfort him," said Theresa. "Kidney-blood pudding. I'll go and cook some kidney-blood pudding."

"Yes," said I. "For he'll never get any money for this dry well."

And I was having to nail new rungs to the ladder all the time.

He didn't eat kidney-blood pudding. He couldn't endure the smell, he said.

When he had got down thirty-five feet, I asked him: "Won't you soon be down to the rock?"

But he answered: "There are ten feet left before I get down to the rock. And on top of the rock there will be water."

But all the same it seemed as if he was a trifle melancholy, when we ate and we drank our coffee he said never a word, and he went to bed immediately after our evening porridge; he slept up in the attic.

On Thursday morning, though, just as he was about to climb down into the well again, he said: "This is serious. There are those who dig wells, as it were, at random. But for me it is a serious business."

And you could see that this was the truth.

But when I could see by the lead line that it was now forty-two feet, I called down to him: "Lidström, this is absolutely futile. Now you must stop."

But he answered, and it was difficult to hear him, forty-two feet is deep down in a well: "Only a few inches more. Or a foot. Then there will be water."

But I called: "You deceive yourself. You deceive yourself. This patch is as dry as the Desert of Sin."

But he called back to me: "Don't be so deadly obstinate, just go on pulling up the buckets."

And I said: "I don't give a damn for this well anymore. Devil take this well."

But then he called: "Who is it who really knows about water? Is it you or I?"

And when he jerked the chain to show that the bucket was full, I pulled it up. One foot more, I thought. But after that it's finished, after that he must climb up the ladder himself with his buckets of gravel.

And on Saturday morning—we were just going to have our midmorning coffee—it was forty-five feet.

"Lidström," I shouted. "Lidström. Not an inch more. Not even a grain of gravel."

But he answered: "Don't you interfere in this. I shall dig as deep as I please."

And I shouted: "You have promised to dig two more wells in Norsjö this summer."

"Yes," he answered. "But I only dig one at a time."

"But I have other things to do than to stand here heaving up buckets," I said. "I haven't got the summer left."

"When there is water," he shouted, "you'll be grateful that I didn't give up just because it was a few inches deeper than one thought."

And I could hear even up there how he continued to dig and delve as we were talking.

"But Lidström," I shouted, "don't you understand what I'm saying to you? Now there must be an end to this. Now you must come up. This is the end of the dig."

And then he called from the bottom of the hole where he was, which was perhaps the deepest well in the Norsjö district:

"You can't order me about. I shall dig as much as I please. I have my freedom. I am a free human being. And a free human being digs as long as he pleases."

And it seemed as if I had no patience left. I felt I was forced to get him out, even if I had to climb down and carry him up the ladder myself.

"But the land is mine," I screamed. "The land you're digging down into. I shall decide myself if some stranger comes here and digs deep dry holes. No outsider shall try to take command over this stony ground."

And I stamped on the ground, I was so provoked, I stamped hard with my right foot on the ground.

And then there was a rumbling down in the well, it sounded like rain on a barn roof, it was the south wall of the well that gave way, it wasn't strutted, and I hastily jumped backward a few paces; the edge above the well was moving too, there was no moisture to hold the gravel and sandy soil together so it rushed and ran like the sand in an hourglass; it was like it is when powder snow fills in a footprint in winter; the whole well disappeared as if it had been dug down in a large lake that had again fallen back into place, all that was left of the well was a sort of hollow in the ground, that forty-five-foot well.

And I was powerless, wasn't I?

And I called to Theresa and she came out and we stood there a while, she had tears in her eyes and she said: "Think if he had to suffer."

"It went so horribly quickly," I said. "I even believe that he is still standing upright. He is standing upright at a depth of forty-five feet."

"He wanted to do his best," she said. "That was all he wanted. To do his best."

"I told him to come up," I said. "If he had done as I told him, this would never have happened."

"Yes," she said. "He was pigheaded. But perhaps they are like that. Well diggers."

And I was obliged to betake myself to Norsjö. I wasn't quite sure how to proceed.

"He is standing upright at a depth of forty-five feet," I said to the parson. "It would take me the whole summer to dig him out again."

And the parson, he turned the matter over in his mind for a bit, then he said: "At sea one commits a dead man to his eternal rest right on the spot. Those who lose their life at sea, they are not fished up from the depths to be sunk into consecrated ground. This well digger Lidström, the man who is standing upright at a depth of forty-five feet, he is like a sailor who has drowned in his ocean."

So I returned home and shoveled back the earth into that hollow. I put back everything that Lidström had dug out, hard packed earth and dry gravel, so that it looked smooth and tidy again, and I planted some raspberry bushes there, and Theresa made a wreath out of rowan twigs, and when two weeks had passed the parson came and carried out the burial service, yes, it was called burial service, he said when I asked if it was really necessary to say: "From earth thou comest, to earth shall thou return." And he had been told by the parson in Vindel that this Lidström had no family nor any kinsfolk in Strycksele, he was a recluse of sorts, and the parson read the verse about water from Matthew: "And whosoever shall give to drink unto one of these little ones a cup of cold water, he shall in no wise lose his reward."

And Theresa said to the parson, "He assured me that he had dug over a hundred."

Nevertheless we were still without water.

And I said to Theresa many times: "If there was only one person who did not mind about water, then we would sell Kläppmyrliden to that person. But we are stuck with Kläppmyrliden."

But Theresa, she said that we only need take one day at a time, we only need carry as much water from Kläppkallkällan or melt as much snow in the washtub as we need for the day. And we are only two, aren't we?

"We are only we two."

But I said: "Think of our old age, Theresa. Who will then carry water for us? And melt snow?"

And she had to admit that I was right.

So I went on digging in various places, though I knew it was in vain. I dug down into the dry gravel and the moraine earth; it was as if I felt obliged to dig a dry hole every summer. Dry gravel is like a colander for water, it's like a sieve and a tub without a bottom.

Our neighbors all had water. In Lakaberg and Inreliden and Böle and Avabäck and Åmträsk, yes even where they had water, people keep a sharp

eye on those who haven't got water. And we were a childless couple who
didn't have water, so that . . .

We were like Kläppmyrliden.

And Kläppmyrliden, it was like the Desert of Sin. Life, too, has an
incurable drought.

After fifteen years had passed since the summer Lidström was with
us—yes, that's what we said, though he was actually with us still—the
fifteen summers, so to say, it was an unbearably dry summer and I was
standing down by the small spruces of the barn sharpening the hay poles.
Then Theresa came out of the house carrying the coffee basket, she had
a bonnet on her head and was wearing a big apron, her baking apron.

And we were no longer young, I was fifty-eight and she was fifty-seven.

I wouldn't tell everyone this. But I will tell the County Council the
truth. Since the County Council have asked about water.

And we didn't have intercourse any longer, that intercourse that man
and wife usually have, we hadn't strength left for everything, and dragging
ourselves along up at Kläppmyrliden had taken it out of us. And besides
it was in a way futile.

We sat down on the grass, she had baked a sponge cake and she had
brought out a jug of fresh water and I drank the water and looked at
her and saw how wrinkled she was and how gray-haired, and that her
cheekbones were much sharper than they had been and that her shoulders
were a bit crooked and that she had a lump on the back of her neck, it
was the yoke. And I thought, Perhaps I should take time off and make a
new one for her, one that lies like a shawl around her neck.

And it was as if she heard my thoughts for she said: "I've been thinking
about the water. Whether we have been too zealous about water. So that
the water has tied itself into a knot. If we hadn't searched for water so
desperately, we might perhaps have found enough and to spare."

She has always been superstitious about water, has Theresa.

But I did not say that. I did not say that to her, I just moved a bit closer
and put my right arm around her, for this thing about water has always
been a sort of sorrow for us; and she leaned her head against me, and we
lay down there on the grass, and then we tried to do what we hadn't done
for years, it was, as it were, unplanned.

It was an inspiration.

And then after a bit I was obliged to say: "It doesn't come for me. I
can't manage anymore."

But then Theresa said: "That doesn't matter. There is so terribly much one can never finish. I only wanted you to taste the sponge cake."

Her patience is like a blessing.

And then she said: "I've got wet behind, on my back."

And I said: "It's not possible. It is as dry here as in the Desert of Sin."

"Feel me, then," she said, and sat up.

And I felt with my hand. And she was as wet as if it had rained.

"You should have a try at digging in this place," she said.

"No," I said. "I'm sure I've dug in this place ten times."

"But if I beg you to," she said.

So I was obliged to fetch the spade, and she stood and watched while I dug, and I dug just where she had lain in the grass, and the grass was shining as if it was dewy, and the water came almost immediately. I had not dug as much as two feet and there was a jet of water as big as a fist, and it spilled over the edges, it was a real spring.

Yes, that's how it's been in the matter of water. It is a good spring, not sweet and not bitter, it does not taste of ice water or of rock, and I've built a frame around it, like a wall around a well, and I shall finish it this summer, and I shall make a lid.

It does not freeze to the bottom in winter so I can answer you like this and tell the County Council that we have water, we have water till our dying day, and we shall leave water behind us, and it is called Theresa's Spring.

Michael Carson, who was born in Cheshire, England, and lives in Ireland, has written about gay life in his fiction. His novels include *Sucking Sherbet Lemons* (1988), *The Knight of the Flaming Heart* (1995), and—in a different genre—*Dying in Style* (1998), an entertainingly offbeat mystery. "Peter's Buddies," originally published in *Gay Times* in 1990 and selected for *Best English Short Stories III* (1991), is also cast as something of a mystery. Opening with the discovery of an unread letter, the story takes us on a search for the letter's writer, Peter Thebus, who seems to have gone missing. Almost from the first, we can surmise that Peter has AIDS, and as a chain of inquiries is forged around the world—epistolary links through which we trace his steps—the real surprise isn't Peter's fate but the way in which it is conveyed as an upbeat tale.

Highgate
1 December 1989

Dear Henry:

Do you remember that part in Tess of the D'Urbervilles where Tess posts a letter and it gets hidden beneath a carpet and is not found until it is far too late? I have always been rather divided about that. On the one hand it seemed a trifle pat. Hardy made his whole plot turn on that one unfortunate incident. But, at the same time, I knew that it was the sort of thing that happens often enough. It had truth all right, though in the novel it did not have the ring of truth.

Well, I have to tell you that the exact same thing has happened to me. As the removers were sliding my hall cupboard onto castors during my move to Highgate, they found a letter. It was from Peter Thebus. I did not get round to reading it until this morning, and it has really taken the wind out of my sails. You will realise why when you read it.

Of course, I am kicking myself for not having been in touch with Peter. It must be at least a year. But he is one of many I have not contacted. These days I fear what I may find, if you understand. Peter's letter also made me feel unutterably sad, though you will probably agree with me that it is far from being a sad letter. But more than anything else I feel unhappy that I did not get in touch with him. It was not that I did not want to, but a day at a time I postponed it. It all slips past so fast, you see, in such tiny moments, and then suddenly there is no more time.

When you have read the letter, please destroy the copy I have sent you. A part of me feels rather guilty in sending it to you at all. However, I am taking the chance because I think that if anyone will know what has happened to Peter, you will.

All the best to you, Henry! Perhaps I shall be able to visit you again soon.

Sincerely,
Barry

181

New York City
14 December 1989

Dear Joel:

I received a rather strange letter from that literary Limey, Barry Coe, we got to know through Peter Thebus a few years ago. He was asking about Peter's whereabouts and enclosed the copy of a letter which he had received some time ago but which had gotten lost in a literary way that would appeal to Barry the Limey. I couldn't decide from his letter whether he was more interested in Peter or in telling me that he was acquainted with Thomas Hardy's novels. I think I already knew that he probably was.

I can't say I noticed anything odd about Peter when he passed through. I was his first stop. He arrived here about a week after he wrote the letter to Barry, stayed a week, did not eat me out of house and home, then was sent on to you. Are you still recovering from the visitation? Our dear brother Brits do seem to think that the colonies owe them extravagant hospitality when they visit our shores—must be a clause in the Marshall Plan with which I am unacquainted—and then treat us to a Gallery seat for *Cats* when we visit their country, staying like any self-respecting tourist, in an hotel.

Still Peter does give good value. Being a New Yorker I'd have thought that I would have instantly recognised the signs. I didn't. He was rather heavily made-up, of course. But one kind of expects that from someone who has trod the boards for half a century.

Excuse the caustic tone. Three friends have succumbed in the last month and I am, as the saying goes, burnt out.

Is he still with you, Joel?

Always,
Henry

San Francisco
17 January 1990

Dear Saul:

I hate writing care of Poste Restantes. I always think American Express drop such letters down the nearest refuse-chute. Still, there's no other way to communicate as far as I can see. If your itinerary has gone according to schedule then you should be arriving in Bali any time now. I've just replied to an enquiry regarding your crewman, Peter Thebus. He's left a trail of anxious friends across Europe and the States, all wondering what's happened to him. Apparently they fear for his health. He seemed pretty robust to me—and to you, I should think—or you wouldn't have taken him on as a member of your crew. I'm not sure whether I was more surprised that you were going to take him or that he wanted to go with you. I did not protest too much because, selfishly, I had feared he might be settling down with me to enjoy his crimson sunset years.

Anyway, I've passed all the intelligence I have about Peter back to his friends. I just hope you may be able to solve the mystery.

Sincerely,
Joel Parker

SS Acqui Me Quedo
Bali
Indonesia
12 February 1990

Dear Sister Margaret Mary Lim:

I am writing to thank you and all the other missionary sisters of St Rapunzel's Convent, Solwezi, for taking in my friend Peter Thebus. I hope he has got over his pneumonia. I also enclose a money order which I hope will cover the costs incurred and leave something left over as a donation to the wonderful work you are doing at the clinic.

It had been my hope that somehow he would have made his way here to Bali and would be awaiting our arrival in port. After a week here there is no sign of him, and I must say I am a little anxious about him. I have been asked by his friends to report back, but failing any communication from you, I am unable to. A note about Peter's progress would be very much appreciated.

Thank you in advance.

Yours sincerely,
Saul Rosenbloom

St Rapunzel's Convent
Mintabo
Solwezi
Indonesia
1 March 1990

Dear Brother De Porres:

What has happened to that poor Englishman to whom you gave a lift that day when he was discharged from St Rapunzel's? The captain of the ship that brought him to Solwezi has written to me asking why he did not rejoin the ship in Bali.

As you will recall, I did not like to think of a man in Peter's condition going off up-country with you, but he was determined and, as you had a spare seat in the landrover, and he so wanted to move on, I did not see any point in objecting too strongly. Now I feel very guilty. Peter Thebus had but a tenuous hold on his life. He seemed set on risking it further, away from all friends and medicine. What has happened to the poor man? Please send your reply with the driver, if he has managed to reach you on the rough roads.

> Yours in Christ's Love.
> Sr Margaret Mary Lim

> Damien Leper Colony
> Port Cecil
> Solwezi
> Indonesia
> 25 March 1990

Dear Cousin:

Can you furnish me with some news regarding our poor brother, Peter Thebus? Sister is worrying. You know how she is. Peter was her pet sparrow. Also mine. I must say that I was greatly encouraged in my work to see such a sick man able to give so much to our poor patients here. The cough he had was like none that I have ever heard from anyone in this tropical climate. I wish that he could have stayed on with us for, despite his terrible illness, he proved a godsend in our work. Many of our patients still ask about him. In a short three months' stay he became beloved of all here.

When I consigned him to your care, I hoped that he would seek medical help in Singapore. I thought that to be his only chance. He did not want to go, but I could not in all conscience allow him to stay. How is he faring, dear cousin?

Keep safe. The typhoon season approaches. Your little plane is such a fragile thing. But then we are all such fragile things, God help us.

> With loving greetings.
> Brother De Porres

Garuda Airlines
Singapore
7 May 1990

Dear Hok Wa Eng:

Do you remember the Englishman Mr Peter Thebus I left in your care at Kota Kinabalu? My cousin in Solwezi has written to ask what has happened to him. He had paid for a flight to Singapore, but during the enforced stopover in Sabah necessitated by Typhoon Maria, he came up to me in the hotel and said he wanted to stay on there.

He seemed to be too sick a man to stay anywhere that did not have a fully-equipped hospital, but he was determined. Did he ever reach his mountain? If ever I saw death on a man's face, I saw it on his. Still, perhaps I was wrong. Please inform me what happened.

Sincerely,
Sumano Ranton (pilot)

National Park Office
Mount Kinabalu
Sabah
Borneo
12 July 1990

Dear Mr Ambassador:

I have just received a letter asking for news about the poor Englishman who died after his ascent of Mount Kinabalu some weeks ago. His name was apparently Peter Thebus, not Peter Smith as he wrote in the park's log book.

As you are aware, our guides did everything they could for him. They felt early on in the climb that he was too sick, but he would not be discouraged. He said that he wanted to reach the summit. It was all he wanted. They informed me that he died immediately. One minute he was standing looking out at the dawn from the summit of the mountain, then he was lying dead.

You are already in possession of all his personal effects. However, I would be grateful to hear of what has happened in this case as there seem to be other concerned people who are anxious for news.

Respectfully,
Hok Wa Eng (National Parks Officer)

British Embassy
Kuala Lumpur
Malaysia
23 September 1990

Dear Bill:

I have a bit of light to shed on the case of Peter Smith. He is (or was) apparently Peter Thebus, whose name rings a vague bell. Wasn't he once an actor of some repute?

You are in receipt of all his personal effects. I hope that my being able to supply you with a proper name for the deceased will help you to contact his next of kin. I am informed that he received a decent burial in the graveyard of St Mary's, Kota Kinabalu. I have the feeling that he died as he wished to die. He must have destroyed all identification prior to making the climb. We all face death in our own way, I suppose. Case closed? Love to Fiona.

Harry Moss

Hampstead
London
1 August 1989

Dear Barry:

Goodbye, old friend. You will not see Peter Thebus again. This is my last stint in life's rep. I am going away and I may be gone—as Captain Oates remarked—for some time. You see, I have caught it. In a way I feel quite flattered that a man of my years could be struck down by a sexual disease. My one great fear is that the lesions now covering me will be mistaken for the Kaposi's Sarcoma that used to only afflict elderly Mediterranean gentlemen. IT IS NOT SO! I am no gentleman! I got it the new-fangled way. I cannot recall the exact circumstances, but let there be no mistake about it!

I could of course stay put and be buddied to death. But I do not choose to. I had thought that I might go out onto the Heath at dead of night with a bottle of pills and ditto of Johnnie Walker, but am either not brave enough or not quite ready for the easy option. I've always been a bit of a travelling thespian. I see no reason to change now.

I intend to drop in on people to bid farewell, though I will not say anything about it. Perhaps on this final journey I may be able to do a few decent acts. I am very aware that my long life has been short on altruism—unless giving my all to the public can be considered as altruism. Also, as Death is a journey into the unknown, perhaps it is better that It finds me while I am embarked on one. A bit like Lear. Also, like Lear, I keep thinking: 'Thou shouldst not have been old, nuncle, until thou hadst first been wise.' Still, I am making a start. I have withdrawn all my money from the Halifax. I do not go gentle into that good night. Rather I go raging towards her screaming 'Who? Me!'

Good night
Peter Thebus

It seems to me a measure of the obscurity of French-Canadian culture in America that Hubert Aquin, so well known in his own country, has been so little known in ours. Born and educated in Montréal, Aquin, by the time he died in 1977, was acclaimed as both an artist and a radical political activist, fighting for the separatist cause. The author of four novels, he also worked in radio, television, and film; wrote plays, screenplays, translations, and essays; and helped found the journal *Liberté* in 1959. It was in *Liberté* that "Back on April Eleventh" first appeared in March 1969. Casting the letter story as a suicide note, Aquin gives it an interesting turn, making us wonder, as we read, how the narrator could be "managing to write this letter from beyond the tomb." A meticulous record of a man's tormented state of mind, the tale suggests Aquin's interest both in narrative forms and in obsession. Reading this story today, it is impossible not to reflect on the author's own suicide eight years after it appeared.

When your letter came I was reading a Mickey Spillane. I'd already been interrupted twice, and was having trouble with the plot. There was this man Gardner, who for some reason always carted around the photo of a certain corpse. It's true I was reading to kill time. Now I'm not so interested in killing time.

It seems you have no idea of what's been going on this winter. Perhaps you're afflicted with a strange intermittent amnesia that wipes out me, my work, our apartment, the brown record-player . . . I assure you I can't so easily forget this season I've passed without you, these long, snowy months with you so far away. When you left the first snow had just fallen on Montréal. It blocked the sidewalks, obscured the houses, and laid down great pale counterpanes in the heart of the city.

The evening you left—on my way back from Dorval—I drove aimlessly through the slippery empty streets. Each time the car went into a skid I had the feeling of going on an endless voyage. The Mustang was transformed into a rudderless ship. I drove for a long time without the slightest accident, not even a bump. It was dangerous driving, I know. Punishable by law. But that night even the law had become a mere ghost of itself, as had the city and this damned mountain that we've tramped so often. So much whiteness made a strong impression on me. I remember feeling a kind of anguish.

You, my love, probably think I'm exaggerating as usual and that I get some kind of satisfaction out of establishing these connections between your leaving and my states of mind. You may think I'm putting things together in retrospect in such a way as to explain what happened after that first fall of cerusian white.

But you're wrong: I'm doing nothing of the kind. That night, I tell you, the night you left, I skidded and slipped on that livid snow, fit to break your heart. It was myself I lost control of each time the Mustang slid softly into the abyss of memory. Winter since then has armed our city with many coats of melting mail, and here I am already on the verge of a burnt-ivory spring . . .

Someone really has to tell you, my love, that I tried twice to take my life in the course of this dark winter.

Yes, it's the truth. I'm telling you this without passion, with no bitterness or depths of melancholy. I'm a little disappointed at having bungled it; I feel like a failure, that's all. But now I'm bored. I've fizzled out under the ice. I'm finished.

Have you, my love, changed since last November? Do you still wear your hair long? Have you aged since I saw you last? How do you feel about all this snow that's fallen on me, drifting me in? I suppose a young woman of twenty-five has other souvenirs of her travels besides these discoloured postcards I've pinned to the walls of our apartment?

You've met women . . . or men; you've met perhaps one man and . . . he seemed more charming, more handsome, more "liberating" than I could ever be. Of course, as I say that, I know that to liberate oneself from another person one has only to be unfaithful. In this case you were right to fly off to Amsterdam to escape my black moods; you were right to turn our liaison into a more relative thing, the kind that other people have, any old love affair, any shabby business of that kind . . .

But that's all nonsense. I'm not really exaggerating, I'm just letting myself go, my love, letting myself drift. A little like the way I drove the Mustang that night last November. I'm in distress, swamped by dark thoughts. And it's no use telling myself that my imagination's gone wild, that I'm crazy to tell you these things, for I feel that this wave of sadness is submerging both of us and condemning me to total desolation. I can still see the snowy streets and me driving through them with no rhyme or reason, as if that aimless motion could magically make up for losing you. But you know, I already had a sedimentary confused desire to die, that very evening.

While I was working out the discords of my loneliness at the steering wheel of the Mustang, you were already miles high in a DC-8 above the North Atlantic. And a few hours later your plane would land gently on the icy runway of Schipol—after a few leisurely manoeuvres over the still plains of the Zuider Zee. By then I would be back in our apartment, reading a Simenon—*The Nahour Affair*—set partly in a Paris blanketed in snow (a rare occurrence), but also in that very city of Amsterdam where you had just arrived. I went to sleep in the small hours of the morning, clutching that bit of reality that somehow reconnected me to you.

The next day was the beginning of my irreversible winter. I tried to act as if nothing had changed and went to my office at the Agency (Place Ville Marie) at about eleven. I got through the day's work one way or another. While I was supposed to be at lunch I went instead to the ground-floor pharmacy. I asked for phenobarbital. The druggist told me, with a big stupid grin, that it called for a prescription. I left the building in a huff, realizing, however, that this needed a little thought.

I had to have a prescription, by whatever means, and information about brand-names and doses. And I needed at least some knowledge of the various barbiturate compounds.

With this drug very much on my mind I went next day or the day after to the McGill medical bookstore. Here were the shelves dealing with pharmacology. I was looking for a trickle and found myself confronted by the sea. I was overcome, submerged, astonished. I made a choice and left the store with two books under my arm: the *Shorter Therapeutics and Pharmacology,* and the *International Vade Mecum* (a complete listing of products now on the market).

That night, alone with my ghosts, I got at the books. To hell with Mickey Spillane, I had better things to read: for example this superbook (the *Vade Mecum*) which has the most delicious recipes going! Your appetite, your tensions, your depressions—they are all at the command of a few grams of drugs sagely administered. And according to this book of magic potions, life itself can be suppressed if only one knows how to go about it. I was passionately engrossed by this flood of pertinent information, but I still had my problem of how to get a prescription. Or rather, how to forge one that wouldn't turn into a passport to prison. A major problem.

His name was in the phone book: Olivier, J.R., internist. I dialled his number. His secretary asked what would be the best time of day for an appointment and specified that it would be about a month as the doctor was very busy. I answered her with a daring that still surprises me.

"It's urgent."

"What is it you have?" asked the secretary.

"A duodenal ulcer."

"How do you know?"

"Well, I've consulted several doctors and they strongly advised me to see Doctor O."

"Tomorrow at eleven," she suggested, struck by my argument. "Will that be convenient?"

"Of course," I replied.

I spent forty-five minutes in the waiting-room with the secretary I'd phoned the day before. I flipped through the magazines on the table searching for subjects of conversation to use on this doctor friend I hadn't seen for so long.

He appeared in the doorway and his secretary murmured my name. I raised my gloomy gaze to greet this smiling friend. He ushered me into his overstuffed office.

After the usual halting exchange of memories from college and university days I took a deep breath and, talking directly to Olivier, J.R., I told him straight out that I was having trouble sleeping. He burst into laughter, while I crouched deeper in the armchair he kept for patients.

"You're living it up too much, old boy," he said, smiling.

Just then his intercom blinked. Olivier lifted the phone.

"What is it?" he asked his secretary.

(I had been hoping for something like this.)

"Just a second. I have something to sign. You know how it is. They're making bureaucrats out of us."

He got up and went out to the reception room, carefully closing the door. At once I spied on his hand-rest the prescription pad with his letterhead. I quickly tore off a number of sheets and stuck them in the left inside pocket of my jacket. I was trembling, dripping with sweat.

"Well, bring me up to date," said Olivier, coming back. "Is she running around on you?"

He obviously found his own humour as irresistible as I found it offensive and our chat didn't get much farther. We fell silent and Olivier took his pen. Before starting to write on his prescription pad he looked up at me.

"What was it, now? You wanted some barbiturates to get you to sleep?"

"Yes," I said.

"Okay, here's some stuff that'll knock out a horse." He tore off the sheet and held it out to me.

"Thanks, thank you very much." I suppose I was a bit emotional.

"I've put *non repetatur* at the bottom for these pills have a tendency to be habit-forming. If you really need more after a couple of weeks come and see me again."

I folded the prescription without even searching out the *non repetatur,* an expression I had learned only a couple of days before. The intercom blinked again. Olivier, annoyed, picked up his phone but I paid no attention. I was already far away. Afterwards Olivier started telling me how his wife complained—or so he said—that she never got to see him any more.

"I'm working too hard," he said, hand on brow. "I probably need a holiday, but there it is. My wife's the one who's off to Europe. And it's only a month or so since she did the Greek Islands."

In my mind I saw you in the streets of Breda and The Hague. I imagined your walks in Scheveningen, your visits to the Maurithuis. I wasn't sure any more just where in Europe you were: at the Hook of Holland, the flying isle of Vlieland, or the seaside suburb of Leiden at Kalwijk aan Zee . . .

I was out again on the chilly street. The sky was dark and lowering. Black clouds scudded by at rooftop level, presaging another snowstorm. Let the snow come to beautify this death-landscape, where I drove in a Mustang while you moved in the clear celestial spaces of the painters of the Dutch school . . .

Back in our apartment I analyzed the prescription I had obtained by trickery. Twelve capsules of sodium amobarbital. I had no intention of remaining the possessor of a non-repeatable number of pills and began practising Olivier's handwriting. On ordinary paper. I had stolen ten sheets of his letterhead but that precious paper must not be wasted. In two or three hours I'd managed four good prescriptions. I fell asleep on the strength of my success.

It took me some days to accumulate a *quoad vitam* dose with the help of my forged scribbles. But I wasn't satisfied with the *quoad vitam* dose indicated in the *Vade Mecum*. I went on accumulating the little sky-blue capsules, each with its three-letter stamp—SK&F. There were nights when I slept not at all rather than dip into my stock of precious sodic torpedoes.

Quite a few days passed this way. Strange days. Knowing that I had my stock of death in hand I felt sure of myself and almost in harmony with life. I knew that I was going to die and at that moment it would have been upsetting to receive a letter from you, my love, for I had come too close to the end of living.

When your letter came on November sixteenth it in no way disturbed this harmony, as I had feared it might. After reading it I still wanted to end my life by using, some evening, my surprising accumulation of sodium amobarbital. You'd written in haste (I could tell by your hand) from the Amstel Hotel, but the postmark said Utrecht. So you'd mailed it from there! What were you doing in Utrecht? How had you gone from Amsterdam to that little town where the treaty was signed ratifying the conquest of French Canada? Symbol of the death of a nation, Utrecht became a premonitory symbol of my own death. Had you gone with someone? A European colleague, as you usually describe the men you meet on your travels? Are there many interior decorators in Utrecht? Or perhaps I should ask if they are friendly and charming. I imagined you sitting in the car of a decorator colleague, lunching on the way and perhaps spending the night in Utrecht. I grew weary of calling back so many memories of you, your charm, your beauty, your hot body in my arms. I tore up your letter to put an end to my despair. By the twenty-eighth of November I'd heard nothing more from you. My days grew shorter and emptier, my nights longer and more sleepless. They finally seemed barely to be interrupted by my days and I was exhausted. Recurrent insomnia had broken my resistance. I was destroyed, hopeless, without the slightest will to organize what was left of my life.

For me an endless night was about to begin, the unique, final, ultimate night. I'd at last decided to put an arbitrary end to my long hesitation, a period to our disordered history; decided, also, no longer to depend on your intermittent grace, which had been cruel only in that I had suffered from it.

That day I made a few phone calls to say that I was not available and spent my time tidying the apartment. When it was evening I took a very hot bath copiously perfumed from the bottle of Seaqua. I soaked for a long time in that beneficent water. Then I put on my burnt-orange bathing trunks and piled a few records on our playback: Ray Charles, Feliciano, Nana Mouskouri. I sprawled on our scarlet sofa, a glass of Chivas Regal in my hand, almost naked, fascinated by the total void that was waiting for me. I put Nana Mouskouri on several times. Then I finally made up my mind and swallowed my little sky-blue capsules four at a time, washing them down with great gulps of Chivas Regal. At the end I took more Scotch to help me absorb the lot. I put the nearly empty bottle on the rug just beside the couch. Still quite lucid, I turned on the radio (without getting up) so that the neighbours would not be alerted by the heavy breathing which, according to my medical sources, would begin as soon as I dropped into my coma.

To tell you the truth I wasn't sad but rather impressed, like someone about to start a long, very long, voyage. I thought of you, but faintly, oh, so faintly. You were moving around in the distance, in a funereal fog. I could still see the rich colours of your dresses and bathrobes. I saw you enter the apartment like a ghost and leave it in slow motion, but eternally in mirror perspective leading to infinity. The deeper I slipped into my comatose feast the less you looked my way, or rather the less I was conscious of you. Melancholy had no grip on me, nor fear. In fact I was blanketed in the solemnity of my solitude. Then, afterwards, obliteration became less complex and I became mortuary but not yet dead, left rocking in a total void.

And now, you ask, how are you managing to write this letter from beyond the tomb?

Well, here's your answer. I failed! The only damage I received in this suicide attempt resulted from the coma that lasted several hours. I was not in the best condition. My failure—even if I had no other devastating clues—would be proof enough of my perfect weakness, that diffuse infirmity that cannot be classified by science but which allows me to ruin everything I touch, always, without exception.

I woke up alive, as it were, in a white ward of the Royal Victoria, surrounded by a network of intravenous tubes that pinned me to the bed and ringed by a contingent of nurses. My lips felt frozen and dried and I remember that one of the nurses sponged my lips from time to time with an anti-herpetic solution.

Outside it was snowing, just as it had been on the day you left. The great white flakes fell slowly and I became aware that the very fact of seeing them silently falling was irrefutable proof that I was still, and horridly, alive. My return to a more articulated consciousness was painful, and took (to my relief) an infinity. As soon as I reached that threshold of consciousness I began to imagine you in the Netherlands or somewhere in Europe. Was there snow in Holland? And did you need your high suede boots that we shopped for together a few days before you left?

Suddenly I feel a great fatigue: these thoughts, returning in all their disorder, are taking me back to my stagnant point again . . .

It was really quite ironic that your telegram from Bruges should have become the means of your tardy (and involuntary) intervention on behalf of my poisoned body. I suppose the message was phoned first. But I didn't hear the ring and Western Union simply delivered the typed message to my address. The caretaker, who has no key to the letter boxes in our building, felt the call of duty and decided to bring me the envelope himself. There is something urgent about telegrams, you can't just leave them lying around. People can't imagine a harmless telegram that might read: HAPPY BIRTHDAY. WEATHER MARVELLOUS. KISSES. And yet that's exactly what was written in that telegram from Bruges.

I suppose the caretaker rapped a few times on our door. He probably couldn't see how I'd be out when the radio was blasting away. Finally, his curiosity must have got the better of him. He opened the door with his pass-key and stepped in to leave the envelope on the Louis XV table under the hall mirror. It's easy to imagine the rest: from the door he saw that I was there, he noted my corpse-like face, etc. Then, in a panic, he phoned the Montréal Police who transported me—no doubt at breakneck speed—to the emergency ward of the Royal Victoria. I spent several days under an oxygen tent. I even underwent a tracheotomy. That, in case the term means nothing to you, involves an incision in the trachea, followed by the insertion of a tracheal drain.

I must tell you everything, my love. I'm alive, therefore I am cured. The only traces are an immense scar on my neck and a general debility. While I was surviving one way or another in Montréal, you were continuing your tour of Europe. You saw other cities, Brussels, Charleroi, Amiens, Lille, Roubaix, Paris . . . Bruges had been just a stopover where you perhaps had dinner with a stranger, but no one hangs around in Bruges when the continent is waiting. Though God knows Bruges is a privileged place, an amorous sanctuary, a fortress that has given up a little terra firma to the insistent North Sea. I feel a soft spot for that half-dead city which you left with no special feeling. I stayed on in Bruges after you left, immured beneath its old and crumbling quays, for that was where you wished me (by telegram) a happy birthday.

There is no end to this winter. I don't know how many blizzards I watched from my hospital window. Around the fifteenth of December some doctor decided I should go home, that I was—so to speak—cured. Easy to say! Can one be cured of having wanted to die? When the ambulance attendants took me up to the apartment I saw myself in a mirror. I thought I would collapse. As a precaution I lay down on the couch where I had almost ended my days in November. Nothing had changed since then, but there was a thin film of dust on our furniture and the photos of you. The sky, lowering and dark, looked like more snow. I felt like a ghost. My clothes hung loose on me and my skin had the colour of a corpse. The sleepless nights again took up their death march but I no longer had my reserve of suicide-blue amobarbital pills. And I'd used up all my blank prescription forms. I couldn't sleep. I stared at the ceiling or at the white snowflakes piling up on our balcony. I imagined you at Rome or Civitavecchia or in the outskirts of Verona, completely surrendered to the intense experience of Europe.

From my calendar I knew that you were coming back to Montréal on April eleventh, on board the *Maasdam*. If I went to meet you that day at the docks of the Holland-American Line I would be in an emotional state. Too emotional, unable to tell you about what I did in November or about my disintegration since. Of course you'd give me a great hug and tell me all about those marvels, the fascinating ruins in Bruges, the baths of Caracalla, the Roman arches of triumph: the Arch of Tiberius, of Constantine, of Trajan, and so on. And all through your euphoric monologue I'd feel the knot at my throat.

It's for that reason—and all sorts of others, all somehow related to cowardice—that I'm writing you this letter, my love. I'll soon finish it and address it to Amsterdam, from which the *Maasdam* sails, so that you can read it during the crossing. That way you'll know that I bungled my first suicide attempt in November.

You'll understand that if I say "first" it means there'll be a second.

Don't you see that my hand is trembling? That my writing is beginning to scrawl? I'm already shaky. The spaces between each word, my love, are merely the symbols of the void that is beginning to accept me. I have ten more lucid minutes, but I've already changed: my mind is slipping, my hand wanders, the apartment, with every light turned on, grows dark where I look. I can barely see the falling snow but what I do see is like blots of ink. My love, I'm shivering with cold. The snow is falling somehow within me, my last snowfall. In a few seconds, I'll no longer exist, I will move no more. And I'm so sorry but I won't be at the dock on April eleventh. After these last words I shall crawl to the bath, which has been standing full for nearly an hour. There, I hope, they will find me, drowned. Before the eleventh of April next.

Julio Cortázar, whose novel *Hopscotch* (1966) helped introduce American readers to Latin American literature in the sixties, brings his characteristic inventiveness to "Letter to a Young Lady in Paris," which appeared in his 1967 story collection, *End of the Game.* The interplay of the fantastic and the real that runs through so much of the Argentine author's fiction permeates this letter tale, in which we find the narrator combining poetic ruminations with a bizarre account of vomiting up bunnies that come to dominate his life. Cortázar plays well here with the unreliable narrator, a familiar figure in the epistolary mode, compelling us to keep trying to sort things out until the final moments, when we grasp just what is reliably real.

Andrea, I didn't want to come live in your apartment in the calle Suipacha. Not so much because of the bunnies, but rather that it offends me to intrude on a compact order, built even to the finest nets of air, networks that in your environment conserve the music in the lavender, the heavy fluff of the powder puff in the talcum, the play between the violin and the viola in Ravel's quartet. It hurts me to come into an ambience where someone who lives beautifully has arranged everything like a visible affirmation of her soul, here the books (Spanish on one side, French and English on the other), the large green cushions there, the crystal ashtray that looks like a soap-bubble that's been cut open on this exact spot on the little table, and always a perfume, a sound, a sprouting of plants, a photograph of the dead friend, the ritual of tea trays and sugar tongs . . . Ah, dear Andrea, how difficult it is to stand counter to, yet to accept with perfect submission of one's whole being, the elaborate order that a woman establishes in her own gracious flat. How much at fault one feels taking a small metal tray and putting it at the far end of the table, setting it there simply because one has brought one's English dictionaries and it's at this end, within easy reach of the hand, that they ought to be. To move that tray is the equivalent of an unexpected horrible crimson in the middle of one of Ozenfant's painterly cadences, as if suddenly the strings of all the double basses snapped at the same time with the same dreadful whiplash at the most hushed instant in a Mozart symphony. Moving that tray alters the play of relationships in the whole house, of each object with another, of each moment of their soul with the soul of the house and its absent inhabitant. And I cannot bring my fingers close to a book, hardly change a lamp's cone of light, open the piano bench, without a feeling of rivalry and offense swinging before my eyes like a flock of sparrows.

You know why I came to your house, to your peaceful living room scooped out of the noonday light. Everything looks so natural, as always when one does not know the truth. You've gone off to Paris, I am left with the apartment in the calle Suipacha, we draw up a simple and satisfactory plan convenient to us both until September brings you back again to

199

Buenos Aires and I amble off to some other house where perhaps . . .
But I'm not writing you for that reason, I was sending this letter to you
because of the rabbits, it seems only fair to let you know; and because I
like to write letters, and maybe too because it's raining.

I moved last Thursday in a haze overlaid by weariness, at five in the
afternoon. I've closed so many suitcases in my life, I've passed so many
hours preparing luggage that never manages to get moved anyplace, that
Thursday was a day full of shadows and straps, because when I look at
valise straps it's as though I were seeing shadows, as though they were parts
of a whip that flogs me in some indirect way, very subtly and horribly.
But I packed the bags, let your maid know I was coming to move in. I
was going up in the elevator and just between the first and second floors
I felt that I was going to vomit up a little rabbit. I have never described
this to you before, not so much, I don't think, from lack of truthfulness
as that, just naturally, one is not going to explain to people at large that
from time to time one vomits up a small rabbit. Always I have managed to
be alone when it happens, guarding the fact much as we guard so many
of our privy acts, evidences of our physical selves which happen to us
in total privacy. Don't reproach me for it, Andrea, don't blame me. Once
in a while it happens that I vomit up a bunny. It's no reason not to live
in whatever house, it's no reason for one to blush and isolate oneself and
to walk around keeping one's mouth shut.

When I feel that I'm going to bring up a rabbit, I put two fingers in my
mouth like an open pincer, and I wait to feel the lukewarm fluff rise in
my throat like the effervescence in a sal hepatica. It's all swift and clean,
passes in the briefest instant. I remove the fingers from my mouth and in
them, held fast by the ears, a small white rabbit. The bunny appears to
be content, a perfectly normal bunny only very tiny, small as a chocolate
rabbit, only it's white and very thoroughly a rabbit. I set it in the palm
of my hand, I smooth the fluff, caressing it with two fingers; the bunny
seems satisfied with having been born and waggles and pushes its muzzle
against my skin, moving it with that quiet and tickling nibble of a rabbit's
mouth against the skin of the hand. He's looking for something to eat,
and then (I'm talking about when this happened at my house on the
outskirts) I take him with me out to the balcony and set him down in the
big flowerpot among the clover that I've grown there with this in mind.
The bunny raises his ears as high as they can go, surrounds a tender clover
leaf with a quick little wheeling motion of his snout, and I know that I

can leave him there now and go on my way for a time, lead a life not very different from people who buy their rabbits at farmhouses.

Between the first and the second floors, then, Andrea, like an omen of what my life in your house was going to be, I realized that I was going to vomit a rabbit. At that point I was afraid (or was it surprise? No, perhaps fear of the same surprise) because, before leaving my house, only two days before, I'd vomited a bunny and so was safe for a month, five weeks, maybe six with a little luck. Now, look, I'd resolved the problem perfectly. I grew clover on the balcony of my other house, vomited a bunny, put it in with the clover and at the end of a month, when I suspected that any moment . . . then I made a present of the rabbit, already grown enough, to señora de Molina, who believed I had a hobby and was quiet about it. In another flowerpot tender and propitious clover was already growing, I waited without concern the morning when the tickling sensation of fluff rising obstructed my throat, and the new little rabbit reiterated from that hour the life and habits of its predecessor. Habits, Andrea, are concrete forms of rhythm, are that portion of rhythm which helps to keep us alive. Vomiting bunnies wasn't so terrible once one had gotten into the unvarying cycle, into the method. You will want to know why all this work, why all that clover and señora de Molina. It would have been easier to kill the little thing right away and . . . Ah, you should vomit one up all by yourself, take it in two fingers and set it in your opened hand, still attached to yourself by the act itself, by the indefinable aura of its proximity, barely now broken away. A month puts a lot of things at a distance; a month is size, long fur, long leaps, ferocious eyes, an absolute difference. Andrea, a month is a rabbit, it really makes a real rabbit; but in the maiden moment, the warm bustling fleece covering an inalienable presence . . . like a poem in its first minutes, "fruit of an Idumean night" as much one as oneself . . . and afterwards not so much one, so distant and isolated in its flat white world the size of a letter.

With all that, I decided to kill the rabbit almost as soon as it was born. I was going to live at your place for four months: four, perhaps with luck three—tablespoonsful of alcohol down its throat. (Do you know pity permits you to kill a small rabbit instantly by giving it a tablespoon of alcohol to drink? Its flesh tastes better afterward, they say, however, I . . . Three or four tablespoonsful of alcohol, then the bathroom or a package to put in the rubbish.)

Rising up past the third floor, the rabbit was moving in the palm of my hand. Sara was waiting upstairs to help me get the valises in . . .

Could I explain that it was a whim? Something about passing a pet store? I wrapped the tiny creature in my handkerchief, put him into my overcoat pocket, leaving the overcoat unbuttoned so as not to squeeze him. He barely budged. His minuscule consciousness would be revealing important facts: that life is a movement upward with a final click, and is also a low ceiling, white and smelling of lavender, enveloping you in the bottom of a warm pit.

Sara saw nothing, she was too fascinated with the arduous problem of adjusting her sense of order to my valise-and-footlocker, my papers and my peevishness at her elaborate explanations in which the words "for example" occurred with distressing frequency. I could hardly get the bathroom door closed; to kill it now. A delicate area of heat surrounded the handkerchief, the little rabbit was extremely white and, I think, prettier than the others. He wasn't looking at me, he just hopped about and was being content, which was even worse than looking at me. I shut him in the empty medicine chest and went on unpacking, disoriented but not unhappy, not feeling guilty, not soaping up my hands to get off the feel of a final convulsion.

I realized that I could not kill him. But that same night I vomited a little black bunny. And two days later another white one. And on the fourth night a tiny grey one.

You must love the handsome wardrobe in your bedroom, with its great door that opens so generously, its empty shelves awaiting my clothes. Now I have them in there. Inside there. True, it seems impossible; not even Sara would believe it. That Sara did not suspect anything, was the result of my continuous preoccupation with a task that takes over my days and nights with the singleminded crash of the portcullis falling, and I go about hardened inside, calcined like that starfish you've put above the bathtub, and at every bath I take it seems all at once to swell with salt and whiplashes of sun and great rumbles of profundity.

They sleep during the day. There are ten of them. During the day they sleep. With the door closed, the wardrobe is a diurnal night for them alone, there they sleep out their night in a sedate obedience. When I leave for work I take the bedroom keys with me. Sara must think that I mistrust her honesty and looks at me doubtfully, every morning she looks as though she's about to say something to me, but in the end she remains silent and I am that much happier. (When she straightens up the bedroom between nine and ten, I make noise in the living room, put on a Benny Carter record which fills the whole apartment, and as Sara is a saetas and pasodobles fan, the wardrobe seems to be silent, and for the most part it is, because for the rabbits it's night still and repose is the order of the day.)

Their day begins an hour after supper when Sara brings in the tray with the delicate tinkling of the sugar tongs, wishes me good night—yes, she wishes me, Andrea, the most ironic thing is that she wishes me good night—shuts herself in her room, and promptly I'm by myself, alone with the closed-up wardrobe, alone with my obligation and my melancholy.

I let them out, they hop agilely to the party in the living room, sniffing briskly at the clover hidden in my pockets which makes ephemeral lacy patterns on the carpet which they alter, remove, finish up in a minute. They eat well, quietly and correctly; until that moment I have nothing to say, I just watch them from the sofa, a useless book in my hand—I who wanted to read all of Giraudoux, Andrea, and López's Argentine history that you keep on the lower shelf—and they eat up the clover.

There are ten. Almost all of them white. They lift their warm heads toward the lamps in the living room, the three motionless suns of their day; they love the light because their night has neither moon nor sun nor stars nor streetlamps. They gaze at their triple sun and are content. That's when they hop about on the carpet, into the chairs, ten tiny blotches shift like a moving constellation from one part to another, while I'd like to see them quiet, see them at my feet and being quiet—somewhat the dream of any god, Andrea, a dream the gods never see fulfilled—something quite different from wriggling in behind the portrait of Miguel de Unamuno, then off to the pale green urn, over into the dark hollow of the writing desk, always fewer than ten, always six or eight and I asking myself where the two are that are missing, and what if Sara should get up for some reason, and the presidency of Rivadavia which is what I want to read in López's history.

Andrea, I don't know how I stand up under it. You remember that I came to your place for some rest. It's not my fault if I vomit a bunny from time to time, if this moving changed me inside as well—not nominalism, it's not magic either, it's just that things cannot alter like that all at once, sometimes things reverse themselves brutally and when you expect the slap on the right cheek—. Like that, Andrea, or some other way, but always like that.

It's night while I'm writing you. It's three in the afternoon, but I'm writing you during their night. They sleep during the day. What a relief this office is! Filled with shouts, commands, Royal typewriters, vice presidents and mimeograph machines! What relief, what peace, what horror, Andrea! They're calling me to the telephone now. It was some friends upset about my monasterial nights. Luis inviting me out for a stroll or Jorge insisting—he's bought a ticket for me for this concert. I hardly dare to say no to them, I invent long and ineffectual stories about my poor health, I'm behind in the translations, any evasion possible. And when I get back home and am in the elevator—that stretch between the first and second floors—night after night, hopelessly, I formulate the vain hope that really it isn't true.

I'm doing the best I can to see that they don't break your things. They've nibbled away a little at the books on the lowest shelf, you'll find the backs repasted, which I did so that Sara wouldn't notice it. That lamp with the porcelain belly full of butterflies and old cowboys, do you like that very much? The crack where the piece was broken out barely shows, I spent a whole night doing it with a special cement that they sold me in an English shop—you know the English stores have the best cements— and now I sit beside it so that one of them can't reach it again with its paws (it's almost lovely to see how they like to stand on their hind legs, nostalgia for that so-distant humanity, perhaps an imitation of their god walking about and looking at them darkly; besides which, you will have observed—when you were a baby, perhaps—that you can put a bunny in the corner against the wall like a punishment, and he'll stand there, paws against the wall and very quiet, for hours and hours).

At 5 A.M. (I slept a little stretched out on the green sofa, waking up at every velvety-soft dash, every slightest clink) I put them in the wardrobe and do the cleaning up. That way Sara always finds everything in order, although at times I've noticed a restrained astonishment, a stopping to look at some object, a slight discoloration in the carpet, and again the desire to ask me something, but then I'm whistling Franck's Symphonic Variations in a way that always prevents her. How can I tell you about it, Andrea, the minute mishaps of this soundless and vegetal dawn, half-asleep on what staggered path picking up butt-ends of clover, individual leaves, white hunks of fur, falling against the furniture, crazy from lack of sleep, and I'm behind in my Gide, Troyat I haven't gotten to translating, and my reply to a distant young lady who will be asking herself already if . . . why go on with all this, why go on with this letter I keep trying to write between telephone calls and interviews.

Andrea, dear Andrea, my consolation is that there are ten of them and no more. It's been fifteen days since I held the last bunny in the palm of my hand, since then nothing, only the ten of them with me, their diurnal night and growing, ugly already and getting long hair, adolescents now and full of urgent needs and crazy whims, leaping on top of the bust of Antinoös (it is Antinoös, isn't it, that boy who looks blindly?) or losing themselves in the living room where their movements make resounding thumps, so much so that I ought to chase them out of there for fear that Sara will hear them and appear before me in a fright and probably in her nightgown—it would have to be like that with Sara, she'd be in her nightgown—and then . . . Only ten, think of that little happiness I have in the middle of it all, the growing calm with which, on my return home, I cut past the rigid ceilings of the first and second floors.

I was interrupted because I had to attend a committee meeting. I'm continuing the letter here at your house, Andrea, under the soundless grey light of another dawn. Is it really the next day, Andrea? A bit of white on the page will be all you'll have to represent the bridge, hardly a period on a page between yesterday's letter and today's. How tell you that in that interval everything has gone smash? Where you see that simple period I hear the circling belt of water break the dam in its fury, this side of the paper for me, this side of my letter to you I can't write with the same calm which I was sitting in when I had to put it aside to go to the committee meeting. Wrapped in their cube of night, sleeping without a worry in the world, eleven bunnies; perhaps even now, but no, not now—In the elevator then, or coming into the building; it's not important now where, if the when is now, if it can happen in any now of those that are left to me.

Enough now, I've written this because it's important to me to let you know that I was not all that responsible for the unavoidable and helpless destruction of your home. I'll leave this letter here for you, it would be indecent if the mailman should deliver it some fine clear morning in Paris. Last night I turned the books on the second shelf in the other direction; they were already reaching that high, standing up on their hind legs or jumping, they gnawed off the backs to sharpen their teeth—not that they were hungry, they had all the clover I had bought for them, I store it in the drawers of the writing desk. They tore the curtains, the coverings on the easy chairs, the edge of Augusto Torres' self-portrait, they got fluff all over the rug and besides they yipped, there's no word for it, they stood in a circle under the light of the lamp, in a circle as though they were adoring me, and suddenly they were yipping, they were crying like I never believed rabbits could cry.

I tried in vain to pick up all the hair that was ruining the rug, to smooth out the edges of the fabric they'd chewed on, to shut them up again in the wardrobe. Day is coming, maybe Sara's getting up early. It's almost queer, I'm not disturbed so much about Sara. It's almost queer, I'm not disturbed to see them gamboling about looking for something to play with. I'm not so much to blame, you'll see when you get here that I've repaired a lot of the things that were broken with the cement I bought in the English shop, I did what I could to keep from being a nuisance . . . As far as I'm concerned, going from ten to eleven is like an unbridgeable chasm. You understand: ten was fine, with a wardrobe, clover and hope, so many things could happen for the better. But not with eleven, because to say eleven is already to say twelve for sure, and Andrea, twelve would be thirteen. So now it's dawn and a cold solitude in which happiness ends, reminiscences, you and perhaps a good deal more. This balcony over the street is filled with dawn, the first sounds of the city waking. I don't think it will be difficult to pick up eleven small rabbits splattered over the pavement, perhaps they won't even be noticed, people will be too occupied with the other body, it would be more proper to remove it quickly before the early students pass through on their way to school.

NADINE GORDIMER
(1923–)

Nobel laureate Nadine Gordimer has devoted much of her fiction to delineating the racist world of her South African homeland. "Letter from His Father" represents a different aspect of her work. Although it reflects many of her concerns as well as her gift for satire and her meticulous style, its setting is not South Africa, nor is its content essentially political. In this story, originally published in the *London Review of Books* in 1983 and included in Gordimer's collection *Something Out There* in 1984, Franz Kafka's father, Hermann, responds to the long "Letter to His Father" that Franz wrote in 1919—but never sent—and which was published posthumously. Context and concept, important in most letter stories, are critical in this self-revelatory portrait, which depends for its impact on Franz Kafka's original letter and on our understanding of Kafka and his work. Although Gordimer cites enough of the original letter so that readers needn't have it at hand to appreciate her story, we do need to be familiar with Kafka. But then, who is not? That celebrity is central to the story and also to its power.

My dear son,

You wrote me a letter you never sent.

It wasn't for me—it was for the whole world to read. (You and your instructions that everything should be burned. Hah!) You were never open and frank with me—that's one of the complaints you say I was always making against you. You write it in the letter you didn't want me to read; so what does *that* sound like, eh? But I've read the letter now, I've read it anyway, I've read everything, although you said I put your books on the night-table and never touched them. You know how it is, here where I am: not something that can be explained to anyone who isn't here—they used to talk about secrets going to the grave, but the funny thing is there are no secrets here at all. If there was something you wanted to know, you should have known, if it doesn't let you lie quiet, then you can *have knowledge of it,* from here. Yes, you gave me that much credit, you said I was a true Kafka in "strength . . . eloquence, endurance, a certain way of doing things on a grand scale" and I've not been content just to rot. In that way, I'm still the man I was, the go-getter. Restless. Restless. Taking whatever opportunity I can. There isn't anything, now, you can regard as hidden from me. Whether you say I left it unread on the night-table or whether you weren't man enough, even at the age of thirty-six, to show me a letter that was supposed to be for me.

I write to you after we are both dead. Whereas you don't stir. There won't be any response from you, I know that. You began that letter by saying you were afraid of me—and then you were afraid to let me read it. And now you've escaped altogether. Because without the Kafka will-power you can't reach out from nothing and nowhere. I was going to call it a desert, but where's the sand, where're the camels, where's the sun—I'm still *mensch* enough to crack a joke—you see? Oh excuse me, I forgot—you didn't like my jokes, my fooling around with kids. My poor boy, unfortunately you had no life in you, in all those books and diaries and letters (the ones you posted, to strangers, to women) you said it a hundred times before you put the words in my mouth, in your literary way, in that letter: you yourself were "unfit for life." So death comes, how would you say, quite naturally to you. It's not like that for a man of vigour like I was, I can tell you, and so here I am writing, talking . . . I don't know if there is a word for what this is. Anyway, it's *Hermann Kafka.* I've outlived you here, same as in Prague.

That is what you really accuse me of, you know, for sixty or so pages (I notice the length of that letter varies a bit from language to language, of course it's been translated into everything—I don't know what—Hottentot and Icelandic, Chinese, although you wrote it "for me" in German). I *outlived* you, not for seven years, as an old sick man, after you died, but while you were young and alive. Clear as daylight, from the examples you give of being afraid of me, from the time you were a little boy: you were not afraid, you were envious. At first, when I took you swimming and you say you felt yourself a nothing, puny and weak beside my big, strong, naked body in the change-house—all right, you also say you were proud of such a father, a father with a fine physique . . . And may I remind you that father was taking the trouble and time, the few hours he could get away from the business, to try and make something of that *nebich,* develop his muscles, put some flesh on those poor little bones so he would grow up sturdy? But even before your barmitzvah the normal pride every boy has in his father changed to jealousy, with you. You couldn't be like me, so you decided I wasn't good enough for you: coarse, loud-mouthed, ate "like a pig" (your very words), cut my fingernails at table, cleaned my ears with a toothpick. Oh yes, you can't hide anything from me, now, I've read it all, all the thousands and thousands of words you've used to shame your own family, your own father, before the whole world. And with your gift for words you turn everything inside-out and prove, like a circus magician, it's love, the piece of dirty paper's a beautiful silk flag, you *loved your father too much,* and so—what? *You* tell me. You couldn't be like him? You wanted to be like *him*? The *ghasa,* the shouter, the gobbler? Yes, my son, these "insignificant details" you write down and quickly dismiss—these details hurt. Eternally. After all, you've become immortal through writing, as you insist you did, only about me, "everything was about you, father"; a hundred years after your birth, the Czech Jew, son of Hermann and Julie Kafka, is supposed to be one of the greatest writers who ever lived. Your work will be read as long as there are people to read it. That's what they say everywhere, even the Germans who burned your sisters and my grandchildren in incinerators. Some say you were also some kind of prophet (God knows what you were thinking, shut away in your room while the rest of the family was having a game of cards in the evening); after you died, some countries built camps where the things you made up for that story *In the Penal Colony* were practised, and ever since then there have been countries in different parts of the world where the devil's work that came into your mind is still carried out—I don't want to think about it.

You were not blessed to bring any happiness to this world with your genius, my son. Not at home, either. Well, we had to accept what God gave. Do you ever stop to think whether it wasn't a sorrow for me (never mind—for once—how you felt) that your two brothers, who might have grown up to bring your mother and me joy, died as babies? And you sitting there at meals always with a pale, miserable, glum face, not a word to say for yourself, picking at your food . . . You haven't forgotten that I used to hold up the newspaper so as not to have to see that. You bear a grudge. You've told everybody. But you don't think about what there was in a father's heart. From the beginning. I had to hide it behind a newspaper—anything. For your sake.

Because you were never like any other child. You admit it: however we had tried to bring you up, you say you would have become a "weakly, timid, hesitant person." What small boy doesn't enjoy a bit of a rough-house with his father? But writing at thirty-six years old, you can only remember being frightened when I chased you, in fun, round the table, and your mother, joining in, would snatch you up out of my way while you shrieked. For God's sake, what's so terrible about that? I should have such memories of my childhood! I know you never liked to hear about it, it bored you, you don't spare me the written information that it "wore grooves in your brain," but when *I* was seven years old I had to push my father's barrow from village to village, with open sores on my legs in winter. Nobody gave me delicacies to mess about on my plate; we were glad when we got potatoes. You make a show of me, mimicking how I used to say these things. But wasn't I right when I told you and your sisters—provided for by me, living like fighting-cocks because I stood in the business twelve hours a day—what did you know of such things? What did anyone know, what I suffered as a child? And then it's a sin if I wanted to give my own son a little pleasure I never had.

And that other business you *schlepped* up out of the past—the night I'm supposed to have shut you out on the *pavlatche*. Because of you the whole world knows the Czech word for the kind of balcony we had in Prague! Yes, the whole world knows that story, too. I am famous, too. You made me famous as the father who frightened his child once and for all: for life. Thank you very much. I want to tell you that I don't even remember that incident. I'm not saying it didn't happen, although you always had an imagination such as nobody ever had before or since, eh? But it could only have been the last resort your mother and I turned to—you know that your mother spoilt you, *over-protected* they would call it, now. You couldn't possibly remember how naughty you were at night, what a little tyrant you were, how you thought of every excuse to keep us sleepless. It was all right for you, you could nap during the day, a small child. But I had my business, I had to earn the living, I needed some rest. Pieces of bread, a particular toy you fancied, make wee-wee, another blanket on, a blanket taken off, drinks of water—there was no end to your tricks and whining. I suppose I couldn't stand it any longer. I feared to do you some harm. (You admit I never beat you, only scared you a little by taking off my braces in preparation to use them on you.) So I put you out of harm's way. That night. Just for a few minutes. It couldn't have been more than a minute. As if your mother would have let you catch cold! God forbid! And you've held it against me all your life. I'm sorry, I have to say it again, that old expression of mine that irritated you so much: I wish I had your worries.

Everything that went wrong for you is my fault. You write it down for sixty pages or so and at the same time you say to me "I believe you are entirely blameless in the matter of our estrangement." I was a "true Kafka," you took after your mother's, the Löwy side etc.—all you inherited from me, according to you, were your bad traits, without having the benefit of my vitality. I was "too strong" for you. You could not help it; I could not help it. So? All you wanted was *for me to admit that,* and we could have lived in peace. You were judge, you were jury, you were accused; you sentenced yourself, first. "At my desk, that is my place. My head in my hands—that is my attitude." (And that's what your poor mother and I had to look at, that was our pride and joy, our only surviving son!) But I was accused, too; you were judge, you were jury in my case, too. Right? By what right? Fancy goods—you despised the family business that fed us all, that paid for your education. What concern was it of yours, the way I treated the shop assistants? You only took an interest so you could judge, judge. It was a mistake to have let you study law. You did nothing with your qualification, your expensive education that I slaved and ruined my health for. Nothing but sentence me.—Now what did I want to say? Oh yes. Look what you wanted me to admit, under the great writer's beautiful words. If something goes wrong, somebody must be to blame, eh? We were not straw dolls, pulled about from above on strings. One of *us* must be to blame. And don't tell me you think it could be you. The stronger is always to blame, isn't that so? I'm not a deep thinker like you, only a dealer in retail fancy goods, but isn't that a law of life? "The effect you had on me was the effect you could not help having." You think I'll believe you're paying me a compliment, forgiving me, when you hand me the worst insult any father could receive? If it's what I am that's to blame, then I'm to blame, to the last drop of my heart's blood and whatever this is that's survived my body, for what *I am,* for being alive and begetting a son! You! Is that it? Because of you *I* should never have lived at all!

You always had a fine genius (never mind your literary one) for working me up. And you knew it was bad for my heart-condition. Now, what does it matter . . . but, as God's my witness, you aggravate me . . . you make me . . .

Well.

All I know is that I am to blame for ever. You've seen to that. It's written, and not alone by you. There are plenty of people writing books about Kafka, Franz Kafka. I'm even blamed for the name I handed down, our family name. *Kavka* is Czech for jackdaw, so that's maybe the reason for your animal obsession. *Dafke!* Insect, ape, dog, mouse, stag, what didn't you imagine yourself. They say the beetle story is a great masterpiece, thanks to me—I'm the one who treated you like an inferior species, gave you the inspiration . . . You wake up as a bug, you give a lecture as an ape. Do any of these wonderful scholars think what this meant to me, having a son who didn't have enough self-respect to feel himself a man?

You have such a craze for animals, but may I remind you, when you were staying with Ottla at Zürau you wouldn't even undress in front of a cat she'd brought in to get rid of the mice . . .

Yet you imagined a dragon coming into your room. It said (an educated dragon, *noch*): "Drawn hitherto by your longing . . . I offer myself to you." Your longing, Franz: ugh, for monsters, for perversion. You describe a person (yourself, of course) in some crazy fantasy of living with a horse. Just listen to you, " . . . for a year I lived together with a horse in such ways as, say, a man would live with a girl whom he respects, but by whom he is rejected." You even gave the horse a girl's name, Eleanor. I ask you, is that the kind of story made up by a normal young man? Is it decent that people should read such things, long after you are gone? But it's published, everything is published.

And worst of all, what about the animal in the synagogue. Some sort of rat, weasel, a marten you call it. You tell how it ran all over during prayers, running along the lattice of the women's section and even climbing down to the curtain in front of the Ark of the Covenant. A *schande*, an animal running about during divine service. Even if it's only a story—only you would imagine it. No respect.

You go on for several pages (in that secret letter) about my use of vulgar Yiddish expressions, about my "insignificant scrap of Judaism," which was "purely social" and so meant we couldn't "find each other in Judaism" if in nothing else. This, from you! When you were a youngster and I had to drag you to the Yom Kippur services once a year you were sitting there making up stories about unclean animals approaching the Ark, the most holy object of the Jewish faith. Once you were grown up, you went exactly once to the Altneu synagogue. The people who write books about you say it must have been to please me. I'd be surprised. When you suddenly discovered you were a Jew, after all, of course your Judaism was highly intellectual, nothing in common with the Jewish customs I was taught to observe in my father's *shtetl*, pushing the barrow at the age of seven. Your Judaism was learnt at the Yiddish Theatre. That's a *nice* crowd! Those dirty-living travelling players you took up with at the Savoy Café. Your friend the actor Jizchak Löwy. No relation to your mother's family, thank God. I wouldn't let such a man even meet her. You had the disrespect to bring him into your parents' home, and I saw it was my duty to speak to him in such a way that he wouldn't ever dare to come back again. (Hah! I used to look down from the window and watch him, hanging around in the cold, outside the building, waiting for you.) And the Tschissik woman, that *nafke*, one of his actresses—I've found out you thought you were in love with her, a married woman (if you can call the way those people live a marriage). Apart from Fräulein Bauer you never fancied anything but a low type of woman. I say it again as I did then: if you lie down with dogs, you get up with fleas. You lost your temper (yes, you, this time), you flew into a rage at your father when he told you that. And when I reminded you of my heart-condition, you put yourself in the right again, as usual, you said (I remember like it was yesterday) "I make great efforts to restrain myself." But now I've read your diaries, the dead don't need to creep into your bedroom and read them behind your back (which you accused your mother and me of doing), I've read what you wrote afterwards, that you sensed in me, your father, "as always at such moments of extremity, the existence of a wisdom which I can no more than scent." So you *knew,* while you were defying me, you knew I was right!

The fact is that you were antisemitic, Franz. You were never interested in what was happening to your own people. The hooligans' attacks on Jews in the streets, on houses and shops, that took place while you were growing up—I don't see a word about them in your diaries, your notebooks. You were only *imagining* Jews. Imagining them tortured in places like your *Penal Colony,* maybe. I don't want to think about what that means.

Right, towards the end you studied Hebrew, you and your sister Ottla had some wild dream about going to Palestine. You, hardly able to breathe by then, digging potatoes on a kibbutz! The latest book about you says you were in revolt against the "shopkeeper mentality" of your father's class of Jew; but it was the shopkeeper father, the buttons and buckles, braid, ribbons, ornamental combs, press-studs, hooks-and-eyes, boot laces, photo frames, shoe horns, novelties and notions that earned the bread for you to dream by. You were antisemitic, Franz; if such a thing is possible as for a Jew to cut himself in half. (For you, I suppose, anything is possible.) You told Ottla that to marry that goy Josef Davis was better than marrying ten Jews. When your great friend Brod wrote a book called "The Jewesses" you wrote there were too many of them in it. You saw them like lizards. (Animals again, low animals.) "However happy we are to watch a single lizard on a footpath in Italy, we would be horrified to see hundreds of them crawling over each other in a pickle jar." From where did you get such ideas? Not from your home, that I know.

And look how Jewish you are, in spite of the way you despised us—Jews, your Jewish family! You answer questions with questions. I've discovered that's your style, your famous literary style: your Jewishness. Did you or did you not write the following story, playlet, wha'd'you-call-it, your friend Brod kept every scribble and you knew he wouldn't burn even a scrap. "Once at a spiritualist seance a new spirit announced its presence, and the following conversation with it took place. The spirit: Excuse me. The spokesman: Who are you? The spirit: Excuse me. The spokesman: What do you want? The spirit: To go away. The spokesman: But you've only just come. The spirit: It's a mistake. The spokesman: No, it isn't a mistake. You've come and you'll stay. The spirit: I've just begun to feel ill. The spokesman: Badly? The spirit: Badly? The spokesman: Physically? The spirit: Physically? The spokesman: You answer with questions. That will not do. We have ways of punishing you, so I advise you to answer, for then we shall soon dismiss you. The spirit: Soon? The spokesman: Soon.

The spirit: In one minute? The spokesman: Don't go on in this miserable way . . ."

Questions without answers. Riddles. You wrote "It is always only in contradiction that I can live. But this doubtless applies to everyone; for living, one dies, dying, one lives." Speak for yourself! So who did you think you were when that whim took you—their prophet, Jesus Christ? What did you *want*? The *goyishe* heavenly hereafter? What did you mean when a lost man, far from his native country, says to someone he meets "I am in your hands" and the other says, "No. You are free and that is why you are lost"? What's the sense in writing about a woman "I lie in wait for her in order not to meet her"? There's only one of your riddles I think I understand, and then only because for forty-two years, God help me, I had to deal with you myself. "A cage went in search of a bird." That's you. The cage, not the bird. I don't know why. Maybe it will come to me. As I say, if a person wants to, he can know everything, here.

All that talk about going away. You called your home (more riddles) "My prison—my fortress." You grumbled—in print, everything ended up in print, my son—that your room was only a passage, a thoroughfare between the livingroom and your parents' bedroom. You complained you had to write in pencil because we took away your ink to stop you writing. It was for your own good, your health—already you were a grown man, a qualified lawyer, but you know you couldn't look after yourself. Scribbling away half the night, you'd have been too tired to work properly in the mornings, you'd have lost your position at the Assicurazioni Generali (or was it by then the Arbeiter-Unfall-Versicherungs-Anstalt für das Königreich Böhmen, my memory doesn't get any better, here). And I wasn't made of money. I couldn't go on supporting everybody for ever.

You've published every petty disagreement in the family. It was a terrible thing, according to you, we didn't want you to go out in bad weather, your poor mother wanted you to wrap up. You with your delicate health, always sickly—you didn't inherit my constitution, it was only a lifetime of hard work, the business, the family worries that got me, in the end! You recorded that you couldn't go for a walk without your parents making a fuss, but at twenty-eight you were still living at home. Going away. My poor boy. You could hardly get yourself to the next room. You shut yourself up when people came to visit. Always crawling off to bed, sleeping in the day (oh yes, you couldn't sleep at night, not like anybody else), sleeping your life away. You invented *Amerika* instead of having the guts to emigrate, get up off the bed, pack up and go there, make a new life!

Even that girl you jilted twice managed it. Did you know Felice is still alive somewhere, there now, in America? She's an old, old woman with great-grandchildren. They didn't get her into the death camps those highly-educated people say you knew about before they happened. America you never went to, Spain you dreamt about . . . your Uncle Alfred was going to find you jobs there, in Madeira, the Azores . . . God knows where else. Grandson of a ritual slaughterer, a *schochet*, that was why you couldn't bear to eat meat, they say, and that made you weak and undecided. So that was my fault, too, because my poor father had to earn a living. When your mother was away from the flat, you'd have starved yourself to death if it hadn't been for me. And what was the result? You resented so much what I provided for you, you went and had your stomach pumped out! Like someone who's been poisoned! And you didn't forget to write it down, either: "My feeling is that disgusting things will come out."

Whatever I did for you was *dreck*. You felt "despised, condemned, beaten down" by me. But you despised *me*; the only difference, I wasn't so easy to beat down, eh? How many times did you try to leave home, and you couldn't go? It's all there in your diaries, in the books they write about you. What about that other masterpiece of yours, *The Judgment*. A father and son quarrelling, and then the son goes and drowns himself, saying "Dear parents, I have always loved you, all the same." The wonderful discovery about that story, you might like to hear, it proves Hermann Kafka most likely didn't want his son to grow up and be a man, any more than his son wanted to manage without his parents' protection. The *meshuggener* who wrote that, may he get rich on it! I wouldn't wish it on him to try living with you, that's all, the way we had to. When your hunchback friend secretly showed your mother a complaining letter of yours, to get you out of your duty of going to the asbestos factory to help your own sister's husband, Brod kept back one thing you wrote. But now it's all published, all, all, all the terrible things you thought about your own flesh and blood. "I hate them all": father, mother, sisters.

You couldn't do without us—without me. You only moved away from us when you were nearly thirty-two, a time when every *man* has a wife and children already, a home of his own.

You were always dependent on someone. Your friend Brod, poor devil. If it hadn't been for the little hunchback, who would know of your existence today? Between the incinerators that finished your sisters and the fire you wanted to burn up your manuscripts, nothing would be left. The kind of men you invented, the Gestapo, confiscated whatever papers of yours there were in Berlin, and no trace of them has ever been found, even by the great Kafka experts who stick their noses into everything. You said you loved Max Brod more than yourself. I can see that. You liked the idea he had of you, that you knew wasn't yourself (you see, sometimes I'm not so *grob,* uneducated, knowing nothing but fancy goods, maybe I got from you some "insights"). Certainly, I wouldn't recognize my own son the way Brod described you: "the aura Kafka gave out of extraordinary strength, something I've never encountered elsewhere, even in meetings with great and famous men . . . the infallible solidity of his insights never tolerated a single lacuna, nor did he ever speak an insignificant word . . . He was life-affirming, ironically tolerant towards the idiocies of the world, and therefore full of sad humour."

I must say, your mother who put up with your faddiness when she came back from a day standing in the business, your sisters who acted in your plays to please you, your father who worked his heart out for his family—we never got the benefit of your tolerance. Your sisters (except Ottla, the one you admit you were a bad influence on, encouraging her to leave the shop and work on a farm like a peasant, to starve herself with you on rabbit-food, to marry that goy) were giggling idiots, so far as you were concerned. Your mother never felt the comfort of her son's strength. You never gave us anything to laugh at, sad or otherwise. And you hardly spoke to me at all, even an insignificant word. Whose fault was it you were that person you describe "strolling about on the island in the pool, where there are neither books nor bridges, hearing the music, but not being heard." You wouldn't cross a road, never mind a bridge, to pass the time of day, to be pleasant to other people, you shut yourself in your room and stuffed your ears with Oropax against the music of life, yes, the sounds of cooking, people coming and going (what were we supposed to do, pass through closed doors?), even the singing of the pet canaries annoyed you, laughter, the occasional family tiff, the bed squeaking where normal married people made love.

What I've just said may surprise. That last bit, I mean. But since I died in 1931 I know the world has changed a lot. People, even fathers and sons, are talking about things that shouldn't be talked about. People aren't ashamed to read anything, even private diaries, even letters. There's no shame, anywhere. With that, too, you were ahead of your time, Franz. You were not ashamed to write in your diary, which your friend Brod would publish—you must have known he would publish everything, make a living out of us—things that have led one of the famous Kafka scholars to *study* the noises in our family flat in Prague. Writing about me: "It would have been out of character for Hermann Kafka to restrain any noises he felt like making during coupling; it would have been out of character for Kafka, who was ultra-sensitive to noise and had grown up with these noises, to mention the suffering they caused him."

You left behind you for everyone to read that the sight of your parents' pyjamas and nightdress on the bed disgusted you. Let me also speak freely like everyone else. You were made in that bed. That disgusts me: your disgust over a place that should have been holy to you, a place to hold in the highest respect. Yet you are the one who complained about my coarseness when I suggested you ought to find yourself a woman—buy one, hire one—rather than try to prove yourself a man at last, at thirty-six, by marrying some Prague Jewish tart who shook her tits in a thin blouse. Yes, I'm speaking of that Julie Wohryzek, the shoemaker's daughter, your second fiancée. You even had the insolence to throw the remark in my face, in that letter you didn't send, but I've read it anyway, I've read everything now, although you said I put *In the Penal Colony* on the bedside table and never mentioned it again.

I have to talk about another matter we didn't discuss, father and son, while we were both alive—all right, it was my fault, maybe you're right, as I've said, times were different . . . Women. I must bring this up because—my poor boy—marriage was 'the greatest terror' of your life. You write that. You say your attempts to explain why you couldn't marry—on these depends the 'success' of the whole letter you didn't send. According to you, marrying, founding a family was "the utmost a human being can succeed in doing at all." Yet you couldn't marry. How is any ordinary human being to understand that? You wrote more than a quarter of a million words to Felice Bauer, but you couldn't be a husband to her. You put your parents through the farce of travelling all the way to Berlin for an engagement party (there's the photograph you had taken, the happy couple, in the books they write about you, by the way). The engagement was broken, was on again, off again. Can you wonder? Anyone who goes into a bookshop or library can read what you wrote to your fiancée when your sister Elli gave birth to our first grand-daughter. You felt nothing but nastiness, envy against your brother-in-law because "I'll never have a child." No, not with the Bauer girl, not in a decent marriage, like anybody else's son; but I've found out you had a child, Brod says so, by a woman, Grete Bloch, who was supposed to be the Bauer girl's best friend, who even acted as matchmaker between you! What do you say to that? Maybe it's news to you. I don't know. (That's how irresponsible you were.) They say she went away. Perhaps she never told you.

As for the next one you tried to marry, the one you make such a song and dance over because of my remark about Prague Jewesses and the blouse etc.—for once you came to your senses, and you called off the wedding only two days before it was supposed to take place. Not that I could have influenced you. Since when did you take into consideration what your parents thought? When you told me you wanted to marry the shoemaker's daughter—naturally I was upset. At least the Bauer girl came from a nice family. What I said about the blouse just came out, I'm human, after all. But I was frank with you, man to man. You weren't a youngster anymore. A man doesn't have to marry a nothing who will go with anybody.

I saw what that marriage was about, my poor son. You wanted a woman. Nobody understood that better than I did, believe me, I was normal man enough, eh! There were places in Prague where one could get a woman. (I suppose whatever's happened, there still are, always will be.) I tried to help you; I offered to go along with you myself. I said it in front of your mother, who—yes, as you write you were so shocked to see, was in agreement with me. We wanted so much to help you, even your own mother would go so far as that.

But in that letter you didn't think I'd ever see, you accuse me of humiliating you and I don't know what else. You wanted to marry a tart, but you were insulted at the idea of buying one?

Writing that letter only a few days after you yourself called off your second try at getting married, aged thirty-six, you find that your father, as a man-of-the-world, not only showed "contempt" for you on that occasion, but that when he had spoken to you as a broad-minded father when you were a youngster, he had given you information that set off the whole ridiculous business of your never being able to marry, ever. Already, twenty years before the Julie Wohryzek row, with "a few frank words" (as you put it) your father made you incapable of taking a wife and pushed you down "into the filth as if it were my destiny." You remember some walk with your mother and me on the Josefsplatz when you showed curiosity about, well, men's feelings and women, and I was open and honest with you and told you I could give you advice about where to go so that these things could be done quite safely, without bringing home any disease. You were sixteen years old, physically a man, not a child, eh? Wasn't it time to talk about such things?

Shall I tell you what *I* remember? Once you picked a quarrel with your mother and me because we hadn't educated you sexually—your words. Now you complain because I tried to guide you in these matters. I did— I didn't. Make up your mind. Have it your own way. Whatever I did, you believed it was *because of what I did* that you couldn't bring yourself to marry. When you thought you wanted the Bauer girl, didn't I give in, to please you? Although you were in no financial position to marry, although I had to give your two married sisters financial help, although I had worries enough, a sick man, you'd caused me enough trouble by persuading me to invest in a *mechulah* asbestos factory? Didn't I give in? And when the girl came to Prague to meet your parents and sisters, you wrote, "My family likes her almost more than I'd like it to." So it went as far as that: you couldn't like anything we liked, was that why you couldn't marry her?

A long time ago, a long way . . . ah, it all moves away, it's getting faint . . . But I haven't finished. Wait.

You say you wrote your letter because you wanted to explain why you couldn't marry. I'm writing this letter because you tried to write it for me. *You would take even that away from your father.* You answered your own letter, before I could. You made what you imagine as my reply part of the letter you wrote me. To save me the trouble . . . Brilliant, like they say. With your great gifts as a famous writer, you express it all better than I could. You are there, quickly, with an answer, before I can be. You take the words out of my mouth: while you are accusing yourself, in my name, of being "too clever, obsequious, parasitic and insincere" in blaming your life on me, you are—yet again, one last time!—finally being too clever, obsequious, parasitic and insincere in the trick of stealing your father's chance to defend himself. A genius. What is left to say about you if—how well you know yourself, my boy, it's terrible—you call yourself the kind of vermin that doesn't only sting, but at the same time sucks blood to keep itself alive? And even that isn't the end of the twisting, the cheating. You then confess that this whole "correction," "rejoinder," as you, an expensively educated man, call it, "does not originate" in your father but in you yourself, Franz Kafka. So you see, here's the proof, something *I* know you, with all your brains, can't know *for me:* you say you always wrote about me, it was all about me, your father; but it was all about you. The beetle. The bug that lay on its back waving its legs in the air and couldn't get up to go and see America or the Great Wall of China. You, you, self, self. And in your letter, after you have defended me against yourself, when you finally make the confession—right again, in the right again, always—you take the last word, in proof of your saintliness I could know nothing about, never understand, a businessman, a shopkeeper. That is your "truth" about us you hoped might be able to "make our living and our dying easier."

The way you ended up, Franz. The last woman you found yourself. It wasn't our wish, God knows. Living with that Eastern Jewess, and in sin. We sent you money; that was all we could do. If we'd come to see you, if we'd swallowed our pride, meeting that woman, our presence would only have made you worse. It's there in everything you've written, everything they write about you: everything connected with us made you depressed and ill. We knew she was giving you the wrong food, cooking like a gypsy on a spirit stove. She kept you in an unheated hovel in Berlin . . . may God forgive me (Brod has told the world), I had to turn my back on her at your funeral.

Franz . . . When you received copies of your book *In the Penal Colony* from Kurt Wolff Verlag that time . . . You gave me one and I said "Put it on the night-table." You say I never mentioned it again. Well, don't you understand—I'm not a literary man. I'm telling you now. I read a little bit, a page or two at a time. If you had seen that book, there was a pencil mark every two, three pages, so I would know next time where I left off. It wasn't like the books I knew—I hadn't much time for reading, working like a slave since I was a small boy, I wasn't like you, I couldn't shut myself up in a room with books, when I was young. I would have starved. But you know that. Can't you understand that I was—yes—not too proud—ashamed to let you know I didn't find it easy to understand your kind of writing, it was all strange to me.

Hah! I know I'm no intellectual, but I knew how to live!

Just a moment . . . give me time . . . there's a fading . . . Yes—can you imagine how we felt when Ottla told us you had tuberculosis? Oh how could you bring it over your heart to remind me I once said, in a temper, to a useless assistant coughing all over the shop (you should have had to deal with those lazy *goyim*), he ought to die, the sick dog. Did I know you would get tuberculosis, too? It wasn't our fault your lungs rotted. I tried to expand your chest when you were little, teaching you to swim; you should never have moved out of your own home, the care of your parents, to that rat-hole in the Schönbornpalais. And the hovel in Berlin . . . We had some good times, didn't we? Franz? When we had beer and sausages after the swimming lessons? At least you remembered the beer and sausages, when you were dying.

One more thing. It chokes me, I have to say it. I know you'll never answer. You once wrote "Speech is possible only where one wants to lie." You were too *ultra-sensitive* to speak to us, Franz. You kept silence, with the truth: those playing a game of cards, turning in bed on the other side of the wall—it was the sound of live people you didn't like. Your revenge, that you were too cowardly to take in life, you've taken here. We can't lie peacefully in our graves; dug up, unwrapped from our shrouds by your fame. To desecrate your parents' grave as well as their bed, aren't you ashamed? Aren't you ashamed—now? Well, what's the use of quarrelling. We lie together in the same grave—you, your mother and I. We've ended up as we always should have been, united. Rest in peace, my son. I wish you had let me.

Your father,
Hermann Kafka

From her early realistic fiction to her more recent works of science fiction, Doris Lessing has used her writing to comment upon society. In her novels and stories, she has addressed such issues as the role and identity of women, violence, and the politics of race in Southern Rhodesia, where she grew up. "A Letter from Home," which was included in *A Man and Two Women* (1963) as well as in *African Stories* (1965), reveals the repressive world of southern Africa through the eyes of a poet and teacher who lives within that world but rejects its values, as his sarcasm and sardonic humor make clear. Lessing uses the letter format, with its implicit division between insiders (correspondents) and outsiders (readers), to evoke the division created by the society itself. The narrator, with his unconventional views, is an outsider within his own homeland. We can assume from the story's title and from the openness with which the narrator speaks—though only "in a whisper," as he says, "under my breath"—that the person to whom he is writing, a former colleague, is also an outsider, and someone who shares his views. This is conversation then between two outsiders who are insiders within their own group, and the letter feels both personal and private. As for readers, we feel transformed by our inclusion into insiders—or fellow outsiders, as it were.

. . . *Ja,* but that isn't why I'm writing this time. You asked about Dick. You're worrying about him?—man! But he's got a poetry scholarship from a Texas University and he's lecturing the Texans about letters and life too in Suid Afrika, South Africa to you (forgive the hostility), and his poems are read, so they tell me, wherever the English read poetry. He's fine, man, but I thought I'd tell you about Johannes Potgieter, remember him? Remember the young poet, The Young Poet? He was around that winter you were here. Don't tell me you've forgotten those big melting brown eyes and those dimples. About ten years ago (*ja*, time flies) he got a type of unofficial grace-gift of a job at St.___ University on the strength of those poems of his, and—God—they were good. Not that you or any other English-speaking *domkop* will ever know, because they don't translate out of Afrikaans. Remember me telling you and everyone else (give me credit for that at least; I give the devil his due, when he's a poet) what a poet he was, how blerry good he was—but several people tried to translate Hans's poems, including me, and failed. Right. *Goed.* Meanwhile a third of the world's population—or is it a fifth, or to put it another way, X5Y59 million people—speak English (and it's increasing by six births a minute) but one million people speak Afrikaans, and though I say it in a whisper, man, only a fraction of them can read it, I mean to read it. But Hans is still a great poet. Right.

He wasn't all that happy about being a sort of unofficial laureate at that university. It's no secret some poets don't make laureates. At the end of seven months he produced a book of poems which had the whole God-fearing place sweating and sniffing out heresy of all kinds, sin, sex, liberalism, brother love, and so forth and so on; but of course in a civilised country (I say this under my breath, or I'll get the sack from my university, and I've got four daughters these days, had you forgotten?) no one would see anything in them but good poetry. Which is how Hans saw them, poor innocent soul. He was surprised at what people saw in them, and he was all upset. He didn't like being called all those names, and the good country boys from their fine farms and the smart town boys from their big houses all started looking sideways, making remarks, and our Hans, he was reduced to pap, because he's not a fighter, Hans; he was never a taker of positions on the side of justice, freedom, and the rest, for tell you the truth, I don't think he ever got round to defining them. *Goed.* He resigned, in what might be called a dignified silence, but his friends knew it was just plain cowardice or, if you like, incomprehension about what the fuss was over, and he went to live in Blagspruit in the Orange Free, where his Tantie Gertrude had a house. He helped her in her store. *Ja,* that's what he did. What did we all say to this? Well, what do you think? The inner soul of the artist (et cetera) knows what is best, and he probably *needed* the Orange Free and his Auntie's store for his development. Well, something like that. To tell the truth, we didn't say much; he simply dropped out. And time passed. *Ja.* Then they made me editor of *Onwards,* and thinking about our indigenous poets, I remembered Johannes Potgieter, and wrote "What about a poem from you?"—feeling bad because when I counted up the years, it was eight since I'd even thought of him, even counting those times when one says drunk at dawn: Remember Hans? Now, there was a poet. . . .

No reply, so I let an editorial interval elapse and I wrote again, and I got a very correct letter back. Well phrased. Polite. But not just that, it took me an hour to work out the handwriting—it was in a sort of Gothic print, each letter a work of art, like a medieval manuscript. But all he said, in that beautiful black art-writing was: he was very well, he hoped I was very well, the weather was good, except the rains were late, his Tantie Gertie was dead, and he was running the store. "*Jou vriend,* Johannes Potgieter."

Right. *Goed.* I was taking a trip up to Joburg, so I wrote and said I'd drop in at Blagspruit on my way back, and I got another Manu Script, or Missal, saying he hoped to see me, and he would prepare Esther for my coming. I thought, he's married, poor *kerel,* and it was the first time I'd thought of him as anything but a born bachelor, and I was right—because when I'd done with Joburg, not a moment too soon, and driven down to the Orange Free, and arrived on the doorstep, there was Hans, but not a sign of a wife, and Esther turned out to be—but first I take pleasure in telling you that the beautiful brown-eyed poet with his noble brow and pale dimpled skin was bald—he has a tonsure, I swear it—and he's fat, a sort of smooth pale fat. He's like a monk, lard-coloured and fat and smooth. Esther is the cook, or rather, his jailor. She's a Zulu, a great fat woman, and I swear she put the fear of God into me before I even got into the house. Tantie Gertie's house is a square brick four-roomed shack, you know the kind, with an iron roof and verandahs—well, what you'd expect in Blagspruit. And Esther stood about six feet high in a white apron and a white *doekie* and she held a lamp up in one great black fist and looked into my face and sighed and went off into her kitchen singing "Rock of Ages." *Ja,* I promise you. And I looked at Hans, and all he said was "It's O.K., man. She likes you. Come in."

She gave us a great supper of roast mutton and pumpkin fritters and samp, and then some preserved fruit. She stood over us, arms folded, as we ate, and when Johannes left some mutton fat, she said in her mellow hymn-singing voice: "Waste not, want not, Master Johannes." And he ate it all up. *Ja.* She told me I should have some more peaches for my health, but I defied her and I felt as guilty as a small kicker, and I could see Hans eyeing me down the table and wondering where I got the nerve. She lives in the *kia* at the back, one small room with four children by various fathers, but no man, because God is more than enough for her now, you can see, with all those kids and Hans to bring up the right way. Auntie's store is a Drapery and General Goods in the main street, called Gertie's Store, and Hans was running it with a coloured man. But I heard Esther with my own ears at supper saying to his bowed bald shamed head: "Master Johannes, I heard from the cook at the predikant's house today that the dried peaches have got worms in them." And Hans said: "O.K., Esther, I'll send them up some of the new stock tomorrow."

Right. We spent all that evening talking, and he was the same old Hans. You remember how he used to sit, saying not a blerry word, smiling that sweet dimpled smile of his, listening, listening, and then he'd ask a question, remember? Well, *do* you? Because it's only just now *I'm* beginning to remember. People'd be talking about I don't know what—the Nats or the weather or the grape crop, anything—and just as you'd start to get nervous because he never said anything, he'd lean forward and start questioning, terribly serious, earnest, about some detail, something not quite central, if you know what I mean. He'd lean forward, smiling, smiling, and he'd say: "You really mean that? It rained all morning? It rained all *morning*? Is that the truth?" That's right, you'd say, a bit uneasy, and he'd say, shaking his head: "God, man, it rained all morning, you say. . . ." And then there'd be a considerable silence till things picked up again. And half an hour later he'd say: "You really mean it? The hanepoort grapes are good this year?"

Right. We drank a good bit of brandewyn that night, but in a civilised way—you know: "Would you like another little drop, Martin?" "*Ja,* just a small tot Hans, thank you"—but we got pretty pickled, and when I woke Sunday morning, I felt like death, but Esther was setting down a tray of tea by my bed, all dressed up in her Sunday hat and her black silk saying: "*Goeie môre,* Master du Preez, it's nearly time for church," and I nearly said: "I'm not a churchgoer, Esther," but I thought better of it, because it came to me, can it be possible, has our Hans turned a God-fearing man in Blagspruit? So I said, "*Goed,* Esther. Thanks for telling me, and now just get out of here so that I can get dressed." Otherwise she'd have dressed me, I swear it. And she gave me a majestic nod, knowing that God had spoken through her to send me to church, sinner that I was and stinking of cheap *dop* from the night before.

Right. Johannes and I went to *kerk,* he in a black Sunday suit, if you'd believe such a thing, and saying: "Good morning, Mr. Stein. *Goeie môre,* Mrs. Van Esslin," a solid and respected member of the congregation, and I thought, poor *kerel,* there but for the grace of God go I, if I had to live in this godforsaken dorp stuck in the middle of the Orange Free State. And he looked like death after the brandewyn, and so did I, and we sat there swaying and sweating in that blerry little church through a sermon an hour and a half long, while all the faithful gave us nasty curious looks. Then we had a cold lunch, Esther having been worshipping at the Kaffir church down in the Location, and we slept it all off and woke covered with flies and sweating, and it was as hot as hell, which is what Blagspruit is, hell. And he'd been there ten years, man, ten years. . . .

Right. It is Esther's afternoon off, and Johannes says he will make us some tea, but I see he is quite lost without her, so I say: "Give me a glass of water, and let's get out from under this iron, that's all I ask." He looks surprised, because his hide is hardened to it, but off we go, through the dusty little garden full of marigolds and zinnias, you know those sun-baked gardens with the barbed-wire fences and the gates painted dried-blood colour in those little dorps stuck in the middle of the veld, enough to make you get drunk even to think of them, but Johannes is sniffing at the marigolds, which stink like turps, and he sticks an orange zinnia in his lapel, and says: "Esther likes gardening." And there we go along the main street, saying good afternoon to the citizens, for half a mile, then we're out in the veld again, just the veld. And we wander about, kicking up the dust and watching the sun sink, because both of us have just one idea, which is: how soon can we decently start sundowning?

Then there was a nasty stink on the air, and it came from a small bird impaled on a thorn on a thorn tree, which was a butcher-bird's cache, have you ever seen one? Every blerry thorn had a beetle or a worm or something stuck on it, and it made me feel pretty sick, coming on top of everything, and I was just picking up a stone to throw at the damned thorn tree, to spite the butcher-bird, when I saw Hans staring at a lower part of this tree. On a long black thorn was a great big brown beetle, and it was waving all its six legs and its two feelers in rhythm, trying to claw the thorn out of its middle, or so it looked, and it was writhing and wriggling, so that at last it fell off the thorn, which was at right angles, so to speak, from the soil, and it landed on its back, still waving its legs, trying to up itself. At which Hans bent down to look at it for some time, his two monk's hands on his upper thighs, his bald head sweating and glowing red in the last sunlight. *Then he bent down, picked up the beetle and stuck it back on the thorn.* Carefully, you understand, so that the thorn went back into the hole it had already made. You could see he was trying not to hurt the beetle. I just stood and gaped, like a *domkop,* and for some reason I remembered how one used to feel when he leaned forward and said, all earnest and involved: "You say the oranges are no good this year? Honestly, is that really true?" Anyway, I said: "Hans, man, for God's sake!" And then he looked at me, and he said, reproachfully: "The ants would have killed it, just look!" Well, the ground was swarming with ants of one kind or another, so there was logic in it, but I said: "Hans, let's drink, man, let's drink."

Well, it was Sunday, and no bars open. I took a last look at the beetle, the black thorn through its oozing middle, waving its black legs at the setting sun, and I said: "Back home, Hans, and to hell with Esther. We're going to get drunk."

Esther was in the kitchen, putting out cold meat and tomatoes, and I said: "Esther, you can take the evening off."

She said: "Master Hans, I have had all the Sunday afternoon off talking to Sister Mary." Hans looked helpless at me, and I said: "Esther, I'm giving you the evening off. Good night."

And Hans said, stuttering and stammering: "That's right, Esther, I'll give you the evening off. Good night, Esther."

She looked at him. Then at me. Hey, what a woman. Hey, what a queen, man! She said, with dignity: "Good night, Mr. Johannes. Good night, Mr. du Preez." Then she wiped her hands free of evil on her white apron, and she strode off, singing "All things bright and beautiful," and I tell you we felt as if we weren't good enough to wash Esther's *broekies,* and that's the truth.

Goed. We got out the brandy, never mind about the cold meat and the tomatoes, and about an hour later I reached my point at last, which was, what about the poems, and the reason I'd taken so long was I was scared he'd say: "Take a look at Blagspruit, man. Take a look. Is this the place for poems, Martin?" But when I asked, he leaned forward and stared at me, all earnest and intent, then he turned his head carefully to the right, to see if the door into the kitchen was shut, but it wasn't; and then left at the window, and that was open too, and then past me at the door to the verandah. Then he got up on tiptoes and very carefully shut all three, and then he drew the curtains. It gave me the *skriks,* man, I can tell you. Then he went to a great old black chest and took out a Manuscript, because it was all in the beautiful black difficult writing, and gave it to me to read. And I sat and slowly worked it out, letter by letter, while he sat opposite, sweating and totting, and giving fearful looks over his shoulders.

What was it? Well, I was drunk, for one thing, and Hans sitting there all frightened scared me, but it was good, it was good, I promise you. A kind of chronicle of Blagspruit it was, the lives of the citizens—well, need I elaborate, since the lives of citizens are the same everywhere in the world, but worse in Suid Afrika, and worse a million times in Blagspruit. The Manu Script gave off a stink of church and right-doing, with the sin and the evil underneath. It had a medieval stink to it, naturally enough, for what is worse than the kerk in this our land? But I'm saying this to you, remember, and I never said it, but what is worse than the stink of the kerk and the God-fearing in this our feudal land?

But the poem. As far as I can remember, because I was full as a tick, it was a sort of prose chronicle that led up to and worked into the poems; you couldn't tell where they began or ended. The prose was stiff and old-fashioned, and formal, monk's language, and the poems too. But I knew when I read it it was the best I'd read in years—since I read those poems of his ten years before, man, not since then. And don't forget, God help me, I'm an editor now, and I read poems day and night, and when I come on something like Hans's poems that night I have nothing to say but—*Goed.*

Right. I was working away there an hour or more because of that damned black ornamented script. Then I put it down and I said: "Hans, can I ask you a question?" And he looked this way and that over his shoulder first, then leaned forward, the lamplight shining on his pate, and he asked in a low trembling sinner's voice: "What do you want to ask me, Martin?"

I said, "Why this complicated handwriting? What for? It's beautiful, but why this monkey's puzzle?"

And he lowered his voice and said: "It's so that Esther can't read it."

I said: "And what of it, Hans? Why not? Give me some more brandewyn and tell me."

He said: "She's a friend of the predikant's cook, and her sister Mary works in the Mayor's kitchen."

I saw it all. I was drunk, so I saw it. I got up, and I said: "Hans, you're right. You're right a thousand times. If you're going to write stuff like this, as true and as beautiful as God and all his angels, then Esther mustn't read it. But why don't you let me take this back with me and print it in *Onwards*?"

He went white and looked as if I might knife him there and then like a *totsi*. He grabbed the manuscript from me and held it against his fat chest, and he said: "They mustn't see it."

"You're right," I said, understanding him completely.

"It's dangerous keeping it here," he said, darting fearful looks all around.

"Yes, you're right," I said, and I sat down with a bump in my *rimpie* chair, and I said: "*Ja,* if they found that, Hans. . . ."

"They'd kill me," he said.

I saw it, completely.

I was drunk. He was drunk. We put the manuscript *boekie* on the table and we put our arms around each other and we wept for the citizens of Blagspruit. Then we lit the hurricane lamp in the kitchen, and he took his *boekie* under his arm, and we tiptoed out into the moonlight that stank of marigolds, and out we went down the main street, all dark as the pit now because it was after twelve and the citizens were asleep, and we went staggering down the tarmacked street that shone in the moonlight between low dark houses, and out into the veld. There we looked sorrowfully at each other and wept some sad brandy tears, and right in front of us, the devil aiding us, was a thorn tree. All virgin it was, its big black spikes lifted up and shining in the devil's moon. And we wept a long time more, and we tore out the pages from his manuscript and we made them into little screws of paper and we stuck them all over the thorns, and when there were none left, we sat under the thorn tree in the moonlight, the black spiky thorns making thin purplish shadows all over us and over the white sand. Then we wept for the state of our country and the state of poetry. We drank a lot more brandy, and the ants came after it and us, so we staggered back down the gleaming sleeping main street of Blagspruit, and that's all I remember until Esther was standing over me with a tin tray that had a teapot, teacup, sugar and some condensed milk, and she was saying: "Master du Preez, where is Master Hans?"

I saw the seven o'clock sun outside the window, and I remembered everything, and I sat up and I said: "My God!"

And Esther said: "God has not been in this house since half past five on Saturday last." And went out.

Right. I got dressed, and went down the main street, drawing looks from the Monday morning citizens, all of whom had probably been watching us staggering along last night from behind their black drawn curtains. I reached the veld and there was Hans. A wind had got up, a hot dust-devilish wind, and it blew about red dust and bits of grit, and leaves, and dead grass into the blue sky, and those pale dry bushes that leave their roots and go bouncing and twirling all over the empty sand, like dervishes, round and around, and then up and around, and there was Hans, letting out yelps and cries and shouts, and he was chasing about after screws of paper that were whirling around among all the dust and stuff.

I helped him. The thorn tree had three squirls of paper tugging and blowing from spikes of black thorn, so I collected those, and we ran after the blowing white bits that had the black beautiful script on them, and we got perhaps a third back. Then we sat under the thorn tree, the hard sharp black shadows over us and the sand, and we watched a dust devil whirling columns of yellow sand and his poems up and off into the sky.

I said: "But Hans, you could write them down again, couldn't you? You couldn't have forgotten them, surely?"

And he said: "But Martin, anyone can read them now. Don't you see that, man? Esther could come out here next afternoon off, and pick any one of those poems up off the earth and read it. Or suppose the predikant or the Mayor got their hands on them?"

Then I understood. I promise you, it had never crossed my *domkop* mind until that moment. I swear it. I simply sat there, sweating out guilt and brandy, and I looked at that poor madman, and then I remembered back ten years and I thought: You idiot. You fool.

Then at last I got intelligent and I said: "But Hans, even if Esther and the predikant and the Mayor did come out here and pick up your poems, like leaves, off the bushes? They couldn't understand one word, because they are written in that *slim* black script you worked out for yourself."

I saw his poor crazy face get more happy, and he said: "You think so, Martin? Really? You really think so?"

I said: "*Ja,* it's the truth." And he got all happy and safe, while I thought of those poems whirling around forever, or until the next rainstorm, around the blue sky with the dust and the bits of shining grass.

And I said: "Anyway, at the best only perhaps a thousand, or perhaps two thousand, people would understand that beautiful *boekie.* Try to look at it that way, Hans, it might make you feel better."

By this time he looked fine; he was smiling and cheered up.

Right.

We got up and dusted each other off, and I took him home to Esther. I asked him to let me take the poems we'd rescued back to publish in *Onwards,* but he got desperate again and said: "No, no. Do you want to kill me? Do you want them to kill me? You're my friend, Martin, you can't do that."

So I told Esther that she had a great man in her charge, through whom Heaven Itself spoke, and she was right to take such care of him. But she merely nodded her queenly white-doeked head and said: "Goodbye, Master du Preez, and may God be with you."

So I came home to Kapstaad.

A week ago I got a letter from Hans, but I didn't see at once it was from him; it was in ordinary writing, like yours or mine, but rather unformed and wild, and it said: "I am leaving this place. They know me now. They look at me. I'm going north to the river. Don't tell Esther. *Jou vriend,* Johannes Potgieter."

Right.

Jou vriend,
Martin du Preez

Tadeusz Borowski was born to Polish parents in the Soviet Ukraine in 1922. Returning to Poland with his parents, he grew up in Warsaw, studied at the university, and had already begun his writing career, publishing a volume of poetry in 1942, when he was arrested by the Nazis; from 1943 to 1945, he was imprisoned in the concentration camps. He survived both Auschwitz and Dachau, and after the war, he published several volumes of stories, including a collection of concentration camp stories written in collaboration with two friends, which was published in 1946, and two volumes of his own camp stories, which were published in 1948. In 1951, at the age of twenty-nine, he committed suicide.

In his introduction to *This Way for the Gas, Ladies and Gentlemen* (1976), the collection in which "Auschwitz, Our Home (A Letter)" appears, Borowski's countryman Jan Kott says that Borowski "was the greatest hope of Polish literature among the generation of his contemporaries decimated by the war." The first of his camp stories to be published "produced a shock," Kott observes: "The public was expecting martyrologies; the Communist party called for works that were ideological, that divided the world into the righteous and the unrighteous, heroes and traitors, Communists and Fascists." As "Auschwitz, Our Home (A Letter)" makes clear, this was not what Borowski gave them. His perspective in these stories, one of "icy detachment," is articulated lucidly in a review Borowski wrote of a book about the camp: "The first duty of Auschwitzers is to make clear just what a camp is," he said. "But let them not forget that the reader will unfailingly ask: But how did it happen that *you* survived? . . . Tell, then, how you bought places in the hospital, easy posts, how you shoved the 'Moslems' [prisoners who had lost the will to live] into the oven, how you bought women, men, what you did in the barracks, unloading the transports, at the gypsy camp; tell about the daily life of the camp, about the hierarchy of fear, about the loneliness of every man. But write that you, you were the ones who did this. That a portion of the sad fame of Auschwitz belongs to you as well."

In reading "Auschwitz, Our Home (A Letter)," it is hard to know where fact leaves off and fiction begins, what is "real" and what is "story." Borowski's fiancée, to whom the letters are addressed, was certainly real: she was in the women's barracks at Birkenau. She too survived. After the war she and Borowski were married, and the couple had just had a child when Borowski took his life. Inseparable from that life, "Auschwitz Our Home (A Letter)" seems at once a document of survival and a testament to what that survival cost.

AUSCHWITZ, OUR HOME
(A LETTER)

I

So here I am, a student at the Auschwitz hospital. From the vast population of Birkenau, only ten of us were selected and sent here to be trained as medical orderlies, almost doctors. We shall be expected to know every bone in the human body, all about the circulatory system, what a peritoneum is, how to cure staphylococcus and streptococcus, how to take out an appendix, and the various symptoms of emphysema.

We shall be entrusted with a lofty mission: to nurse back to health our fellow inmates who may have the "misfortune" to become ill, suffer from severe apathy, or feel depressed about life in general. It will be up to us—the chosen ten out of Birkenau's twenty thousand—to lower the camp's mortality rate and to raise the prisoner's morale. Or, in short, that is what we were told by the S.S. doctor upon our departure from Birkenau. He then asked each of us our age and occupation, and when I answered "student" he raised his eyebrows in surprise.

"And what was it you studied?"

"The history of art," I answered modestly.

He nodded, but had obviously lost interest; he got into his car and drove away.

Afterwards we marched to Auschwitz along a very beautiful road, observing some very interesting scenery en route. Then we were assigned guest quarters at one of the Auschwitz hospital blocks, and as soon as this dreary procedure was over, Staszek (you know, the one who once gave me a pair of brown trousers) and I took off for the camp; I in search of someone who might deliver this letter to you, and Staszek to the kitchens and the supply rooms to round up some food for supper—a loaf of white bread, a piece of lard and at least one sausage, since there are five of us living together.

I was, naturally, entirely unsuccessful, my serial number being over one million, whereas this place swarms with very "old numbers" who look down their noses at million-plus fellows like me. But Staszek promised to take care of my letter through his own contacts, provided it was not too heavy. "It must be a bore to write to a girl every day," he told me.

So, as soon as I learn all the bones in the human body and find out what a peritoneum is, I shall let you know how to cure your skin rash and what the woman in the bunk next to yours ought to take for her fever. But I know that even if I discovered the remedy for *ulcus duodeni,* I would still be unable to get you the ordinary Wilkinson's itch ointment, because there just is none to be had at the camp. We simply used to douse our patients with mint tea, at the same time uttering certain very effective magic words, which, unfortunately, I cannot repeat.

As for lowering the camp's mortality rate: some time ago one of the "bigwigs" in our block fell ill; he felt terrible, had a high fever, and spoke more and more of dying. Finally one day he called me over. I sat down on the edge of the bed.

"Wouldn't you say I was fairly well known at the camp, eh?" he asked, looking anxiously into my eyes.

"There isn't one man around who wouldn't know you . . . and always remember you," I answered innocently.

"Look over there," he said, pointing at the window.

Tall flames were shooting up in the sky beyond the forest.

"Well, you see, I want to be put away separately. Not with all the others. Not on a heap. You understand?"

"Don't worry," I told him affectionately. "I'll even see to it that you get your own sheet. And I can put in a good word for you with the morgue boys."

He squeezed my hand in silence. But nothing came of it. He got well, and later sent me a piece of lard from the main camp. I use it to shine my shoes, for it happens to be made of fish oil. And so you have an example of my contribution to the lowering of the camp's mortality rate. But enough of camp talk for one day.

For almost a month now I have not had a letter from home . . .

II

What delightful days: no roll-call, no duties to perform. The entire camp stands at attention, but we, the lucky spectators from another planet, lean out of the window and gaze at the world. The people smile at us, we smile at the people, they call us "Comrades from Birkenau," with a touch of pity—our lot being so miserable—and a touch of guilt—theirs being so fortunate. The view from the window is almost pastoral—not one cremo in sight. These people over here are crazy about Auschwitz. "Auschwitz, our home . . ." they say with pride.

And, in truth, they have good reason to be proud. I want you to imagine what this place is like: take the dreary Pawiak, add Serbia,[1] multiply them by twenty-eight and plant these prisons so close together that only tiny spaces are left between them; then encircle the whole thing with a double row of barbed wire and build a concrete wall on three sides; put in paved roads in place of the mud and plant a few anaemic trees. Now lock inside fifteen thousand people who have all spent years in concentration camps, who have all suffered unbelievably and survived even the most terrible seasons, but now wear freshly pressed trousers and sway from side to side as they walk. After you had done all this you would understand why they look down with contempt and pity on their colleagues from Birkenau— where the barracks are made of wood, where there are no pavements, and where, in place of the bathhouses with hot running water, there are four crematoria.

From the orderlies' quarters, which have very white, rustic-looking walls, a cement floor, and many rows of triple-deck bunks, there is an excellent view of a "free-world" road. Here sometimes a man will pass; sometimes a car will drive by; sometimes a horse-drawn cart; and sometimes—a lonely bicycle, probably a labourer returning home after a day's work.

In the far distance (you have no idea what a vast expanse can fit between the frames of one small window; after the war, if I survive, I would like to live in a tall building with windows facing open fields), there are some houses, and beyond them a dark-blue forest. There the earth is black and it must be damp. As in one of Staff's[2] sonnets—"A Walk in Springtime," remember?

Another window looks out on a birch-lined path—the *Birkenweg*. In the evening, after the roll-call, we stroll along this path, dignified and solemn, and greet friends in passing with a discreet bow. At one of the crossings stands a road marker and a sculpture showing two men seated on a bench, whispering to each other, while a third leans over their shoulders and listens. This means: beware . . . every one of

1. Two Warsaw prisons.
2. A Polish lyrical poet.

your conversations is overheard, interpreted and reported to the proper authorities. In Auschwitz one man knows all there is to know about another: when he was a "Muslim," how much he stole and through whom, the number of people he has strangled, and the number of people he has ruined. And they grin knowingly if you happen to utter a word of praise about anyone else.

Well then, imagine a Pawiak, multiplied many times, and surrounded with a double row of barbed wire. Not at all like Birkenau, with its watch-towers that really look like storks perched on their high, long legs, with searchlights at only every third post, and but a single row of barbed wire.

No, it is quite different here: there are searchlights at every other post, watch-towers on solid cement bases, a double-thick fence, plus a high concrete wall.

So we stroll along the *Birkenweg,* clean-shaven, fresh, carefree. Other prisoners stand about in small groups, linger in front of block No. 10 where behind bars and tightly boarded-up windows there are girls—experimental guinea-pigs; but mostly they gather around the "educational" section, not because it houses a concert hall, a library, and a museum, but because up on the first floor there is the Puff. But I shall tell you about that in my next letter.

You know, it feels very strange to be writing to you, you whose face I have not seen for so long. At times I can barely remember what you look like—your image fades from my memory despite my efforts to recall it. And yet my dreams about you are incredibly vivid; they have an almost physical reality. A dream, you see, is not necessarily visual. It may be an emotional experience in which there is depth and where one feels the weight of an object and the warmth of a body . . .

It is hard for me to imagine you on a prison bunk, with your hair shaved off after the typhoid fever. I see you still as I saw you the last time at the Pawiak prison: a tall, willowy young woman with sad eyes and a gentle smile. Later, at the Gestapo headquarters, you sat with your head bent low, so I could see nothing but your black hair that has now been shaven off.

And this is what has remained most vivid in my memory: this picture of you, even though I can no longer clearly recall your face. And that is why I write you such long letters—they are our evening talks, like the ones we used to have on Staryszewska Street. And that is why my letters are not sad. I have kept my spirit and I know that you have not lost yours either. Despite everything. Despite your hidden face at the Gestapo headquarters, despite the typhoid fever, despite the pneumonia—and despite the shaved head.

But the people here . . . you see, they have lived through and survived all the incredible horrors of the concentration camp, the concentration camp of the early years, about which one hears so many fantastic stories. At one time they weighed sixty pounds or less, they were beaten, selected for the gas chamber—you can understand, then, why today they wear ridiculous tight jackets, walk with a characteristic sway, and have nothing but praise of Auschwitz.

We stroll along the *Birkenweg,* elegant, dressed in our civilian suits; but alas—our serial numbers are so high! And around us are nothing but one-hundred-and-three thousand, one-hundred-and-nineteen thousand . . . What a pity we did not get here a little sooner! A man in prison stripes approaches us: his number is twenty-seven thousand—it almost makes your head swim! A young fellow with the glassy stare of a masturbator and the walk of a hunted animal.

"Where're you from, comrades?"

"From Birkenau, friend."

"From Birkenau?" He examines us with a frown. "And looking so well? Awful, awful . . . How do you stand it over there?"

Witek, my skinny, tall friend and an excellent musician, pulls down his shirt cuffs.

"Unfortunately we had some trouble getting a piano, but otherwise we managed," he retorts.

The "old number" looks at us as though he were looking through dense fog.

"Because . . . around here we're afraid of Birkenau . . ."

III

Again the start of our training has been postponed, as we are awaiting the arrival of orderlies from neighbouring camps: from Janin, Jaworzyn and Buna, and from some more distant camps that are nevertheless part of Auschwitz. Meanwhile, we have had to listen to several lofty speeches made by our chief, black, dried-up little Adolf, who has recently come from Dachau and exudes *Kameradschaft.* By training orderlies, he expects to improve the camp's health, and by teaching us all about the nervous system, to reduce the mortality rate. Adolf is extremely pleasant and really out of another world. But, being a German, he fails to distinguish between reality and illusion, and is inclined to take words at their face value, as if they always represented the truth. He says *Kameraden* and thinks that such a thing is possible. Above the gates leading to the camp, these words are inscribed on metal scrolls: "Work makes one free." I suppose they believe it, the S.S. men and the German prisoners—those raised on Luther, Fichte, Hegel, Nietzsche.

And so, for the time being we have no school. I roam around the camp, sightseeing and making psychological notes for myself. In fact, three of us roam together—Staszek, Witek and I. Staszek usually hangs around the kitchens and the supply rooms, searching for men whom he has helped in the past and who he now expects will help him. And, sure enough, towards evening the procession begins. Odd, suspicious-looking characters come and go, their clean-shaven faces smiling compassionately. From the pockets of their tightly fitted jackets they pull out a piece of margarine, some white hospital bread, a slice of sausage, or a few cigarettes. They set these down on the lower bunk and disappear, as in a silent film. We divide the loot, add to it what we have received in our packages from home, and cook a meal on our stove with the colourful tiles.

Witek spends his time in a tireless search for a piano. There is one large black crate in the music room, which is located in the same block as the Puff, but playing during work hours is forbidden, and after the roll-call the piano is monopolized by the musicians who give symphony concerts every Sunday. Some day I must go to hear them.

Across from the music room we have spotted a door with "Library" written on it, but we have heard through reliable sources that it is for the *Reichsdeutsch* only, and contains nothing but mystery stories. I have not been able to verify this, for the room is always locked up as tight as a coffin.

Next door to the library is the political office, and beyond it, to complete the "cultural section," the museum. It houses photographs confiscated from the prisoners' letters. Nothing more. And what a pity— for it would have been interesting to have on exhibit that half-cooked human liver, a tiny nibble of which cost a Greek friend of mine twenty-five lashes across his rear-end.

But the most important place of all is one flight up. The Puff. Its windows are left slightly open at all times, even in winter. And from the windows—after roll-call—peek out pretty little heads of various shades of colour, with delicate shoulders, as white and fresh as snow, emerging from their frilly blue, pink and sea-green robes (the green is my favourite colour). Altogether there are, I am told, fifteen little heads, not counting the old Madame with the tremendous, legendary breasts, who watches over the little heads, the white shoulders, etc. . . . The Madame does not lean out of the window, but, like watchful Cerberus, officiates at the entrance to the Puff.

The Puff is for ever surrounded by a crowd of the most important citizens of the camp. For every Juliet there are at least a thousand Romeos. Hence the crowd, and the competition. The Romeos stand along the windows of the barracks across the street; they shout, wave, invite. The Camp Elder and the Camp Kapo are there, and so are the doctors from the hospital and the Kapos from the Kommandos. It is not unusual for a Juliet to have a steady admirer, and along with promises of undying love and a blissful life together after the war, along with reproaches and bickering, one is apt to hear exchanges of a more basic nature, concerning such particulars as soap, perfume, silk panties, or cigarettes.

But there is a great deal of loyalty among the men: they do not compete unfairly. The girls at the windows are tender and desirable, but, like goldfish in an aquarium, unattainable.

This is how the Puff looks from the outside. To get inside you need a slip of paper issued by the clerical office as a reward for good conduct and diligent work. As guests from Birkenau, we were offered priority in this regard also, but we declined the favour; let the criminals use the facilities intended for them. Forgive me, therefore, but my report must be of necessity only second-hand, although it relies on such excellent witnesses as, for example, old prisoner M from our barracks, whose serial number is almost three times lower than the last two figures in mine. One of the original founding fathers, you know! Which is why he rocks from side to side like a duck when he walks, and wears wide, carefully pressed trousers secured in front with safety pins. In the evening he returns to the barracks excited and happy. His system is to go to the clerical office when the numbers of the "elect" are being called, waiting to see if there will be an absentee. When this happens, he shouts *hier,* snatches the pass and races over to the Madame. He slips several packets of cigarettes in her hand, undergoes a few treatments of a hygienic nature, and, all sprayed and fresh, leaps upstairs. The Juliets stroll along the narrow hallway, their fluffy robes carelessly wrapped around them. In passing, one of them may ask prisoner M indifferently:

"What number have you got?"

"Eight," he answers, glancing at his slip to make sure.

"Ah, it's not for me, it's for Irma, the little blonde over there," she will mutter and walks back to the window, her hips swaying softly.

Then prisoner M goes to room No. 8. Before he enters, he must read a notice on the door saying that such and such is strictly forbidden, under severe penalty, that only such and such (a detailed list follows) is allowed, but only for so many minutes. He sighs at the sight of a spy-hole, which is occasionally used for peeping by the other girls, occasionally by the Madame, or the Puff's Kommandoführer, or the camp Kommandant himself. He drops a packet of cigarettes on the table, and . . . oh, at the same time he notices two packets of English cigarettes on top of the dresser. Then he does what he has come for and departs . . . absent-mindedly slipping the English cigarettes into his pocket. Once more he undergoes a disinfecting treatment, and later, pleased with himself and cheerful, he relates his adventure to us blow by blow.

But once in a while all the precautions fail . . . only recently the Puff again became contaminated. The place was locked up, the customers, traced through their numbers, were called in and subjected to a radical treatment. But, because of the flourishing black-market in passes, in most cases the wrong men underwent the cure. Ha, such is life. The Puff girls also used to make trips inside the camp. Dressed in men's suits, they would climb down a ladder in the middle of the night to join a drinking brawl or an orgy of some kind. But an S.S. guard from a near-by sector did not like it, and that was the end of that.

There is another place where women may be found: No. 10, the experimental block. The women in No. 10 are being artificially inseminated, injected with typhoid and malaria germs, or operated on. I once caught a glimpse of the man who heads the project: a man in a green hunting outfit and a gay little Tyrolian hat decorated with many brightly shining sports emblems, a man with the face of a kindly satyr. A university professor, I am told.

The women are kept behind barred and boarded-up windows, but still the place is often broken into and the women are inseminated, not at all artificially. This must make the old professor very angry indeed.

But you must not misunderstand—these men are not maniacs or perverts. Every man in the camp, as soon as he has had enough food and sleep, talks about women. Every man in the camp dreams about women. Every man in the camp tries to get hold of a woman. One camp Elder wound up in a penal transport for repeatedly climbing through the window into the Puff. A nineteen-year-old S.S. man once caught the orchestra conductor, a stout, respectable gentleman, and several dentists inside an ambulance in unambiguous positions with the female patients who had come to have their teeth pulled. With a club which he happened to have in his hand, the young S.S. man administered due punishment across the most readily available parts of their anatomy. An episode of this sort is no discredit to anyone: you are unlucky if you are caught, that is all.

The woman obsession in the camp increases steadily. No wonder the Puff girls are treated like normal women with whom one talks of love and family. No wonder the men are so eager to visit the F.K.L. in Birkenau. And stop to think, this is true not only of Auschwitz, it is true also of hundreds of "great" concentration camps, hundreds of *Oflags* and *Stalags* . . .

Do you know what I am thinking about as I write to you?

It is late evening. Separated by a large cabinet from the rest of the huge sick-ward full of heavily breathing patients, I sit alone by a dark window which reflects my face, the green lampshade, and the white sheet of paper on the table. Franz, a young boy from Vienna, took a liking to me the very first evening he arrived—so now I am sitting at his table, under his lamp, and am writing this letter to you on his paper. But I shall not write about the subjects we were discussing today at the camp: German literature, wine, romantic philosophy, problems of materialism.

Do you know what I am thinking about?

I am thinking about Staryszewska Street. I look at the dark window, at my face reflected in the glass, and outside I see the blackness occasionally broken by the sudden flash of the watch-tower searchlight that silhouettes fragments of objects in the dark. I look into the night and I think of Staryszewska Street. I remember the sky, pale and luminous, and the bombed-out house across the street. I think of how much I longed for your body during those days, and I often smile to myself imagining the consternation after my arrest when they must have found in my room, next to my books and my poems, your perfume and your robe, heavy and red like the brocades in Velazquez's paintings.

I think of how very mature you were; what devotion and—forgive me if I say it now—selflessness you brought to our love, how graciously you used to walk into my life which offered you nothing but a single room without plumbing, evenings with cold tea, a few wilting flowers, a dog that was always playfully gnawing at your shoes, and a paraffin lamp.

I think about these things and smile condescendingly when people speak to me of morality, of law, of tradition, of obligation . . . Or when they discard all tenderness and sentiment and, shaking their fists, proclaim this the age of toughness. I smile and I think that one human being must always be discovering another—through love. And that this is the most important thing on earth, and the most lasting.

And I think about my cell at the Pawiak prison. During the first week I felt I would not be able to endure a day without a book, without the circle of light under the paraffin lamp in the evening, without a sheet of paper, without you . . .

And indeed, habit is a powerful force: will you believe it, I paced up and down the cell and composed poems to the rhythm of my steps. One of them I wrote down in a cellmate's copy of the Bible, but the rest—and they were poems conceived in the style of Horace—I no longer remember.

IV

Today is Sunday. In the morning we made another little sightseeing tour, took a look at the exterior of the women's experimental block (they push out their heads between the bars, just like the rabbits my father used to keep; do you remember—grey ones with one floppy ear?), and then we toured the S.K. block (in its courtyard is the famous Black Wall where mass executions used to be carried out; today such business is handled more quietly and discreetly—in the crematoria). We saw some civilians: two frightened women in fur coats and a man with tired, worried eyes. Led by an S.S. man, they were being taken to the city jail which is temporarily located in the S.K. block. The women gazed with horror at the prisoners in stripes and at the massive camp installations: the two-storey barracks, the double row of barbed wire, the concrete wall beyond it, the solid watch-towers. And they did not even know that the wall extends two yards into the ground, to prevent us from digging our way out! We smiled to cheer them up: after all, in a few weeks they will be released. Unless, of course, it is proved that they did indeed dabble in black marketeering. In that case they will go to the cremo. But they are really quite amusing, these civilians. They react to the camp as a wild boar reacts to firearms. Understanding nothing of how it functions, they look upon it as something inexplicable, almost abnormal, something beyond human endurance. Remember the horror you felt when they arrested you?

Today, having become totally familiar with the inexplicable and the abnormal; having learned to live on intimate terms with the crematoria, the itch and the tuberculosis; having understood the true meaning of wind, rain and sun, of bread and turnip soup, of work to survive, of slavery and power; having, so to say, daily broken bread with the beast— I look at these civilians with a certain indulgence, the way a scientist regards a layman, or the initiated an outsider.

Try to grasp the essence of this pattern of daily events, discarding your sense of horror and loathing and contempt, and find for it all a philosophic formula. For the gas chambers and the gold stolen from the victims, for the roll-call and for the Puff, for the frightened civilians and for the "old numbers."

If I had said to you as we danced together in my room in the light of the paraffin lamp: listen, take a million people, or two million, or three, kill them in such a way that no one knows about it, not even they themselves, enslave several hundred thousand more, destroy their mutual loyalty, pit man against man, and . . . surely you would have thought me mad. Except that I would probably not have said these things to you, even if I had known what I know today. I would not have wanted to spoil our mood.

But this is how it is done: first just one ordinary barn, brightly whitewashed—and here they proceed to asphyxiate people. Later, four large buildings, accommodating twenty thousand at a time without any trouble. No hocus-pocus, no poison, no hypnosis. Only several men directing traffic to keep operations running smoothly, and the thousands flow along like water from an open tap. All this happens just beyond the anaemic trees of the dusty little wood. Ordinary trucks bring people, return, then bring some more. No hocus-pocus, no poison, no hypnosis.

Why is it that nobody cries out, nobody spits in their faces, nobody jumps at their throats? We doff our caps to the S.S. men returning from the little wood; if our name is called we obediently go with them to die, and—we do nothing. We starve, we are drenched by rain, we are torn from our families. What is this mystery? This strange power of one man over another? This insane passivity that cannot be overcome? Our only strength is our great number—the gas chambers cannot accommodate all of us.

Or here is another way: the spade handle across the throat—that takes care of about a hundred people daily. Or, first nettle soup and dry bread and a number tattooed on your arm, and then a young, beefy S.S. man comes around with a dirty slip of paper in his hand, and then you are put in one of those trucks . . . Do you know when was the last time that the "Aryans" were selected for the gas chamber? April 4th. And do you remember when we arrived at the camp? April 29th. Do you realize what would have happened—and you with pneumonia—if we had arrived just a few months earlier?

The women who share your bunk must find my words rather surprising. "You told us he was so cheerful. And what about this letter? It's so full of gloom!" And probably they are a little bit shocked. But I think that we should speak about all the things that are happening around us. We are not evoking evil irresponsibly or in vain, for we have now become a part of it . . .

Once again it is late evening after a day full of curious happenings.

In the afternoon we went to see a boxing match in the huge *Waschraum* barracks used in the old days as the starting point for transports going to the gas chamber. We were led up to the front, although the hall was packed to capacity. The large waiting-room had been turned into a boxing ring. Floodlights overhead, a real referee (an Olympic referee from Poland, in fact), boxing stars of international fame, but only Aryans—Jews are not allowed to participate. And the very same people who knock out dozens of teeth every day or who themselves have no teeth left inside their mouths, were now enthusiastically cheering Czortek, or Walter from Hamburg, or a young boy trained at the camp who has apparently developed into a first-class fighter. The memory of No. 77, who once fought and mercilessly defeated the Germans in the ring, revenging there what the other prisoners had to endure in the field, is still very much alive. The hall was thick with cigarette smoke and the fighters knocked each other around to their heart's content. A bit unprofessionally perhaps, but with considerable perseverance.

"Just take a look at old Walter!" cried Staszek. "At the Kommando he can strike down a "Muslim" with one blow whenever the spirit moves him! And up here—it's already the third round and nothing happens! He's really getting a beating! Too many spectators I reckon, don't you think?"

The spectators indeed seemed to be in their seventh heaven, and there were we, seated, sure enough, in the front row, as befitted important guests.

Right after the boxing match I took in another show—I went to hear a concert. Over in Birkenau you could probably never imagine what feats of culture we are exposed to up here, just a few kilometres away from the smouldering chimneys. Just think—an orchestra playing the overture to *Tancred*, then something by Berlioz, then some Finnish dances by one of those composers with many 'a's in his name. Warsaw would not be ashamed of such music! But let me describe the whole thing from the beginning: I walked out of the boxing match, exhilarated and pleased, and immediately made way to the Puff block. The concert hall, located directly below the Puff, was crowded and noisy. People stood against the walls; the musicians, scattered throughout the room, were tuning their instruments. Over by the window—a raised platform. The kitchen Kapo (who is the orchestra conductor) mounted it; whereupon the potato peelers and cart pushers (I forgot to tell you that the orchestra members spend their days peeling potatoes and pushing carts) began to play. I sank into an empty chair between the clarinet and the bassoon and became lost in the music. Imagine—a thirty-piece orchestra in one ordinary room! Do you know what a volume of sound that can produce? The Kapo-conductor waved his arms with restraint, trying not to strike the wall, and clearly shook his fist at anyone who happened to hit a sour note, as if to warn him: "You'll pay for it in the potato field!" The players at the far end of the room (one at the drums, the other with the viola) tried to improvise as best they could. But almost all the instruments seemed drowned out by the bassoon, maybe because I was seated right by it. An audience of fifteen (there was no room for more) listened with the air of connoisseurs and rewarded the musicians with a little scattered applause . . . Somebody once called our camp *Betrugslager*—a fraud and a mockery. A little strip of lawn at the edge of the barracks, a yard resembling a village square, a sign reading "bath," are enough to fool millions of people, to deceive them until death. A mere boxing match, a green hedge along the wall, two deutsche marks per month for the more diligent prisoners, mustard in the canteen, a weekly delousing inspection, and the *Tancred* overture suffice to deceive the world—and us. People on the outside know that, of course, life over here is terrible; but after all, perhaps it is not really so bad if there is a symphony orchestra, and boxing, and green little lawns, and blankets on the bunks . . . But a bread ration that is not sufficient to keep you alive—is a mockery.

Work, during which you are not allowed to speak up, to sit down, to rest, is a mockery. And every half empty shovelful of earth that we toss on to the embankment is a mockery.

Look carefully at everything around you, and conserve your strength.

For a day may come when it will be up to us to give an account of the fraud and mockery to the living—to speak up for the dead.

Not long ago, the labour Kommandos used to march in formation when returning to camp. The band played and the passing columns kept step with its beat. One day the D.A.W.[3] Kommando and many of the others—some ten thousand men—were ordered to stop and stood waiting at the gate. At that moment several trucks full of naked women rolled in from the F.K.L. The women stretched out their arms and pleaded:

"Save us! We are going to the gas chambers! Save us!"

And they rode slowly past us—the ten thousand silent men—and then disappeared from sight. Not one of us made a move, not one of us lifted a hand.

V

Our medical training has now been in progress for some time, but I have written little to you about it, because the attic where we work is very cold. We sit on "organized" stools and have a tremendously good time, particularly when we can fool around with the large models of the human body. The more serious students try to learn what this is all about, but Witek and I spend most of our time hurling sponges at one another or duelling with rulers, which brings Black Adolf close to despair. He waves his arms above our heads and talks about *Kameradschaft* and about the camp in general. We retreat quietly into a corner; Witek pulls a photograph of his wife out of his pocket, and asks in a muffled tone:

"I wonder how many men he's murdered over in Dachau? Otherwise, why would he be carrying on in this way? . . . How would you like to strangle him? . . ."

"Uhm . . . a good-looking woman, your wife. How did you ever get her?"

"One day we went for a walk in Pruszkow.[4] You know how it is—everything fresh and green, narrow winding paths, woods all around. We were walking along, happy and relaxed, when all at once an S.S. dog jumped out of the bushes and came straight at us."

3. Scrap and demolition Kommando.
4. A wooded suburb of Warsaw.

"Liar! That was Pruszkow, not Auschwitz."

"An S.S. dog, I mean it—because the house near by had been taken over by the S.S. And the cur came straight at my girl! Well, what was I to do? I shot a few slugs into his hide, I grabbed the girl and said: 'Come on, Irene, we'd better get out of here!' But she did not budge an inch—just stood there, stupefied, and stared at the revolver. 'Where did you get that!' I barely managed to drag her away, I could already hear voices approaching. We ran straight across the fields, like two scared rabbits. It took me some time before I was able to convince Irene that this piece of iron was indispensable in my work."

Meanwhile another doctor had begun to lecture about the oesophagus and other such things found inside the human body, but Witek went on, unruffled:

"Once I had a fight with a friend of mine. It's got to be him or me, I thought to myself. And the same idea, I felt certain, had occurred to him. I tailed him for about three days, but always taking care that there was nobody behind me. Finally I cornered him one evening over on Chmielna Street and I let him have it, except that I missed the right spot. The next day I went around—his arm was all bandaged up and he stared at me grimly. 'I've fallen down,' he said."

"And so what did you do?" I asked, finding the story rather timely.

"Nothing, because immediately after that I was locked up."

Whether his friend had anything to do with it or not is difficult to say, but Witek nevertheless refused to let fate get the better of him. At the Pawiak prison he became washroom attendant—a kind of helper to Kronschmidt who, together with one Ukrainian, used to amuse himself torturing Jews. You remember the cellars of Pawiak; the metal floors they had down there. Well, the Jews, naked, their bodies steaming after a hot bath, were forced to crawl over them, back and forth, back and forth. And have you ever seen the soles of military boots, studded with heavy nails? Well, Kronschmidt, wearing such boots, would climb on top of a naked man and make him crawl while he rode on his back. The Aryans were not treated quite as badly, although I too crawled on the floor, but in a different section, and nobody climbed on top of me; and it was not an ordinary occurrence but rather punishment for misbehaviour. In addition, we had physical training: one hour every two days. First running around the yard, then falling to the ground and push-ups. Good, healthy exercise!

My record—seventy-six push-ups, and terrible pain in the arms until the next time. But the best exercise of all was the group game "Air raid, take cover!" Two rows of prisoners, chests pressed against backs, hold a ladder on their shoulders, supporting it with one hand. At the call "Air raid, take cover!" they fall to the ground, still holding the ladder on their shoulders. Whoever lets go, dies under the blows of the club. And then an S.S. man starts walking back and forth on the rungs of the ladder lying across your body. Then you must stand up and, without changing formation, fall down again.

You see, the inexplicable actually happens: you do miles of somersaults; spend hours simply rolling on the ground; you do hundreds of squat-jumps; you stand motionless for endless days and nights; you sit for a full month inside a cement coffin—the bunker; you hang from a post or a wooden pole extended between two chairs; you jump like a frog and crawl like a snake; drink bucketfuls of water until you suffocate; you are beaten with a thousand different whips and clubs, by a thousand different men. I listen avidly to tales about prisons—unknown provincial prisons like Malkini, Suwalki, Radom, Pulawy, Lublin—about the monstrously perfected techniques for torturing man, and I find it impossible to believe that all this just sprang suddenly out of somebody's head, like Minerva out of Jove's. I find it impossible to comprehend this sudden frenzy of murder, this mounting tide of unleashed atavism . . .

And another thing: death. I was told about a camp where transports of new prisoners arrived each day, dozens of people at a time. But the camp had only a certain quantity of daily food rations—I cannot recall how much, maybe enough for two, maybe three thousand—and Herr Kommandant disliked to see the prisoners starve. Each man, he felt, must receive his allotted portion. And always the camp had a few dozen men too many. So every evening a ballot, using cards or matches, was held in every block, and the following morning the losers did not go to work. At noon they were led out behind the barbed-wire fence and shot.

And in the midst of the mounting tide of atavism stand men from a different world, men who conspire in order to end conspiracies among people, men who steal so that there will be no more stealing in the world, men who kill so that people will cease to murder one another.

Witek, you see, was such a man—a man from a different world—so he became the right-hand man to Kronschmidt, the most notorious killer at the Pawiak prison. But now he sat next to me, listening to what is inside the human body and how to cure whatever ails it with home-made remedies. Later there was a small row in the classroom. The doctor turned to Staszek, the fellow who is so good at "organizing," and asked him to repeat everything he had been taught about the liver. Staszek repeated, but incorrectly.

"What you have just said is very stupid, and furthermore you might stand up when you answer," said the doctor.

"I'll sit if I want to,' retorted Staszek, his face reddening. "And furthermore, you don't have to insult me, Herr Doktor."

"Quiet, you're in a classroom!"

"Naturally you want me to keep quiet, or I might say too much about some of your activities at the camp . . ."

Whereupon all of us started banging against the stools, screaming "yes! yes!" and the doctor flew out of the door. Adolf arrived, thundered for a few minutes about *Kameradschaft,* and we were sent back to our barracks—right in the middle of the digestive system. Staszek immediately rushed out in search of his friends, just in case the doctor should try to make trouble for him. But I am convinced he will not, because Staszek has powerful backing. One thing we have learned well about anatomy: at the camp you are not likely to trip if you stand on the shoulders of men who have influence. As for the doctor, many of his camp activities are common knowledge. It seems that he learned surgery experimenting with the sick. Who knows how many patients he has slashed to bits in the name of scientific research, and how many through sheer ignorance. No doubt quite a few, for the hospital is always crowded and the mortuary always full.

As you read this letter you must be thinking that I have completely forgotten the world we left behind. I go on and on about the camp, about its various aspects, trying to unravel their deeper significance, as though there were to be no future for us except right here . . .

But I do remember our room. The little Thermos bottle you once bought for me. It did not fit inside my pocket, so—to your dismay—it ended up under the bed. Or the round-up of civilians at Zoliborz, the course of which you kept reporting to me all through the day on the telephone—that the Germans were dragging people out of the trolley buses but you had got off at the previous stop; that the entire block was surrounded, but you managed to escape across the fields, all the way to the Vistula. Or what you used to say to me when I complained about the war, about the inhumanity of man, and worried that we should grow up to be a generation of illiterates:

"Think of those who are in concentration camps. We are merely wasting time, while they suffer agonies."

Much of what I once said was naïve, immature. And it seems to me now that perhaps we were not really wasting time. Despite the madness of war, we lived for a world that would be different. For a better world to come when all this is over. And perhaps even our being here is a step towards that world. Do you really think that, without the hope that such a world is possible, that the rights of man will be restored again, we could stand the concentration camp even for one day? It is that very hope that makes people go without a murmur to the gas chambers, keeps them from risking a revolt, paralyses them into numb inactivity. It is hope that breaks down family ties, makes mothers renounce their children, or wives sell their bodies for bread, or husbands kill. It is hope that compels man to hold on to one more day of life, because that day may be the day of liberation. Ah, and not even the hope for a different, better world, but simply for life, a life of peace and rest. Never before in the history of mankind has hope been stronger than man, but never also has it done so much harm as it has in this war, in this concentration camp. We were never taught how to give up hope, and this is why today we perish in gas chambers.

Observe in what an original world we are living: how many men can you find in Europe who have never killed; or whom somebody does not wish to kill?

But still we continue to long for a world in which there is love between men, peace, and serene deliverance from our baser instincts. This, I suppose, is the nature of youth.

P.S. And yet, first of all, I should like to slaughter one or two men, just to throw off the concentration camp mentality, the effects of continual subservience, the effects of helplessly watching others being beaten and murdered, the effects of all this horror. I suspect, though, that I will be marked for life. I do not know whether we shall survive, but I like to think that one day we shall have the courage to tell the world the whole truth and call it by its proper name.

VI

For some days now we have had regular entertainment at midday: a column of men marches out of the *für Deutsche* block and, loudly singing

Morgen Nach Heimat, tramps round and round the camp, with the Camp Elder in the lead, marking time with his cane.

These men are the criminals, or army "volunteers." Those who are guilty of petty crimes will be shipped to the front lines. But the fellow who butchered his wife and mother-in-law, and then let the canary out of its cage so that the poor little creature should not be unhappy in captivity, is the lucky one—he will remain in the camp. Meanwhile, however, all of them are here. One happy family!

They are being taught the art of marching and are watched for any signs that they may be developing a sense of social responsibility. As a matter of fact, they have exhibited a considerable amount of "social" initiative and have already managed to break into the supply rooms, to steal some packages, destroy the canteen and demolish the Puff (so it is closed again, to everyone's sorrow). "Why in hell," they say—and very wisely—"should we go and fight and risk our necks for the S.S.? . . . And who is going to polish our boots out there? We're quite satisfied to stay right here! Our glorious Fatherland? It will fall to pieces without any assistance from us . . . and out there, who will polish our boots, and how are we going to get pretty young boys?"

So the gang marches along the road singing "Tomorrow we march home." Notorious thugs, one and all: Seppel, the terror of the *Dachdecker,* who mercilessly forces you to work in rain, snow and freezing weather and shoves you off the roof if you hammer a nail in crookedly; Arno Böhm, number eight, an old-time Block Elder, Kapo and Camp Kapo, who used to kill men for selling tea in the black market and administered twenty-five lashes for every minute you were late and every word you uttered after the evening gong; he is also the man who always wrote short but touching letters, filled with love and nostalgia, to his old parents in Frankfurt. We recognize all of them: that one beat the prisoners at the D.A.W.; this one was the terror of Buna; the one next to him, the weakling, used to steal regularly and was therefore sent to the camp and put in charge of some miserable Kommando. There they go—one after the other—well-known homosexuals, alcoholics, dope addicts, sadists; and way in the back marches Kurt—well dressed, looking carefully around. He is not in step with the others, and he is not singing. After all, I thought to myself, it was he who managed to find you for me and who then carried our letters. So I raced downstairs and said to him: "Kurt, I am sure you must be hungry. Why don't you come up—you enlisted criminal?" And I pointed at our windows. And indeed he showed up at our place in the evening, just in time for the dinner which we had cooked on our big tile stove.

Kurt is very nice (it sounds odd, but I cannot think of a better word) and really knows how to tell stories. He once wanted to be a musician, but his father, a prosperous storekeeper, threw him out of the house. Kurt went to Berlin. There he met a girl, the daughter of another storekeeper, lived with her, did some writing for the sports magazines, spent a month in jail after a row with a *Stahlhelm,* and afterwards never went back to see the girl. He managed to acquire a sports car and he smuggled currency. He saw the girl once on the street, but he did not have the nerve to speak to her. Then he took trips to Yugoslavia and Austria until he was caught and put in jail. And since he already had a record (that unfortunate first month), after the jail it was the concentration camp for him and the waiting for the war to end.

It is late evening—way past roll-call. Several of us sit around the table, telling stories. Everybody here tells stories—on the way to work, returning to the camp, working in the fields and in the trucks, in the bunks at night, standing at roll-call. Stories from books and stories from life. And almost always about the world outside the barbed-wire fence. But somehow today we cannot get away from camp tales, maybe because Kurt is about to leave.

"Actually, people on the outside knew very little about the camp. Sure, we had heard about the pointless work, paving roads, for example, only to tear them up again, or the endless spreading of gravel. And, of course, about how terrible it all is. Various tales were circulated. But, to tell the truth, we weren't particularly interested in all this. We were certain of only one thing—once you got in, you didn't get out."

"If you'd been here two years ago, the wind would have blown your ashes out of the chimney long ago," interrupted Staszek (the one who is such an expert at "organizing").

I shrugged. "Maybe it would have, and maybe not. It hasn't blown yours out, so it might not have blown mine out either. You know, back in Pawiak we once had a fellow from Auschwitz."

"Sent back for a trial, I suppose."

"Exactly. So we started asking him questions, but he wouldn't talk, oh no. All he'd say was: 'Come and you'll see for yourself. Why should I waste my breath? It would be like talking to children.' "

"Were you afraid of the camp?"

"Yes, I was afraid. We left Pawiak in the morning, and were driven to the station in trucks. It's not good—the sun is behind our backs, we thought. That means the West station. Auschwitz. They loaded us quickly into the freight trains, sixty in each car, in alphabetical order. It wasn't even too crowded."

"Were you allowed to bring some of your things?"

"Yes, I was. I took a blanket and a robe given to me by my girl, and two sheets."

"You were a fool. You should have left them for your friends. Didn't you know they'd take everything away?"

"I suppose so, but . . . And then we pulled all the nails out of one wall, tore the planks away, and started to climb out! But up on the roof they had a machine gun and promptly cut down the first three men. The fourth foolishly stuck his head out of the car and got a bullet right in the back of the neck. Immediately the train was stopped and we squeezed ourselves against the corners of the car. There were screams, curses—total hell! 'Didn't I tell you not to do it?' 'Cowards!' 'They'll kill us all!' and swearing, but what swearing!"

"Not worse than in the woman's section?"

"No, not worse, but very strong stuff, believe me. And there I sat, under the heap of people, at the very bottom. And I thought to myself: Good, when they start shooting I won't be the first to get it. And it was good. They did shoot. They fired a series of bullets right into the heap, killed two, wounded one in the abdomen, and *los, aus,* without our belongings! Well, I thought, that's it. Now they'll finish us all off. I was a little sad about leaving the robe, since I had a Bible hidden in the pocket, and anyway, you see, it was from my girl."

"Didn't you say the blanket too was from your girl?"

"It was. I also regretted leaving the blanket. But I couldn't take anything because they threw me down the steps. You have no idea how tremendous the world looks when you fall out of a closed, packed freight car! The sky is so high . . ."

" . . . and blue . . ."

"Exactly, blue, and the trees smell wonderful. The forest—you want to take it in your hand! The S.S. men surrounded us on all sides, holding their automatics. They took four men aside and herded the rest of us into another car. Now we travelled one hundred and twenty of us in one car, plus three dead and one wounded. We nearly suffocated. It was so hot that water ran from the ceiling, literally. Not one tiny window, nothing, the whole car was boarded up. We shouted for air and water, but when they started shooting, we shut up instantly. Then we all collapsed on the floor and lay panting, like slaughtered cattle. I took off first one shirt, then the other. Sweat streamed down my body. My nose bled continuously. My ears hummed. I longed for Auschwitz, because it would mean air. Finally the doors were thrown open alongside a ramp, and my strength returned completely with the first whiff of fresh air. It was an April night—starlit, cool. I did not feel the cold, although the shirt I had put on was soaking wet. Someone behind me reached forward and embraced me. Through the thick, heavy darkness I could see in the distance the gleaming lights of the concentration camp. And above them flickered a nervous, reddish flame. The darkness rose up under it so that it seemed as though the flame were burning on top of a gigantic mountain. 'The crematorium'—passed a whisper through the crowd."

"How you can talk! It's evident that you're a poet . . ." said Witek approvingly.

"We walked to the camp carrying the dead. Behind I could hear heavy breathing and I imagined that perhaps my girl was walking behind me. From time to time there came the hollow thud of a falling blow. Just before we reached the gate somebody struck my thigh with a bayonet. It didn't hurt, only my leg became very warm. Blood was streaming down my thigh and leg. After a few steps my muscles became stiff and I began to limp. The S.S. man escorting us struck a few other men who were up front and said as we were entering the camp:

'Here you will have a good long rest.'

"That was on Thursday night. On Monday I joined a labour Kommando in Budy, several kilometres outside the camp, to carry telegraph poles. My leg hurt like the devil. It was quite a rest!"

"Big deal," said Witek, "the Jews travel in much worse conditions, you know. So what do you have to brag about?"

Opinions were divided as to modes of travel and as to the Jews.

"Jews . . . you know what the Jews are like!" said Staszek. "Wait and see, they'll manage to run a business in any camp! Whether it's the cremo or the ghetto, every one of them will sell his own mother for a bowl of turnips! One morning our labour Kommando was waiting to leave for work, and right next to us stood the *Sonder*. Immediately I saw Moise, a former bookkeeper. He's from Mlawa, I'm from Mlawa, you know how it is. We had palled around together and done business together—mutual confidence and trust. 'What's the trouble, Moise?' I said. 'You seem out of sorts.' 'I've got some new pictures of my family.' 'That's good! Why should it upset you?' 'Good? Hell! I've sent my own father to the oven!'

'Impossible!' 'Possible, because I have. He came with a transport, and saw me in front of the gas chamber. I was lining up the people. He threw his arms around me, and began kissing me and asking, what's going to happen. He told me he was hungry because they'd been riding for two days without any food. But right away the Kommandoführer yells at me not to stand around, to get back to work. What was I to do? "Go on, Father," I said, "wash yourself in the bath-house and then we'll talk. Can't you see I'm busy now?" So my father went on to the gas chamber. And later I found the pictures in his coat pocket. Now tell me, what's so good about my having the pictures?' "

We laughed. "Anyway, it's lucky they don't gas Aryans any longer. Anything but that!"

"In the old days they did," said one of the Auschwitz old-timers who always seemed to join our group. "I've been in this block a long time and I remember a lot of things. You wouldn't believe how many people have passed through my hands, straight to the gas chamber—friends, school-mates, acquaintances from my home town! By now I have even forgotten their faces. An anonymous mass—that's all. But one episode I will undoubtedly remember for the rest of my life. At the time I was an ambulance orderly. I can't say I was any too gentle when it came to dressing wounds—there was no time for fooling around, you know. You scraped a little at the arm, the back, or whatever—then cotton, bandages, and out! Next! You didn't even bother to look at the face. Nor did anyone bother to thank you; there was nothing to thank you for. But once, after I had dressed a phlegmon wound, all of a sudden a man said to me, pausing at the door: 'Spasibo, thank you, Herr Flager!' The poor devil was so pale, so weak, he could barely hold himself up on his swollen legs. Later I went to visit him and took him some soup. He had the phlegmon on his right buttock, then his entire thigh became covered with running sores. He suffered horribly. He wept and spoke of his mother. 'Stop it,' I would say to him. 'All of us have mothers, and we're not crying.' I tried to console him as best I could, but he lamented that he would never go home again. But what was I able to give him? A bowl of soup, a piece of bread once in a while . . . I did my best to protect little Toleczka from being selected for the gas, but finally they found him and took down his name. One day I went to see him. He was feverish. 'It doesn't matter that I'm going to the gas chamber,' he said to me. 'That's how it has to be, I reckon. But when the war is over and you get out . . .' 'I don't know whether I'll survive,

Toleczka,' I interrupted. 'You will survive,' he went on stubbornly, 'and you will go to see my mother. There will be no borders after the war, I know, and there will be no countries, no concentration camps, and people will never kill one another. *Wied' eto poslednij boj,*' he repeated firmly. 'It is our last fight, you understand?' 'I understand,' I told him. 'You will go to my mother and tell her I died. Died so that there would be no more borders. Or wars. Or concentration camps. You will tell her?' 'I'll tell her.' 'Memorize this: my mother lives in Dalniewostoczny County, the city of Chabrowsk, Tolstoy Street, number 24. Now repeat it.' I repeated it. I went to see Block Elder Szary who still might have been able to save Toleczka. He struck me across the mouth and threw me out of his shack. Toleczka went to the gas chamber. Several months later Szary was taken out in a transport. At the moment of his departure he pleaded for a cigarette. I tipped the men not to give him any. And they didn't. Perhaps I did a wrong thing, for he was on his way to Mauthausen to be killed. But I memorized Toleczka's mother's address: Dalniewostoczny County, the city of Chabrowsk, Tolstoy Street . . ."

We were silent. Kurt, who understood nothing of what was said, wondered what was going on. Witek explained:

"We're talking about the camp and wondering whether there will be a better world some day. How about you, have you something to say about it?"

Kurt looked at us with a smile and then spoke slowly, so we should all understand:

"I have only a short tale to tell. I was in Mauthausen. Two prisoners had escaped and were caught on Christmas Eve itself. The entire camp stood at roll-call to watch them hang. The Christmas tree was lighted. Then the Lagerführer stepped forward, turned to the prisoners and barked a command:

" '*Haftlinge, Mützen ab!*'

"We took our caps off. And then, for the traditional Christmas message, the Lagerführer spoke these words:

'Those who behave like swine will be treated like swine. *Haftlinge, Mützen auf!*'

"We put our caps on.

" '*Dismissed!*'

"We broke up and lighted our cigarettes. We were silent. Everyone began thinking of his own problems."

VII

If the barrack walls were suddenly to fall away, many thousands of people, packed together, squeezed tightly in their bunks, would remain suspended in mid-air. Such a sight would be more gruesome than the medieval paintings of the Last Judgment. For one of the ugliest sights to a man is that of another man sleeping on his tiny portion of the bunk, of the space which he must occupy, because he has a body—a body that has been exploited to the utmost: with a number tattooed on it to save on dog tags, with just enough sleep at night to work during the day, and just enough time to eat. And just enough food so it will not die wastefully. As for actual living, there is only one place for it—a piece of the bunk. The rest belongs to the camp, the Fatherland. But not even this small space, nor the shirt you wear, nor the spade you work with are your own. If you get sick, everything is taken away from you: your clothes, your cap, your "organized" scarf, your handkerchief. If you die—your gold teeth, already recorded in the camp inventory, are extracted. Your body is burned and your ashes are used to fertilize the fields or fill in the ponds. Although in fact so much fat and bone is wasted in the burning, so much flesh, so much heat! But elsewhere they make soap out of people, and lampshades out of human skin, and jewellery out of the bones.

We work beneath the earth and above it, under a roof and in the rain, with the spade, the pickaxe and the crowbar. We carry huge sacks of cement, lay bricks, put down rails, spread gravel, trample the earth . . . We are laying the foundation for some new, monstrous civilization. Only now do I realize what price was paid for building the ancient civilizations. The Egyptian pyramids, the temples, and Greek statues— what a hideous crime they were! How much blood must have poured on to the Roman roads, the bulwarks, and the city walls. Antiquity— the tremendous concentration camp where the slave was branded on the forehead by his master, and crucified for trying to escape! Antiquity—the conspiracy of freemen against slaves!

You know how much I used to like Plato. Today I realize he lied. For the things of this world are not a reflection of the ideal, but a product of human sweat, blood and hard labour. It is we who built the pyramids, hewed the marble for the temples and the rocks for the imperial roads, we who pulled the oars in the galleys and dragged wooden ploughs, while they wrote dialogues and dramas, rationalized their intrigues by appeals in the name of the Fatherland, made wars over boundaries and democracies.

We were filthy and died real deaths. They were "aesthetic" and carried on subtle debates.

There can be no beauty if it is paid for by human injustice, nor truth that passes over injustice in silence, nor moral virtue that condones it.

What does ancient history say about us? It knows the crafty slave from Terence and Plautus, it knows the people's tribunes, the brothers Gracchi, and the name of one slave—Spartacus.

They are the ones who have made history, yet the murderer—Scipio—the lawmakers—Cicero or Demosthenes—are the men remembered today. We rave over the extermination of the Etruscans, the destruction of Carthage, over treason, deceit, plunder. Roman law! Yes, today too there is a law!

If the Germans win the war, what will the world know about us? They will erect huge buildings, highways, factories, soaring monuments. Our hands will be placed under every brick, and our backs will carry the steel rails and the slabs of concrete. They will kill off our families, our sick, our aged. They will murder our children.

And we shall be forgotten, drowned out by the voices of the poets, the jurists, the philosophers, the priests. They will produce their own beauty, virtue and truth. They will produce religion.

Where Auschwitz stands today, three years ago there were villages and farms. There were rich meadows, shaded country lanes, apple orchards. There were people, no better nor worse than any other people.

And then we arrived. We drove the people out, demolished their houses, levelled the earth, kneaded it into mud. We built barracks, fences, crematoria. We brought scurvy, phlegmon and lice.

Now we work in mines and factories, and the fruit of our labour brings enormous profits to somebody.

The story of the building of Auschwitz is an interesting one. A German Company built our camp—the barracks, halls, shacks, bunks, chimneys. When the bill was presented, it turned out to be so fantastic that it stunned not only the Auschwitz officials but Berlin itself. Gentlemen—they said—it is not possible, you are making much too much profit, there must be a mistake! Regrettably—replied the Company—here are the bills. Well yes—said Berlin—but we simply cannot . . . In that case, half—suggested the patriotic Company. Thirty per cent—haggled Berlin manfully, and that is what was finally agreed upon. Since then all the bills are cut accordingly. But the Company is not worried: like all German companies, it is increasing its capital. It has done fantastic business at

Auschwitz and is now waiting calmly for the war to end. The same goes for the companies in plumbing, in well-drilling, in electrical appliances; for the producers of brick, cement, metal and lumber, the makers of barracks parts and striped prison suits. The same thing is true of the huge automobile company, and of the scrap demolition outfit. And of the owners of the coalmines in Myslawice, Gliwice, Janin and Jaworzna. Those of us who survive will one day demand compensation for our work. Not in money, or goods, but in hard, relentless labour.

When the patients finally fall asleep, I have time to talk with you. In the darkness, I can see your face, and although my words are full of bitterness and hatred that must be foreign to you, I know you listen carefully.

Your fate has now become a part of my own. Except that your hands are not suited to the pickaxe and your body not accustomed to scurvy. We are bound together by our love and by the love of those who have stayed behind, those who live for us and who constitute our world. The faces of our parents, friends, the shapes of objects we left behind— these are the things we share. And even if nothing is left to us but our bodies on the hospital bunk, we shall still have our memories and our feelings.

VIII

You cannot imagine how very pleased I am!

First of all—the tall electrician. I go to him every morning with Kurt (because he is Kurt's contact), bringing along my letters to you. The electrician, a fantastically old serial number, just a bit over one thousand, loads up on sausage, sugar and lingerie, and slides a stack of letters somewhere in his shoe. The electrician is bald and has no particular sympathy for our love. The electrician frowns upon every letter I bring. The electrician declares when I want to give him some cigarettes:

"Look pal, here in Auschwitz we don't accept payment for letters! And I'll bring the reply, if I can."

So I go to see him again in the evening. The reverse procedure takes place: the electrician reaches inside his shoe, produces a card from you, hands it to me with a bitter frown. Because the electrician has no sympathy for our love. Besides, I am sure he is very unhappy living in a bunk—that one by one-and-a-half metre cage. Since the electrician is very tall, it must be quite uncomfortable for him.

So, first of all—the tall electrician. Secondly—the wedding of the Spaniard. The Spaniard fought defending Madrid, then escaped to France and ended up at Auschwitz. He had found himself a Frenchwoman, as a Spaniard would, and had had a child by her. The child grew. The Spaniard stayed on and on behind the barbed-wire. So the Frenchwoman started clamouring for a wedding. Out goes a petition to H. himself. H. is indignant: "Is there no *Ordnung* in the new Europe? Marry them immediately!"

So they shipped the Frenchwoman, together with the child, to the camp, hurriedly pulled the stripes off the Spaniard's back, fitted him into an elegant suit pressed personally by the Kapo in the laundry room, carefully selected a tie and matching socks from the camp's abundant supplies, and married them.

Then the newlyweds went to have their pictures taken: she with the child at her side and a bouquet of hyacinths in her arms, he standing close to her on the other side. Behind them—the orchestra *in corpore*, and behind the orchestra the S.S. man in charge of the kitchen, furious:

"I'll report this, that you're playing music during working hours instead of peeling potatoes! I've got the soup all ready, and no potatoes! I fuck all weddings!"

"Calm down . . ." some of the other "bigwigs" tried to pacify him. "It's orders from Berlin. We can have soup without potatoes."

The newlyweds, meanwhile, had finished the picture-taking ceremony and were sent to a Puff suite for their wedding night. The regular Puff residents were temporarily exiled to Block 10. The following day the Frenchwoman returned to France, and the Spaniard, again in his stripes, returned to a labour Kommando.

But now everyone at the camp walks proudly, head high.

"We even have weddings in Auschwitz!"

So, first of all—the tall electrician. Secondly—the wedding of the Spaniard. And thirdly—school is almost over. The F.K.L. girls were the first to finish. We bid them farewell with a chamber music concert. They sat at the windows of Block 10 and out of our windows flowed the sounds of the saxophone, the drum, the violins. To me, the loveliest is the saxophone, as it sobs and weeps, laughs and giggles!

What a pity Slowacki[5] died so early, or he would most certainly have become a saxophone player.

5. A Polish romantic poet.

After the women it was our turn. Everybody assembled in our attic classroom. *Lagerarzt* Rhode (the "decent" one who makes no distinction between Jews and Aryans) came in, took a look at us and our work, said he was very pleased and quite certain that the situation in Auschwitz would greatly improve from now on, and left quickly, for the attic was cold.

All day they have been saying goodbye to us here in Auschwitz. Franz, the fellow from Vienna, gave me a last-minute lecture on the meaning of war. Stuttering a little, he spoke of the people who build, and the people who destroy. Of victory for the former and defeat for the latter; of the comrades from the Urals and London, Chicago and Calcutta, on land and sea, who are fighting for our cause. Of the future brotherhood of all creative men. Here, I thought to myself, is a messianic vision emerging out of the surrounding death and destruction—a characteristic process of the human mind. Then Franz opened the package which he had just received from Vienna and we had our evening tea. Franz sang Austrian songs and I recited poems that he did not understand.

Then I was given some medicine and a few books for the road. I squeezed them inside my bundle, underneath the food. Would you believe it—the works of Angelus Silesius! So I am quite pleased, because of everything combined: the tall electrician, the Spaniard's wedding, the school being over. And in addition—I received letters from home. They had strayed a long time, but found me at last.

I had not heard a word from home for almost two months and I worried terribly. Fantastic tales have been circulating as to the conditions in Warsaw, and I had already started writing desperate letters. And then yesterday, just think, two letters! One from Staszek and one from my brother.

Staszek writes very simply, like a man who wishes to convey something straight from the heart in a foreign tongue. "We love you and think of you," he says, "and we also think of Tuska, your girl. We live, we work and write." They live, work and write, except that Andrzej has been shot and Wacek is dead.

What a pity that the two most talented men of our generation, with the most passionate desire to create, were the ones who had to die!

You probably remember how strongly I always opposed them—their imperialistic conception of an omnivorous state, their dishonest approach to society, their theories on state art, their muddled philosophy, their futile poetry, their whole style of living and their unconscious hypocrisy.

And today, separated as we are by the barrier between two worlds, the barrier which we too will cross some day, I reopen our dispute about the meaning of the world, the philosophy of living, and the nature of poetry. And today I shall still challenge their acceptance of the infectious idea of the all-powerful, aggressive state, their awe for the evil whose only defect is that it is not our own. And even today I shall challenge their unrealistic poetry, void of all human problems.

But across the barrier that divides us I can still see their faces, and I think about them, the young men of my generation; and I feel a growing emptiness around me. They went away while still so much alive, so much in the very centre of the world that they were building. I bid them farewell, my friends on the opposite side of the barricades. May they find in that other world the truths and the love that they failed to find here!

Eva, the girl who recited such beautiful poems about harmony and stars, and who used to say that "things aren't really that bad . . ." was also shot. A void, an ever-growing void. And I had thought that all this would be limited to us. That when we return, we should be returning to a world which would not have known the horrors and the atmosphere that are killing us. That we alone had hit bottom. But it seems that they too are being taken away—out of the very centre of life.

We are as insensitive as trees, as stones. And we remain as numb as trees when they are being cut down, or stones when they are being crushed.

The other letter was from my brother. You know how affectionate Julek has always been in his letters. This time too he tells me that they are thinking of us and waiting, that they have hidden all my books and poems . . .

When I return I shall find on my shelves a new little volume of my poems. "They are your love poems," writes my brother. I think it is somehow symbolic that our love is always tied to poetry and that the book of poems which were written for you and which you had with you at the time of your arrest is a kind of victory *in absentia*. Perhaps they were published in memory of us? But I am grateful to the friends who keep alive our poetry and our love and recognize our right to them.

Julek also writes about your mother, that she prays for us and trusts that we shall return and that we will always be together . . . Do you recall what you wrote in the very first card I received from you, only a few days after arriving at the camp? You wrote that you were sick and were desperate because you felt responsible for my being thrown into the concentration camp. That had it not been for you, etc . . . . Do you want to know how it really happened?

It happened this way: I was waiting for your promised telephone call from Maria's. That afternoon, as on every Wednesday, the underground school held a class at my place. I spoke, I think, about linguistics, and I think that the paraffin lamp went out.

Then again I waited for you to call. I knew you would, because you had promised. But you did not. I cannot remember if I went out to dinner. If so, then on returning I sat again by the telephone, afraid I might not hear it from the other room. I looked through some newspaper clippings and read a story by Maurois about a man who weighed human souls in order to learn how to keep them captive for ever in imperishable receptacles, and thus find a way to unite his own soul with that of his beloved for all eternity. But he only succeeded in accidentally capturing the souls of two circus clowns, whereas his own soul and the soul of the woman in question continued to float separately in space . . . It was getting light when I fell asleep.

In the morning as usual I went home with my briefcase and books. I had my breakfast, said I must rush off but would be back for dinner, ruffled the ears of the dog, and went to see your mother. She was worried about you. I took the trolley-bus to Maria's and on the way down looked long and intently at the trees of Lazienki Park, of which I am very fond. Then I walked up Pulawska Street. The staircase was covered with cigarette butts, and, if I remember correctly, had some traces of blood. But it may have been only my imagination. I went up and rang the doorbell, using our code. Men with revolvers in their hands opened the door.

Since then, a year has passed. But I am writing about it so that you will know I have never regretted that we are here together. It has never even occurred to me that it could be any other way. And I often think about the future. About the life we shall have, if . . . About the poems I am going to write, the books we shall read together, the objects that will be around us. I know these are small things, but I think about them nevertheless.

IX

We are back. As in the old days, I went over to my block, rubbed some of the patients with mint tea and stood around for a while, a knowing expression on my face, watching the doctor operate. Then I helped myself to the last two shots of Prontisil which I am sending to you. Finally I went to see our block barber, Hank Liberfreund (a restaurant owner from Krakow), who decided that I shall certainly be the best writer among the orderlies.

Apart from that, I spent all day long snooping around the camp, carrying my letter to you. In order to reach their destination, these few pieces of paper must have a pair of feet. It is the feet that I have been hunting for. I finally located a pair—in high, red, laced-up boots. The feet, besides, wear dark glasses, have broad shoulders, and march daily to the F.K.L. to collect corpses of male infants which must be processed through our office of male statistics and our male mortuary, and examined personally by our S.D.G. Order is the essence of the universe, or, less poetically—*Ordnung muss sein*!

And so the feet march to the F.K.L. and are, for a change, fairly sympathetic. They too, they tell me, have a wife among the female prisoners, and understand how it is. They will deliver my letter free of charge. And perhaps smuggle me in too, should an opportunity arise. Actually, I feel rather in the mood for travelling, though my colleagues suggest I take along a heavy blanket and—wrap it around me where it may afford the most protection . . . With my luck and resourcefulness, they figure, I am bound to be caught on the first try. I told them to go and smear themselves with Peruvian itch ointment!

I am still examining the surrounding landscape. Nothing has changed, only there is somehow even more mud. Spring is in the air. Soon people will start drowning in mud. The breezes from the forest now carry a whiff of pine, now of smoke. Cars drive by, now loaded with bundles, now with Muslims from Buna; now with dinner for the offices, now with S.S. men on their way to change the guard.

Nothing has changed. Yesterday was Sunday and we went to the camp for a delousing inspection. The barracks seem even more terrible in the winter! The dirty bunks, the black, damp earth floors, swept clean, the stale odour of human bodies. The blocks are packed with people, but there is not one louse inside. The never-ending delousing treatments have not been in vain. After the inspections, just as we started to leave, a *Sonderkommando* marched back to camp returning from the cremo. Black with smoke, looking fat and prosperous, the men were loaded down with heavy sacks. There is no limit to what they may take; anything except gold, but this is what they smuggle the most of.

Small groups of people began stealing out of the barracks, rushing over to the marching column and snatching the awaited packages from their hands. The air became filled with shouts, cursing and the sound of blows. At last the *Sonder* disappeared behind the gate leading to their quarters, which are separated from the rest of the camp by a stone wall. But it was not long before the Jews started sneaking out to trade, "organize" and visit with friends.

I cornered one of them, an old pal from my previous Kommando. I became ill and landed at the K.B. He was "luckier," and joined the *Sonder,* which is certainly better than swinging a pickaxe on nothing but one bowl of soup a day. He shook my hand warmly.

"Ah, it's you! Want to buy anything? If you've got some apples . . ."

"No, I haven't any apples for you," I replied affectionately. "So, you're still alive, Abbie? And what's new with you?"

"Not much. Just gassed up a Czech transport."

"That I know. I mean personally?"

"Personally? What sort of 'personally' is there for me? The oven, the barracks, back to the oven . . . Have I got anybody around here? Well, if you really want to know what 'personally'—we've figured out a new way to burn people. Want to hear about it?"

I indicated polite interest.

"Well then, you take four little kids with plenty of hair on their heads, then stick the heads together and light the hair. The rest burns by itself and in no time at all the whole business is *gemacht.*"

"Congratulations," I said drily and with very little enthusiasm.

He burst out laughing and with a strange expression looked right into my eyes.

"Listen, doctor, here in Auschwitz we must entertain ourselves in every way we can. Otherwise, who could stand it?"

And putting his hands in his pockets he walked away without saying goodbye.

But this is a monstrous lie, a grotesque lie, like the whole camp, like the whole world.

RECOMMENDED LETTER STORIES

Aldrich, Thomas Bailey. "Marjorie Daw." In *119 Years of the Atlantic*. Boston: Little, Brown, 1977.

Aleichem, Sholom. "In Haste." In *The Old Country*. New York: Crown, 1946.

Auchincloss, Louis. "The Penultimate Puritan." In *The Winthrop Covenant*. Boston: Houghton Mifflin, 1976.

Barstow, Stan. "The Middle of the Journey." In *The Glad Eye*. London: Michael Joseph, 1984.

Barthelme, Donald. "Letters to the Editor." In *Forty Stories*. New York: G. P. Putnam's Sons, 1987.

Benét, Stephen Vincent. "The Curfew Tolls." In *Selected Works*. New York: Farrar and Rinehart, 1942.

Borges, José Carlos Cavalcanti. "With God's Blessing, Mom." In *Modern Brazilian Short Stories*. Berkeley: University of California Press, 1967.

Bowles, Paul. "In Absentia." In *A Distant Episode*. New York: Ecco Press, 1988.

Brown, Rosellen. "Re: *Femme*." In *A Rosellen Brown Reader*. Hanover, N.H.: University Press of New England, 1992.

Carr, John Dickson. "The Gentleman from Paris." In *The Mammoth Book of Historical Whodunnits*. New York: Carroll and Graf, 1993.

Cisneros, Sandra. "Little Miracles, Kept Promises." In *Woman Hollering Creek*. New York: Random House, 1991.

Collins, Wilkie. "The Biter Bit." In *The Complete Shorter Fiction*. New York: Carroll and Graf, 1995.

Dazai, Osamu. "The Sound of Hammering." In *Crackling Mountain*. Rutland, Vt.: Charles E. Tuttle, 1989.

Drake, Mary. "The Feast to End All Feasts." In *Short Story International.* No. 50. Great Neck, N.Y.: International Cultural Exchange, June 1985.

Ellison, Ralph. "Backwacking, a Plea to the Senator." In *Children of the Night.* Boston: Little, Brown, 1995.

Greenberg, Joanne. "De Rerum Natura." In *High Crimes and Misdemeanors.* New York: Holt, Rinehart and Winston, 1980.

Hall, James B. "The Executive Touch." In *New Directions in Prose and Poetry.* No. 32. New York: New Directions, 1976.

Higgins, Anne. "In Search of a Missing IUD." In *Many Windows: 22 Stories from American Review.* New York: Harper and Row, 1982.

James, Henry. "A Bundle of Letters." In *Complete Stories.* New York: Library of America, 1999.

Jolley, Elizabeth. "Wednesdays and Fridays." In *Woman in a Lampshade.* New York: Penguin Books, 1986.

Lardner, Ring. "Some Like Them Cold." In *The Best Short Stories of Ring Lardner.* New York: Charles Scribner's Sons, 1957.

Marsella, Anne. "The Mission San Martin." In *The Lost and Found.* New York: New York University Press, 1994.

Maurois, André. "Ariane, My Sister." In *Collected Stories.* New York: Washington Square Press, 1967.

Mistral, Frédéric. "The Complaint of the Bulls of the Camargue." In *Voices from France.* New York: Doubleday, 1969.

Munro, Alice. "Before the Change." In *The Love of a Good Woman.* New York: Alfred A. Knopf, 1998.

Narayan, R. K. "Uncle's Letters." In *Under the Banyan Tree.* New York: Viking Press, 1985.

O'Faolain, Julia. "Man in the Cellar." In *Bitches and Sad Ladies.* New York: Dell, 1975.

O'Hara, John. "Pal Joey." In *Collected Stories.* New York: Random House, 1984.

Roditi, Edouard. "The Vampires of Istanbul: A Study in Modern Communications Methods." In *New Directions in Prose and Poetry.* No. 24. New York: New Directions, 1972.

Rodoreda, Mercè. "The Dolls' Room." In *My Christina.* Port Townsend, Wash.: Graywolf Press, 1984.

Still, James. "Pattern of a Man." In *Short Story International.* No. 43. Great Neck, N.Y.: International Cultural Exchange, April 1984.

Taylor, Kressmann. "Address Unknown." In *Address Unknown.* Cincinnati: Story Press, 1995.

Hubert Aquin, "Back on April Eleventh," translated by Alan Brown, from *The Oxford Book of French-Canadian Short Stories*. Originally published as "De retour le 11 avril" in *Liberté* and in *Point de Fuite*. Copyright © by Andrée Yanacopoulo. Reprinted by permission of Andrée Yanacopoulo.

Tadeusz Borowski, "Auschwitz, Our Home (A Letter)" from *This Way for the Gas, Ladies and Gentlemen*, translated by Barbara Vedder. Copyright © 1959 by Maria Borowski. English translation copyright © 1967 by Penguin Books, Ltd. Reprinted by permission of Viking Penguin, a division of Penguin Putnam Inc. and Penguin Books Ltd.

Michael Carson, "Peter's Buddies" from *Gay Times*. Copyright by Michael Carson. Reprinted by permission of the author.

Julio Cortázar, "Letter to a Young Lady in Paris," from *Bestiary, Selected Stories,* first published in Great Britain in 1998 by Harvill Press. Copyright © the Estate of Julio Cortázar 1969, 1974, 1977, 1979, 1980, 1982, 1998. Copyright © in the English translation, Paul Blackburn, 1963, 1967. Copyright © 1967 by Random House, Inc. Reprinted by permission of Pantheon Books, a division of Random House, Inc., and the Harvill Press.

Stephen Dixon, "Man of Letters" from *The Stories of Stephen Dixon.* (New York: Henry Holt, 1994). Originally published in *Quite Contrary* (New York: Harper & Row, 1979). Copyright © 1979 by Stephen Dixon. Reprinted by permission of the author.

Gail Godwin, "False Lights" from *Dream Children*. Copyright © 1976 by Gail Godwin. Reprinted by permission of Alfred A. Knopf, Inc., and the John Hawkins Agency.

Virginia Moriconi, "Simple Arithmetic" from *The Mark of St Crispin* (London: Gerald Duckworth, 1978). Originally published in *Transatlantic Review* (1964). Copyright © 1964, renewed 1992 by the Estate of Virginia Moriconi. Reprinted by permission of the literary executor.

Alice Munro, "A Wilderness Station" from *Open Secrets*. Copyright © 1994 by Alice Munro. Reprinted by permission of Alfred A. Knopf, Inc., McClelland & Stewart, Ltd., and Chatto & Windus, Ltd.

Ray Russell, "Evil Star" from *Paris Review* 17, no. 68 (winter 1976). Copyright © 1976 by Ray Russell. Reprinted by permission of the author.

As a book critic, Gail Pool has long been fascinated by letter stories. As a reader, she has enjoyed them. And as a writing instructor, she has used them for reading and writing assignments. She is currently an instructor for the Radcliffe Seminars at Radcliffe College in Cambridge, Massachusetts.